Sports Coach

MW01518088

Routledge Research in Sport, Culture and Society

Sports Coaching Research
Context, Consequences, and Consciousness

**Anthony Bush, Michael Silk,
David Andrews and Hugh Lauder**

Routledge
Taylor & Francis Group
NEW YORK LONDON

First published 2013
by Routledge
711 Third Avenue, New York, NY 10017

Simultaneously published in the UK
by Routledge
2 Park Square, Milton Park, Abingdon, Oxfordshire OX14 4RN

First issued in paperback 2014

*Routledge is an imprint of the Taylor and Francis Group,
an informa business*

Library of Congress Cataloging-in-Publication Data
Bush, Anthony.
  Sports coaching research : context, consequences, and consciousness /
by Anthony Bush ... [et al.].
      p. cm. — (Routledge research in sport, culture and society ; v.20)
  Includes bibliographical references and index.
  1. Coaching (Athletics)—Research. I. Title.
  GV711.B87 2012
  796.07'7—dc23
  2012021772

ISBN 978-0-415-89026-7 (hbk)
ISBN 978-1-138-92065-1 (pbk)
ISBN 978-0-203-07922-5 (ebk)

Typeset in Sabon
by IBT Global.

Contents

1 Introduction

Nothing can exist as an element of knowledge if, on the one hand, it does not conform to a set of rules and constraints characteristic, for example, of a given type of scientific discourse in a given period, and if, on the other hand, it does not possess the effects of coercion or simply the incentives peculiar to what is scientifically validated or simply rational or simply generally accepted. (Foucault, 1997, p.52)

This book is a response to the growing consensus that sports coaching research "needs to extend its physical and intellectual boundaries" (Potrac et al., 2007, p.34). Indeed, despite considerable research from a number of theoretical and empirical perspectives, "it is arguable that sports coaching continues to lack a sound conceptual base" (Cushion et al., 2006, pp.83–84). The aim of this book is to contextualize the current 'moment' in which sports coaching research is undertaken, and then offer a directional purview of the ontological, epistemological, and methodological boundaries—the conceptual base—of a reconceptualized 'field' of sports coaching research.

This book is framed by a Physical Cultural Studies (PCS) approach. We mobilize a reconceptualized 'field' of sports coaching, building upon the evolutionary shift away from 'sport' as the sole, and privileged, focus of academic study in allied fields such as the sociology or psychology of sport. Rather, and embracing the nomenclature of physical cultural studies—which not only decenters sport and opens enquiry to a multitude of physical cultural forms, experiences, structures, and subjectivities, but also has clear communitarian, political, moral, and ethical concerns at its heart which we delineate through this text (Silk and Andrews, 2011)—we provide a critical, and hopefully challenging (and thus healthy) explication of sports coaching research and scholarship. In doing so, it is hoped that the progressive potential of a 'field in tension' (Silk and Andrews, 2011) can be realized, resulting in the evolution of a socially and culturally responsive, communitarian, justice-oriented agenda; in essence, an approach that can 'do coaching justice'.

In order to study and offer a reconceptualization of a discipline or 'field' such as sports coaching, we examine the workings of the discipline as it currently stands and is historically situated in an effort to develop a rigorous understanding of the ways that the discipline has, and continues, to traditionally operate (Kincheloe, 2001). To invoke and paraphrase Kincheloe (2001), scholarly activity in sports coaching operates in a power-saturated and regulatory manner, with disciplinarians having developed a methodical, persistent, and well-coordinated process of knowledge production. Of course, these disciplinarians have exhibited genius within these domains and great triumphs of scholarly breakthrough that have resulted in improvements in the knowledge base of sports coaching; and our humble efforts clearly do not leave behind these insights and contributions. Indeed, they are the very basis from which we begin to (re)conceptualize the field; this book will thus work with extant sports coaching knowledges and thereby avoid any form of disciplinary parochialism and domination that delimits knowledge in, and indeed the (potential) impact of, the 'field'. In essence, through the text, we call for questions of disciplinarity—the consistent division between disciplinarians and interdisciplinarians[1]—not to detract from the efforts to understand and theorize the research bricolage in a reconceptualized 'field' of sports coaching and the multiple contributions that coaching can make to a more socially just world.

Deploying the theory and method of articulation (Hall, 1996b) and Foucault's (1969) genealogical method, we map out the critical history of the sports coaching present through consideration of the social forces that comprise our conjunctural moment (Grossberg, 2006) allowing the social construction of the discipline's knowledge bases, epistemologies, and knowledge production methodologies to be studied. Importantly, this genealogical context facilitates the exploration of the "discipline as a discursive system of regulatory power with its propensity to impound knowledge within arbitrary and exclusive boundaries" (Kincheloe, 2001, p. 684). By pursuing this dialectic of disciplinarity, it is envisaged that practitioners in the reconceptualized 'field'—the 'bricoleurs'—would develop a power literacy to better understand the nature and effects of the web of power relations that have shaped sports coaching's official research methodologies, and also the ways that these power dynamics have shaped the knowledge produced. In essence, this is a field in which sports coaching is understood with respect to the ways in which knowledges are *articulated* into a particular set of complex relationships that comprise the social context (Silk and Andrews, 2011). In doing so, the sports coaching 'bricoleur':

> . . . becomes an expert on the relationships connecting cultural context, meaning making, power, and oppression within disciplinary boundaries. Their rigorous understanding of these dynamics possibly makes them more aware of the influence of such factors on the everyday practices of the discipline than those who have traditionally operated as scholars within the discipline. (Kincheloe, 2001, p.684)

Such an understanding of the boundaries, constraints and possibilities of ones academic field is of course in many respects liberating; yet, in and of itself, however is not enough. Rather, through the methodological approach that runs through the text, we work not just to delineate these disciplinary power structures and prestige hierarchies but to provide insights into what a de-blinkered field *might* (not *ought* to) look like. In essence, with and through articulation, "we engage the concrete in order to change it, that is, to *rearticulate* it" (Slack, 1996, p.114, emphasis added). This is of course, an unfinished project and not one that will be tidied up within the confines of this provocative text. Yet we hope it is a project others will engage with, challenge, contest, revise, and 'play with' in an effort to 'do coaching justice'.

By putting our collective heads above the disciplinary parapets, we of course risk being deemed as brave by some or foolish by others—it is likely that both are, in differential ways, appropriate. Indeed, through the book, and in arguing for theoretical and methodological approaches that tend to center on social justice, ethics, morality, communities, exposing power relations—approaches that tend to favor qualitative, localized, and community based methodologies as opposed to the gold standard of scientific enquiry, evidence—we are perhaps more foolish than brave given the political and economic context of such approaches within corporatized, McDonaldized, higher education institutions (see e.g. Giroux, 2009; Hayes and Wynard, 2002; Ritzer, 2002). St. Pierre and Roulston (2006, p.674) argue that the politics of this historical 'moment' have qualitative researchers concerned that qualitative inquiry is under siege and that some in positions of power have either never heard or choose now to ignore the victory narrative of the paradigm wars of the 1980s. This victory narrative is one in which qualitative inquiry cleared a space for itself and became legitimate. The 'moment,' termed our 'proto-fascist present' (Giroux, 2005) or the 'pernicious present' (Silk and Andrews, 2011), means that qualitative research exists in a time of global uncertainty (Denzin et al., 2006) where government agencies are attempting to regulate scientific enquiry by defining what counts as 'good' science (Denzin et al., 2006). 'Good' science is based on the desire for research that is replicable, generalizable, empirical, and experimental, which results in 'scientifically-based research' (SBR) or evidence-based research (EBR) being heralded as the gold standard for research practices.[2]

The 'moment' is shaped by the dominant political and ideological form of capitalist globalization—neoliberalism—which due to the global hegemony of this mode of rationality, has become omnipresent and a common-sense of the times (Brenner and Theodore, 2002a; Peck and Tickell, 2002). Neoliberalism is *everywhere* and has been referred to as a "new religion" (Peck and Tickell, 2002, p.381) and through the adoption of the neoliberal policy agenda, the contemporary higher education system is a 'locality' in a globalized world that demonstrates subservience to commercialization, vocationalization, privatization, militarization, marketization and managerialism. This rise in 'corporate power' (Giroux, 1999), 'governmentality' (Olssen and Peters, 2005), an 'audit culture' (Frith, 2001), and 'profit-driven instrumental rationality'—McDonaldization (Ritzer, 2004)—has impacted on the core functions of universities and the academic community. It is within this context, we argue that sports coaching research has become part of an episteme guided by the controlling yardstick of profit, knowledge instrumentalization, and a climate of responsibility which has diverted acadehme from broader public good towards narrow specialties (Dimitriadis, 2006; Giroux, 1999). However, we assert that the sports coaching knowledges can, and should, be far more than a handmaiden for a neoliberal, corporate and high-performance agenda. Sports coaching knowledges have the potential to be meaningful, have important social, political and economic impacts that contribute towards socially just societal goals—scholarly activity in the 'field' of sports coaching could be characterized by a more productive vision in which Universities encourage *creative* effort and the formation of multidisciplinary groupings, and which result in the formation of inventive problem nets, research programs and ideas (Barnett, 2000a); in other words an environment conducive for meaningful investigation in the reconceptualized 'field'.

Chapter 2 of the book offers what Lawrence Grossberg (2006) has termed a critical history of the present through consideration of the social forces that comprise our conjunctural moment. It explicates the rise and adoption of neoliberalism, from its genealogy as a strategic political response to the global recession in the late fifties, to its global hegemonic omnipresence of current times. Although seen as a 'commonsense of the times' (Peck and Tickell, 2002), by invoking and deploying Lauder et al. (2006), the *success* of the market economy is critiqued in order to highlight the issues with the corporate capitalist 'fairytale' of neoliberalism (Giroux, 2005). Once the oppositional mobilization has been mapped, the impact of neoliberalism on the higher education sector in the United Kingdom is unpicked, using historical 'moments' to frame the discussion. Ending with the recent white paper, *Higher Education: Students at the Heart of the System* (Department for Business, Innovation and Skills [BIS], 2011), the current 'moment' of capitalist order dominant in the 'locality' of the higher education system is presented.

Chapter 3 illuminates the impact that neoliberalism has had on the core functions of universities and the academic community. It maps out how the theory of 'academic capitalism' (Slaughter and Rhoades, 2004)—based on the analysis of the changing relations between higher education institutions and society—best describes how universities have actively positioned themselves *in* the new economy and are driving corporate dispositions. The resultant 'academic revolution' (Etzkowitz et al., 1998) in higher education has led to a commodification of teaching and research activities; in essence, a shift towards corporate principles of efficiency, accountability, and profit maximization, and away from social responsibility. Further, we draw upon Max Weber's notion of 'iron cage' and George Ritzer's updating of this view to the ubiquitous 'Golden Arches' to frame the bureaucratic and commercially rationalized efficiencies—termed McDonaldization—that has crept out of the fast-food franchise and into all aspects of life, including the public university. In doing so, we will frame how McDonaldization—a metaphor that speaks to a set of principles of profit-driven instrumental rationality—has contributed to a particular understanding and way of doing 'science' within [Mc]universities. Although knowledge has been instrumentalized and academics' work hyper-professionalized (Dimitriadis, 2006; Slaughter and Rhoades, 2004), this context does afford possibilities of new networks for socially productive purposes and a diversification of higher education knowledges (David, 2007; Kincheloe and Steinberg, 2006; Slaughter and Rhoades, 2004). Thus, the corporatization of the higher education system can be seen to be an *opportunity* for scholars to mobilize a critical pedagogy to empower the powerless and to transform social inequalities and injustices within the context of neoliberal influences (Barnett, 2000a; McLaren, 2003).

Building on the previous chapters that illuminated the influence of neoliberal ideology on higher education policy in tandem with the impact that this has had on scholarly activity, Chapter 4 situates the 'theme field' of sports coaching research within the wider context of the critical academy study of sport. As sport policy occupies a contested space with the same ideological influences as those located in higher education, this chapter maps the impact this has had on sports policy, and then situates this within a global context. The importance that is placed on sport by nation states and global associations *must* be mapped out to fully appreciate the conjunctural history of the sports coaching present. Then, locating this within higher education, academia, and sport, the rise of sports coaching as an academic endeavor, the current sports coaching landscape, and the *influence* of sports coaching research is mapped. As a result, there is a need to overcome the invisible networks of prestige afforded to the 'elders' or 'gatekeepers' of sports coaching knowledge that prevail over a one-dimensional, evidence-based portrait of sports coaching, and evolve the field in order to gain a fuller understanding of its complexity and contribute to wider social issues. In doing so, the evolution of sports coaching knowledge becomes "attuned to dynamic relationships connecting individuals, their contexts, and their activities instead of focusing on these separate entities in isolation from one another" (Kincheloe, 2001, p.689).

Chapter 5 provides a brief genealogy of cultural studies and its widespread and often superficial appropriation by sport-focused scholars. Cultural studies of sport can be considered a critical and contextually-driven intellectual project prefigured on furthering the understanding of the politics of contemporary sport culture. At the definitional core is the intellectual practice and praxis of 'radical contextualism' (Grossberg, 2010), and within this chapter, we unpick what this means by drawing on the work of Stuart Hall. Following this, we map the marked physical culturalization of the sociology of sport and the move towards a *physical* cultural studies (PCS); a position that has encouraged some critical scholars to question the value of the term sport, as a descriptor of their intellectual focus and practice. We identify the three main characteristics of PCS scholarship; the ontological complexity and interrelatedness of physical culture, radical contextualism, and, the assumption that societies are fundamentally divided along hierarchically ordered lines of differentiation (i.e. those based on class, ethnic, gender, ability, generational, national, racial, and/or sexual norms), as realized through the operations of power and power relations within the social formation. PCS therefore is motivated by a commitment to social change and to produce the type of knowledge through which it would be in a position to intervene into the broader social world, and *make a difference.*

PCS—albeit a relatively embryonic and constantly morphing project—has largely overlooked sports coaching as a site of inquiry; something this book seeks to address. Chapter 6 delineates an 'inconvenient truth': in order to challenge the epistemological hierarchy that privileges positivist, quantitative, predictive ways of knowing (Andrews, 2008), the 'field' of sports coaching fundamentally needs to embrace a fresh *modus operandi.* After critiquing the evangelical status afforded to evidence-based research (EBR), we develop a line of thinking that embraces a physical cultural studies (PCS) sensibility to frame the ontological, epistemological, and axiological praxis underpinning the reconceptualized 'field' of sports coaching research. In doing so, the commitment of PCS to progressive social change locates the reconceptualized 'field' as a 'performative pedagogy' (Giroux, 2001) with an underlying intent based on a 'moral ethic' (Denzin and Lincoln, 2005a). The chapter also considers how best to focus and magnify events of inquiry, and discusses the expansive and flexible methodological toolbox available to practitioners in the reconceptualized 'field'. The concept of the researcher-as-methodological bricoleur (Denzin and Lincoln, 2005b) is deployed, and we explicate that the ontological, epistemological, and methodological advances *must* be accompanied by similar advances in expression and (re)presentation (Amis and Silk, 2008). In this reconceptualized 'field', building upon the work of sports coaching scholars such as Jones (2009; 2007; 2006), we explore new territories of expression, arguing that the reconceptualized 'field' considers democratizing writing practices and moves beyond persuasive fictions (Sparkes, 1995) or 'classic' forms of representations in the production of more self-conscious texts.

While a conclusion is offered in Chapter 7, we are at pains to point out that our conclusion, rather ironically, does not signifying any form of end point. Rather, it marks the beginning of a project concerned with the progressive potential of a 'field in tension' (Silk and Andrews, 2011). In this coda, we return to the impreciseness, limiting, and somewhat misleading terms 'sport' and 'coaching'. In so doing, and through holding together the potentialities of sports coaching as it articulates and contests a physical cultural studies sensibility, we tentatively propose a new nomenclature for the 'field' of sports coaching. We call for practitioners working in the reconceptualized 'field'—the *bricoleurs*—to challenge the corporate dispositions that are driving academics' work, to become 'border intellectuals' (Giroux, 1995), and use the monikers of multidisciplinarity, interdisciplinarity, and intellectual integration to guide their scholarly activity. Of course, we fully recognize the limits of such a clarion call—not least the disciplinary demarcations of Departments, of research excellence panels (such as the REF in the UK), of tenure/promotion committees, of graduate programs, of journals and of scholarly 'elders'. Yet, in 'doing coaching justice', academics need to escape from their ascribed label and dispositions of neo-liberal subjects, and instead of focusing on survival as being an *individual* responsibility—survival (of the field, of meaningful, productive and impactful knowledge, of a legitimate field) in the current 'moment' should be viewed in terms of *social* responsibility (Dimitriadis, 2006).

2 Towards a Corporate Culture in Higher Education

> Neoliberalism is in the first instance a theory of political economic practices that proposes that human well-being can best be advanced by liberating individual entrepreneurial freedoms and skills within an institutional framework characterised by strong private property rights, free markets, and free trade. The role of the state is to *create* and *preserve* an institutional framework appropriate to such practices. (Harvey, 2005, p.2, emphasis added)

INTRODUCTION

Giroux (2004a) suggests that we are living in dangerous times in which a new type of society is emerging unlike anything we have seen in the past. These dangerous times are shaped by the evolution of the liberal capitalist order that, in turn, frames the subjective and material experience of our current moment. This 'moment'—referred to as the 'proto-fascist present' (Giroux, 2005a) or the 'pernicious present' (Silk and Andrews, 2011)—is symbolized by a society in which symbolic capital and political power reinforce each other through a public pedagogy produced by a concentrated media, which has become a cheerleading section for dominant elites and corporate ruling interests (Giroux, 2004a). The consequence of this is a society which is "increasingly marked by a poverty of critical public discourse, thus making it more difficult for young people and adults to appropriate a critical language outside of the market that would allow them to translate private problems into public concerns or to relate public issues to private considerations. This is also a social order that seems incapable of questioning itself, just as it wages war against the poor, youth, women, people of colour, and the elderly" (Giroux, 2004a, pp.206–207).

This chapter aims to frame the climate/context in society and higher education. In order to locate the current social and economic context, this chapter will be divided into three sections. The first section will trace the emergence and ascendancy of neoliberalism in which the market is seen as delivering prosperity and social justice with the wider framework of economic globalization. Section two will deploy the work of Lauder et al. (2006) to challenge the assumption that prosperity, democracy and social justice can be delivered by a market economy. Section three will chart the development of the dominant discourse(s) surrounding the evolution of the liberal capitalist order prevalent in higher education in the United

Kingdom. This genealogy will specifically look at the period of time from the Black Paper produced by Cox and Dyson in 1969 for the Conservative government led by Edward Heath[1]—aimed at dealing with the problem of universities and falling standards—through the developments proposed by 'New' Labour in their third term in office under the premiership of Gordon Brown, to the recent White Paper, *Higher Education: Students at the Heart of the System* (Department for Business, Innovation and Skills [BIS], 2011) that places students as consumers at the heart of the system. It will illuminate the key players, policy initiatives, and ideological assumptions that have contributed to the development of the 'corporate culture' (Giroux, 1999) in higher education over that period of time.

THE RISE OF NEOLIBERALISM

Before proceeding it is important to emphasize that although neoliberalism promulgates the unitary logic of the market as a universal cure it is in fact variegated in character with its ideology and implementation in policy have quite different forms in different countries. Undoubtedly, the powerful family resemblances necessitate conceptualizations that "must be attentive to *both* the local peculiarities *and* the generic features of neoliberalism" (Peck and Tickell, 2002, p.388).

The dismantling of the Berlin Wall in 1989 was the dramatic moment that assigned communism to the archives of world history and offered vindication that a market economy was the only way to deliver prosperity, democracy and social justice (Brown and Lauder, 2001). It is events dating back ten years prior to this moment that future historians may well view as the crossroads in the world's social and economic history (Harvey, 2005). Harvey (2005) cites Deng Xiaoping's steps towards the liberalization of the communist-ruled economy in China in 1978, Paul Volcker taking command at the U.S. Federal reserve in 1979, Margaret Thatcher being elected Prime Minister of Britain in 1979, and Ronald Reagan being elected as President of the U.S. in 1980 as the epicenters from which "revolutionary impulses seemingly spread and reverberated to remake the world around us in a totally different image" (p.1). It was the late 1970s that saw the shift[2] as neoliberalism moved from the philosophical project and abstract intellectualism of Hayek[3] (1933; 1941; 1944; 1948; 1952; 1960; 1973; 1976; 1979, 1988) and Friedman[4] (1948; 1953; 1956; 1959; 1963; 1982) to the state-authored restructuring projects of Thatcher and Reagan.

Hall (1983, p.19)[5] explains that although Margaret Thatcher gave the swing to the right "a powerful impetus and a distinctive personal stamp." However, when properly analyzed the deeper movement has a much longer trajectory. Hall (1983) writes that economic decline in Britain dates back at least a century, yet this was not inevitable. It is worth noting the post-war context that was the precursor to Thatcherism:

The 1945 Labour Government, under the impact of war and the radicalisation of the working class, carried through a series of major structural changes including nationalisation, the welfare state and full employment. At the same time, it sought to restore Britain's international position in the context of the new post-war situation. This involved the maintenance of the Empire and its legacy together with a major international military and financial role for Britain. The key here was the relationship with the United States, which, given the weaknesses of other western powers and the onset of the cold war, was seeking a special relationship with Britain. (Jacques, 1983, p.40)

The fifties[6] saw a period of rapid economic growth, rising living standards, full employment, and relative social stability. However by the late fifties this picture of social harmony was being undermined by the first cracks in the Cold War, the rapid growth of Britain's competitors, a reduction in traditional imperial markets, and a growing concern about the economy. It is important to emphasize that as welfare state provision increased for workers and families, so there was a squeeze on profitability. This was a fundamental problem for both Britain and the United States (Brenner and Theodore, 2002a). Hence, if capitalism was to overcome this Keynesian form of social democracy, there was a need for a strategic political response to the "declining profitability of traditional mass-production industries and the crisis of Keynesian welfare policies" (Brenner and Theodore, 2002a, p.350).

Successive changes in government[7] prior to Margaret Thatcher being elected Prime Minister of Britain in 1979, served only to emphasize that "the new dawn of the fifties had only been a temporary interregnum" (Jacques, 1983, p.41). The 'modernist' approach of Wilson's labour government, the 'laissez-faire' conceptions of economic and industrial policy[8] of Heath's conservative government, and the 'working class quiescence' of the returning labour government in 1974 did nothing to halt the relative decline of Britain. In describing the 'decay' of British society, the adverse economic environment, and the transition to the Thatcher government, Bleaney (1983) maps the emergence of a new direction in economic management:

Public services were cut back to make room for tax cuts, but private incomes were controlled (or at least meant to be) by an endless succession of incomes policies. Labour, once it became 'the natural party of government' in Harold Wilson's famous phrase, had almost inadvertently become the main bulwark of an unsatisfactory status quo. Meanwhile the Conservatives, under the leadership of Mrs. Thatcher since 1975, had developed a coherent and strident political challenge . . . they argued the whole drift of British society since around 1960 (or even before) had been for the worse, and that economic revival required radical changes which would reverse that drift. In particular, drastic reductions in the economic role of the state and the burden of taxation were necessary to liberate private enterprise. (pp.134–135)

The belief that the optimal mechanism for economic development is through the liberation of state interference in the economy—resulting in open, competitive, and unregulated markets—is the linchpin of neoliberal ideology (Brenner and Theodore, 2002a).

Although Britain through 'Thatcherism,' and the United States through 'Reaganism,' were exposed to particularly aggressive programs of neoliberal restructuring during the 1980s, the global influence (or imposition?) of a more moderate form of neoliberal ideology spread to other Anglophone countries, including Australia, Canada, and New Zealand (Brenner and Theodore, 2002a). "By the mid-1980s . . . neoliberalism had become the dominant political and ideological form of capitalist globalisation" (Brenner and Theodore, 2002a, p.350) and due to the global hegemony of this mode of political rationality it has become omnipresent, a commonsense of the times (Peck and Tickell, 2002). Neoliberalism has been referred to as a "new religion" (Peck and Tickell, 2002, p.381), a "new planetary vulgate" (Bourdieu and Wacquant, 2001, p.2) and an ideological "thought virus" (Beck, 2000, p.122). However, the rise of the Asian Tigers and now China have fundamentally changed the nature and structures of economic globalization, because in these countries the aim is emphatically to 'govern the market' to use Robert Wade's (2004) phrase rather than to be governed by it. Neo-liberal ideology may still hold sway in Britain and America in the light of the rise of China and the Great Recession but it has less purchase, elsewhere.

THE *SUCCESS* OF THE MARKET ECONOMY

Brown and Lauder (2001) suggest that the euphoria following the dismantling of the Berlin Wall in 1989 led a number of commentators to announce the 'end of history.'[9] In essence, "Western capitalism had not only assigned communism to the archives of world history, but had also offered a final vindication that a market economy was the only way to deliver prosperity, democracy and social justice" (Brown and Lauder, 2001, p.99). It could be argued that since the dismantling of the Berlin Wall, the communist crackdown in Tiananmen Square, the Iraqi invasion of Kuwait, the two Gulf wars, and the terrorist attacks on the World Trade Center, to name a few, history was in fact continuing and that Fukuyama could have been wrong. Bates (2002a) suggests that this could be the case:

> Could it be that the End of History was simply the passing of a particular phase of history—the end of the Enlightenment project of the universal rationally ordered society? Could it be the Death of Ideology was simply the end of US liberal pragmatism and the European project

of social democracy? Could it be that the coming Global Civilization is simply a western fantasy based upon an exaggerated assessment of the success of its missionary project among the natives? (p.139)

However, Fukuyama (1992, p.xii) states that what he "suggested had come to an end was not the occurrence of events, even large and grave events, but History: that is, history understood as a single, coherent, evolutionary process, when taking into account the experience of all peoples in all times." Invoking and paraphrasing Tamboukou (1999), in the context of this text, theorizing the present as an 'episode,' a result of struggle and relations of force and domination, is important when undertaking a genealogical exploration. There is a need to ensure that the *disruptions* that call in to question the linear evolution of history are explored. Despite the 'euphoria' surrounding the end of *History*, Lauder et al. (2006) illuminate three fundamental problems–or *disruptions*–confronting individuals and societies that place a challenge to the assumption that a market economy delivers prosperity, democracy and social justice, namely: the control of technological and economic forces that threaten global environmental catastrophe, the paradox of prosperity, and the opportunity trap. The importance of highlighting these challenges to the dominant view of the *success* of the global market economy is that the rhetoric of national prosperity, justice, and social cohesion—now taken as a matter of common sense—has direct consequences on the roles and functions ascribed to (higher) education. Thus, by elucidating the challenge to the *success*, it affords the possibility to challenge "the education gospel" (Grubb and Lazerson, 2006).

DISRUPTIONS TO THE MARKET ECONOMY

In considering "the control of technological and economic forces that threaten global catastrophe," Lauder et al. (2006) cite powerful factors such as potential nuclear holocaust,[10] sustainability of the planet and advances in genetics as indicators of our inability to control the forces we have unleashed. This loss of control is attributed to an imbalance between the historically counteracted forces driving the transformation of *Homo sapiens* from Neolithic to nuclear humanity, and the counter forces associated with ensuring stability in human social environments (Hobsbawm, 2005).[11] This imbalance, resulting from the globalization of the free market, produces a "condition of polarization and maldistributions, of privilege and exclusion which is unstable and unsustainable economically, ecologically, socially and politically" (Bates, 2002a, p.141). Importantly, Hobsbawm (2005, p.4) intimates that the imbalance or disequilibrium has been tilted so far in one direction that it "is almost certainly beyond the ability of human social and political institutions to control."

The challenge of environmental sustainability is one where it seems Hobsbawm may be right. Especially since there is a high degree of inequality in that it is the West and latterly China who use the majority of ecological resources. As Bates (2002a, p.140) suggests, the consequences of the policies from a global market economy have resulted in a 20:80 world in which "the wealthiest 20 percent of nations control 80 percent of the wealth and the poorest 80 percent make do with 20 percent of the wealth." This disequilibrium in a global 20:80 world is further illuminated when consideration is given to the emerging ecological 'catastrophe':

THE PARADOX OF PROSPERITY

According to Lauder et al. (2006) the second problem challenging the assumption that a market economy delivers prosperity, democracy, and social justice is 'the paradox of prosperity':

> This paradox refers to the growing inequalities both within and between nations at a time when the global economy is wealthier than it has ever been. During the twentieth century the gross domestic product (GDP) of Britain increased more than sevenfold but income inequalities within Britain are as wide today as they were in the late nineteenth century (Halsey and Webb, 2000). The gap has also widened between rich and poor nations. Landes (1999) suggests that the gap between Switzerland and Mozambique is roughly 400 to 1, whereas the gap between the richest and poorest 250 years ago was around 5 to 1. (p.4)

Indeed, Chossudovsky (1996) suggests that the policies driven by capitalism have led to the burden of two trillion dollars of external debt in the developing world, effectively globalizing poverty and destabilizing entire countries resulting in the outbreak of social discord, ethnic conflicts, and civil war. At this time when the global economy is wealthier than it has ever been, the exponential rise in the gap between the richest and poorest nations can be accurately measured by monitoring the status of children in relation to time-sensitive benchmarks such as the Millennium Development Goals (UNICEF, 2007). The Millennium Development Goals evolved out of the largest gathering of world leaders in human history in September 2000. The convened leaders set down the Millennium Declaration which represented the collective priorities for peace and security, human rights, the environment and poverty reduction. The Millennium Development Goals are the blueprint of how the world would achieve measurable improvements in these most critical areas of human development. The stark reality of 'the paradox of prosperity' is emphasized by the following quotation:

> If the entire population of Seoul (Republic of Korea) died within one year, shock waves would reverberate throughout the world. Yet, the more than 10 million deaths each year of children under age five barely evokes a tremor . . . Nearly 4 million infants do not survive their first month of

life. Half a million women die in pregnancy each year . . . more than 1 billion people do not have access to potable water. 2.3 million children are infected with HIV, millions more are affected due to parental illness, and 15 million have been orphaned. (UNICEF, 2007, p.4)

THE OPPORTUNITY TRAP

The third problem that confronts individuals and societies is 'the opportunity trap' (Lauder et al., 2006), and can be found to be inter-linked with 'the paradox of prosperity.' This inexorable link between 'opportunity' and 'prosperity' is highlighted by Brown (2006) who states that "the opportunity to make a better life is enshrined in democratic societies. It is one of the few constants in a maelstrom of technological, economic, and social change" (p.381). In democratic societies, education sits at center stage of social and policy agendas, with the growing importance attached to grades and credentials indicating a tightening bond between education, jobs, and rewards (Brown, 2006). The logic behind the linking of education, jobs, and rewards is emphasized by the Department of Work and Pensions (2007):

> Work is the best route out of poverty for most parents and their children. This is not only because children in families where parents are in work are much less likely to be poor in income terms, although this is of course the case. It is also because it is paid employment that offers the most sustainable route out of poverty for the longer term; because work is good for the physical and psychological health of parents and hence their children; and because children who grow up in workless households are themselves much more likely to be poor in adulthood. (p.3)

The rise of mass higher education, the drive for lifelong learning, the emphasis on individualization, and the policy focus on the knowledge driven economy are part of the official mantra believed to deliver opportunity, prosperity, and justice. Brown (2006) challenges this account of education due to the *opportunity gap* widening between the rich and the poor in countries such as the United States, Britain, and Australia.

Not only is the 'opportunity trap' an issue in the western, industrialized nations but is also evident on a wider world level in the economically poorer countries of the 'third' world. In the western, industrialized nations "there are too many contestants chasing credentials, jobs, and rewards that only a few can attain" (Brown, 2006, p.381) and in the poorer countries unemployment is substantially higher and much of the employment is low-paid and "does not meet the requirement of adequacy to ensure that people can access what is required to live life with dignity" (Reynolds, 2005, p.12). This is reinforced by Chakraborty and Lahiri (2007) who state that there is an observable 33-fold income difference between the richest and poorest countries in the world. In the context of the global economy being wealthier than it has ever been, prosperity, democracy, and social justice is a distant, unobtainable fantasy for a significant proportion of the population in economically poorer countries. In addition to this and essentially framing the 'opportunity trap' Reynolds (2005) is skeptical about the possibility of change:

> The world's population is rising at the rate of a quarter of a million every day and is set to continue rising at this rate at least until 2040. If the numbers of unemployed are not to rise in that period the *net gain* in jobs would have to be 1,750,000 a week for every week of every year for the next thirty five years (p.12)

OPPOSITIONAL MOBILIZATION

In light of the documented challenges to the assumption that a market economy delivers, prosperity, democracy, and social justice—what Giroux (2005b) would describe as the 'corporate capitalist fairy-tale' of neoliberalism—it is not surprising to find a wide range of anticapitalist movements that have emerged over that last decade:

> From the Zapatista rebellion in Chiapas, the subsequent series of Gatherings for Humanity and Against Neoliberalism, and the December 1995 mass strikes in France to the mass protests against the WTO, the IMF, the World Bank, and the World Economic Forum in locations such as Davos, Genoa, London, Melbourne, Mumbai, Nice, Prague, Seattle, Sydney, Washington DC, and Zurich, among many others. As such struggles continue to proliferate in the new millennium, anticapitalist forces throughout the world have come to identify neoliberalism as a major target for oppositional mobilization. (Brenner and Theodore, 2002a, p. 352)

There seems to be an important disjuncture between the ideology of neoliberalism and its everyday political operations and societal effects (Moody, 1997). Brenner and Theodore (2002a) explain how the aspiration of neoliberalism to create a 'utopia' of free markets liberated from state interference, has in reality instigated a rise in coercive, disciplinary forms of state intervention in order to impose market rule on all aspects of social life. In addition to this, instead of neoliberal ideology facilitating a self-regulatory market with optimal allocation of investment and resources, the reality is that the "neoliberal shift in government policies has tended to subject the majority of the population to the power of market forces whilst preserving social protection for the strong" (Gill, 1995, p. 407). The unrelenting pace of globalization and the entrenched political hegemony of a neoliberal ideology (Macleod, 2002) have unquestionably led to more pronounced social difference and an increased polarization of society; this is the context in which higher education institutions are operating.

THE CHANGING ROLE OF THE STATE IN EDUCATION: THE DEVELOPMENT OF A CORPORATE CULTURE IN HIGHER EDUCATION

Invoking Evans (2005), "the British Labour government has *adopted* a policy agenda, which in most crucial aspects reflects the continuing transformation of the British state into a competition state" (p.69, emphasis added). In using the term 'adopted,' Evans is inferring that the Labour government reinforced the neoliberal marketizing trends of the Thatcher (and later John Major) period. To appreciate how the competition state—which can be seen as a form of the neo-liberal state—underwrites current development in Higher Education it is necessary to outline the changing role of the state during the preceding conservative government in relation to education in the higher education (HE) sector.

'CONSERVATIVE MODERNIZATION' AND THE 'RIGHT APPROACH' TO EDUCATION

In 1969 Cox and Dyson produced a Black Paper to deal with the problem of universities and falling standards, although the remit was expanded to primary and secondary schools. This corresponded with Edward Heath being returned as Conservative Prime Minister with Margaret Thatcher as Secretary of State for Education. The Black Paper provided right wing ammunition ('Black Paper ideology') to the Conservative party and in 1970 this ammunition was fueled by the Council for Preservation of Educational Standards (CPES, later re-named the National Council for Educational Standards). Lawton (1992) sees this as the start of right wing influence on policy formulation and the answer to left-wing progressivism, with the concepts of choice and preservation of traditional standards being core themes:

> But others were wanting much more radical policies, namely to move the discussion away from the state system to the desirability of choice outside state schools, for example, by means of vouchers. These two ideas—traditional standards and parental choice—were not unconnected: There was the assumption (partly but not entirely correct) that traditional standards were most likely to be found in independent schools. (p.36)

The appointment of a right-wing junior Education minister in 1973 (Norman St. John Stevas), the establishment of the 'Think Tank' (Centre for Policy Studies, CPS) founded by Sir Keith Joseph in 1974, and the appointment of Margaret Thatcher to Conservative Party leader in opposition in 1975 all contributed to the growing momentum towards right-wing, neoliberal educational policies. During the Conservative opposition period a paper titled 'The Right Approach' was published indicating the desire to implement vouchers in the form of an Assisted Places Scheme that subsidized places in independent schools, and the publication of school examination reports in the form of league tables.

In 1979 Margaret Thatcher was elected Prime Minister and shortly after, Sir Keith Joseph was appointed Secretary of State. The momentum of right-wing policy influence was now irresistible in the field of educational policy. The policy direction was one that would bring all sectors of the education system more into line with the free market. Writing in 1976, Sir Keith Joseph wrote:

> The blind, unplanned, uncoordinated wisdom of the market . . . is overwhelmingly superior to the well-researched, rational, systematic, well meaning, cooperative, science-based, forward looking, statistically respectable plans of the government . . . The market system is the greatest generator of national wealth known to mankind: coordinating and fulfilling the diverse needs of countless individuals in a way which no human mind or minds could ever comprehend, without coercion, without direction, without bureaucratic interference. (Cited in Lawton, 1992, p.6)

Lawton (1992) argues that neo-liberal Hayekian thinking is evident in Thatcherism, and that human selfishness is not a problem as it is eventually transformed into a public good. Apple (2001, pp.38–39) analyses the important factors that lay behind the neoliberal influence on conservative modernization, these can be summarized as follows: guided by the vision of a weak state (what is private is necessarily good and what is public is necessarily bad); economic rationality (efficiency and an 'ethic' of cost-benefit analysis are the dominant norms); students' as human capital (students to be given requisite skills to compete efficiently and effectively); educational institutions waste economic resources that could be applied elsewhere (educational institutions are 'black holes' into which money is poured); 'producer capture' (educational institutions respond to the demands of teachers, administrators and other state bureaucrats, not the consumer); consumer choice (the ideal of the citizen is that of a purchaser/consumer); democracy an economic rather than a political concept (policies give a message best called 'arithmetical particularism' in which the individual as a consumer, is deraced, declassed and degendered).

In addition to neoliberal economic theories, the Thatcher educational policies also demonstrated neoconservative 'cultural rightism,' and together these demonstrated the twin New Right ideological bases of Thatcherism:

> The neo-liberals tend to talk about choice, competition and the market in education, the neo-conservatives are more likely to advocate traditional values, traditional subjects, and less educational theory in the training of teachers, but greater immersion into the traditional values of good schools. (Lawton, 1992, p.7)

The increasing influence of the New Right, with its seemingly contradictory twin ideological bases were woven cleverly into Conservative education policy, what Gamble (1988) refers to as "the free economy and the strong state" (p.115). Indeed, Apple (2001) captures this by articulating that:

> Unlike the neo-liberal emphasis on the weak state, neo-conservatives are usually guided by a vision of a strong state. This is especially true surrounding issues of knowledge, values and the body. Whereas neoliberalism may be seen as being based in what Raymond Williams would call an 'emergent' ideological assemblage, neoconservatism is grounded in 'residual' forms. It is largely, though not totally based in a romantic appraisal of the past. (p.47)

Lawton (1992) infers that Thatcher managed to reduce the scope of government but maintain its strength, thus enabling conservative policy to encompass New Right ideology. It had been ideologically presumed that in the early 1980s, that if the government 'got out of the way' then the spontaneous operation of market forces would be sufficient for economic regulation (Peck and Tickell, 2002). Relative failures in the labor market, financial markets, transport, food systems and pollution were the precursors to the need for government intervention beyond deregulation and marketization, "hence the deliberate stretching of the neoliberal policy repertoire (and its associated rhetoric) to embrace a range of extramarket forms of governance and regulation" (Peck and Tickell, 2002, p.390). The neoconservative ideology manifested itself with the emergence of strong state control of higher education but also other educational policies demonstrated this ideology through the implementation of mandatory national curricula, national testing and a repetitive call for raising standards (Apple, 2001). Apple (2005) terms these evaluative and measurement pressures introduced as a result of neoconservative ideology, an 'auditing culture,' which ensured the *strength* of government in education:

> The ultimate result of an audit culture of this kind is not the promised de-centralisation that plays such a significant role rhetorically in most neo-liberal self-understandings, but what seems to be a massive

re-centralisation and what is best seen as a process of de-democratisation. (p.15, emphasis added)

This re-centralization—or de-democratization—created the climate for the exponential rise in education policies in the 1980's and the "introduction of market forces and competition, the license given to people to pursue personal and familial profit, and a diminished emphasis on redistribution, equity and social justice" (Tomlinson, 2001, p.3). According to Fowler (1994) the United Kingdom was the leader in market-oriented education reforms in the 1980's. Fowler cites the Assisted Places Scheme (1981), quasi-private City Technology Colleges (1986), and the Education Reform Act (1988) as key examples of reforms designed to increase competition and choice.

Lawton (1992, p.56) documents some of the changes brought about by the Education Reform Act (1988), and can be summarized to demonstrate the 'New Right' influences that resulted in significant changes in the higher and further education sectors.

NEO-LIBERALISM AND HIGHER EDUCATION IN BRITAIN

The first clear step in the strong state seizing greater control over high education was in relation to funding. The University Grants Committee (UGC) consisting mainly of university professors was replaced by the Universities Funding Council (UFC), which integrated a higher number of members from industry and commerce with academics; polytechnics and larger colleges financed by the new Polytechnics and Colleges Funding Council (PCFC) which had a similar mix of academic and business experience as the newly formed UFC were removed from Local Education Authority control and became part of the national system of higher education, and; emergence of the concept of 'managerialism' and an increased dependence on the state. Higher education institutions would receive contracted funding from UFC and PCFC based on formulae that took into account the number of students and also research.

It was the concept of 'managerialism' that drew a great deal of criticism, the idea of the Secretary of State controlling the funding distributed by the UFC would inevitably lead to the reward of institutional entrepreneurship by an administration that encouraged market forces. Maclure (1989) commented on the magnitude of the change in the management of British higher education:

> The foundations have shifted. The idea of universities as independent centres of learning and research, capable of standing out against government and society, and offering critical judgements of varying objectivity, informed by learning and protected by the autonomy of historic

institutions, is discarded. Instead universities are to be made servants of the State and its priorities. (Cited in Lawton, 1992, p.57)

In November 1990, Margaret Thatcher resigned from her position as leader of the Conservative Party and was replaced by John Major. John Major was elected Prime Minister and launched a White Paper, *Higher Education: A New Framework* (Department for Education and Science [DES], 1991) and proposed the abolition of the binary line. The binary policy sought to safeguard the universities' privileged scholarly activities in the face of growing demands of increasing numbers in higher education:

> The polytechnics and other public service institutions should leave to the universities the essential function of pursuing and transmitting specialist knowledge through research and scholarship and that, drawing on this knowledge should concentrate on the no less difficult and important task of meeting this wider demand from potential learners from 18–30. (Sir Toby Weaver, 1982, cited in Silver 1990, p.69)

The Polytechnics main function was teaching and any research undertaken would be to fulfill one of the following two functions: research for industry, and; research to improve teaching. The argument for the removal of the binary line is also a reflection of the New Right ideologies shaping higher education policies. The removal of the binary line was not designed to improve the self-esteem of non-university higher education institutions or to make improvements to the quality of higher education. According to Lawton (1992, pp.74–75), it was justified in terms of competition: "institutions were expected to expand by competing for funds and students, and it was therefore desirable that this competition should not be artificially constrained by the binary distinction." In 1992 the binary line was abolished and over forty institutions were designated universities (McNay, 1999) leading to the appointment of a review chaired by Ron Dearing to investigate the nature, purpose and funding of universities as well as the issues of teaching and research. The Dearing Report (*Higher Education in the Learning Society*) was published in 1997, now under a New Labour Government with Tony Blair as Prime Minister and David Blunkett as Secretary of State for Education with the following recommendations: raising the participation rate to 45% of young people; more sub-degree courses provided in FE colleges; substantial increase in public spending on higher education, and; graduates in work to contribute 25% of their tuition costs. New Labour had embraced the Dearing Report, except his recommendations on fees and student support, whilst simultaneously completing the Conservative project of turning all student grants in to loans. According to Watson (2006, p.2) "New Labour was too greedy," and it was this precipitate decision that has become the 'Achilles heel' of subsequent New Labour policy for higher education.

In July 1998 the government passed the Teaching and Higher Education Act which clearly established who was going to pay for the expanded access. Expansion to the student loans and abolition of maintenance grants coupled with the introduction of up-front tuition fees signaled that students were to become increasingly responsible for investing in their own education. Funding of higher education has always been a crucial issue, the Department for Education and Skills (DfES) state that there had been a 36% reduction in student funding between 1989 and 1997 (DfES, 2003). Coupled with the reduction in student funding, the DfES (2003) estimate that the backlog accumulated in teaching and research facilities during the rapid expansion of higher education in the 1990s to be at around £8 billion pounds.

THE 'THIRD WAY' AND THE 'NEW MODERNIZERS'

Tomlinson (2001) alludes to the continuities and similarities in post-16 and higher education policies (and in educational policies across the whole spectrum) marking the transition in 1997 between Conservative and New Labour governments. The ideology guiding both governments was, according to Giddins (1998), an investment in human capital wherever possible:

> Governments of varying political persuasions around the world rediscovered human capital theory, a theory which is suggested that improving people's skills and capabilities makes them act in more productive ways, and assumed that investment in education will improve the quality of the workforce, which will in turn improve economic growth and productivity. (Tomlinson, 2001, p.4)

Bottery (2000) sees the New Labour educational policies as a clear example of a nation state treating its educational system as a tool for national and economic development driven by global influences:

> Learning is the key to prosperity—for each of us as individuals, as well as for the nation as a whole. Investment in human capital will be the foundation of success in the knowledge-based global economy of the twenty-first century. This is why the government has put learning at the heart of its ambition. (Blunkett, 1998, cited in Bottery 2000, p.19)

Interestingly in the take up of the term *human capital*, not only is there a new conception of economic processes behind this politics, but a new conception of moralizing explanations "of individual and collective pathologies underpin[ning] political strategies to regulate crime, enhance individual competencies, and administer security through activating the responsibilities of communities for their own well-being" (Rose, 2000a, p.1408). This represents a reframing of society and the emergence of community as an object of government policy, and a new politics that aims to reconstruct citizens as moral subjects of responsible communities. The need to frame values in which this politics is grounded is important, Rose (2000a) argues that reference to civil society, civic activism, strong communities, rights, duties and responsibilities are recurrent themes in Blair's vision of the Third Way,[12]

New Labour policies reflect a divergence from the New Right viewpoint, referred to by some as the "Blairite 'Third Way' rhetoric" (Menz, 2005, p.50) implemented by the New Modernizers. The debate over a credible Third Way in British politics between the traditional positions of the Old Right (anti-state and pro-market) and the Old Left (pro-public ownership and state intervention and anti-market), "emerged within the context of trying to establish a more coherent future for social democratic politics" (Evans, 2005, p.73). Bottery (2000)suggests that New Right policies neglected social responsibility and resulted in an ironic expansion of the public sector, New Modernizers perceived that the market could be part of the problem rather than part of the solution:

> If the first part of the Third Way agenda meant accepting the reality of the market, the second part of this agenda meant devising policies that would bring the losers along. Thus, the phrase the 'inclusive society' came to be a popular term, even though it would not mean a return to the old redistributivist politics . . . What was required was a 'Social Investment State' to replace the old welfare state, one which subscribed to investment in human capital wherever possible, rather than the direct provision of economic maintenance. (p.33)

It is interesting to note that one of the immediate effects of the Teaching and Higher Education Act (1998) was to cause a reduction in applications, identified by the Universities and Colleges Admissions Service (UCAS), from under-represented groups applying to university: mature students; ethnic minorities, and; working class (Tomlinson, 2001). Targett (1998) reiterates the findings of UCAS, by stating in the Financial Times:

> Across the UK, applications for degree courses have fallen by 2.1% and applications for HND courses by 15.2%. With universities also suffering a drop in overseas applicants, fee reforms could halt the expansion of higher education and threaten the financial stability of some institutions. (p.12)

As New Modernizers placed more of an emphasis on an 'inclusive society' and the creation of a 'Social Investment State' in their policies in comparison to policies formulated by the New Right, one would have expected to see the pivotal White Paper[13], *The Future of Higher* Education (DfES, 2003) to

have addressed this issue. The White Paper 2003 stipulates that massifica-
tion of higher education will continue, and participation is to be increased
towards 50% of those aged 18–30 (DfES, 2003) through the development
of two-year work focused degrees -foundation degrees- developed with
employers, and increased flexibility of courses. These structural changes
were designed to encourage certain groups disadvantaged by the 1998 Act
into higher education (some ethnic minorities and mature students), and in
combination with the following economic concessions (DfES, 2003), the
New Modernizers perceived that they were creating the environment of a
'Social Investment State' allowing disadvantaged individuals to invest in
themselves and contribute to the country as a whole:

- Restoring grants from students from lower income families
- Universities to be required to draw up an Access Agreement
- Access Agreements overseen by an independent Access Regulator
  (Office for Fair Access, OFFA)
- Expansion of national AimHigher program to develop links between
  universities and schools
- Universities reimbursed for additional costs of attracting students
  from non-traditional backgrounds
- New package of grant support for part-time students
- Abolish up-front payment of tuition fees (i.e. allow students to defer
  payment until after graduation and linked to their ability to pay)

This commitment to the social aspect to higher education is reiterated in
the 'values' that the DfES (2003, p.10) stated that higher education sub-
scribes to: contribution to the economic and social well-being of the nation
is of vital importance; wide access to higher education makes for a more
enlightened and socially just society, and; equipping the workforce with
appropriate and relevant skills.

There was no mention of standards or quality in the 'value' section of
the White Paper 2003, the competing values of choice, efficiency and equity
that Silver (1990) alluded to seem to have taken on a far greater prominence
than quality. This New Modernizers drive to a 'Social Investment State'
through the proposed strategies highlighted above angered the 'new universities' because according to MacLeod (2003) they perceived that their
track record in widening access to working class and ethnic minority students had been ignored. MacLeod (2003) inferred that the government had
missed the point in considering the 'fear of rejection' as a deterrent factor in
attending a top university and that it is the 'fear of debt.' Diana Green (vice
chancellor of Sheffield Hallam University) says:

> The proposals imply that the reason these people do not apply to the
> 'top' universities is because they believe they won't be admitted. In fact
> a major disincentive to participation generally is worry about finance

and the fear of debt—which doesn't figure in the government analysis at all . . . where there has been success in attracting students from these backgrounds, they have tended to study at local universities on cheaper courses . . . On the face of it, these proposals are focused on the top universities, but by applying them across the board it creates difficulties for universities like mine, where widening participation is not an issue. (Cited in MacLeod, 2003, p.1)

The primary incentive of the Access Agreements was to ensure that the prestigious Russell Group[14] institutions and Oxbridge appeased the widening access rhetoric, and with its implementation, placed extra stresses on universities already fulfilling OFFA standards. MacLeod (2003) also cites vice-chancellors from other institutions (Coventry University and Westminster University) who argued that their widening access programs are the envy of other academic institutions but have concerns that generating bursaries to subsidize course fees could prove difficult (if not impossible) and that the increase in paperwork and administration required by OFFA will detract from investment into teaching and research.

It should be remembered that the social is subordinate to the economic (Bottery, 2000) and again demonstrates the influence of the New Modernizers in shaping the White Paper 2003. The DfES (2003) summarize the contribution that universities make to the national economy:

In 1999—2000 they [universities] generated directly and indirectly over £34.8 billion of output and over 562,000 full time equivalent jobs throughout the economy. This is equivalent to 2.7 per cent of the UK workforce in employment. For every 100 jobs within the HEIs themselves, a further 89 were generated through knock on effects throughout the economy; and for every £1 million of economic output from higher education, a further £1.5 million is generated in other sectors of the economy. (p.10)

Funding was not just an issue for students; it was also an issue for universities in a market economy. The universities had an investment backlog in teaching and research facilities of £8 billion due to decades of underinvestment. The Government argued that they wished to continue to be the major financial sponsor of universities:

Government funding will increase to around £10 billion a year by 2005—06 to support university students, teaching and research—a rise of over 6% a year in real terms. This is equivalent to around £400 a year paid by every income tax payer in England, whether or not they personally gained from a university education. We believe that state support at this level is justified by the contribution of universities to the economy and society. (DfES, 2003, p.77)

The figures presented by the DfES (2003) highlight a good rate of return for the government: £10 billion investment into higher education in return for the generation of over £34 billion of output directly and indirectly. It is interesting to note at this point that many of the governments' economic competitors (France, Germany, the Netherlands, the United States, and Japan) all invest more in higher education than the United Kingdom (1 % of GDP in comparison to 0.8% of GDP respectively), in fact Watson (2006) indicates that the public funding of higher education as a proportion of GDP remains in the bottom third of the Organization for Economic Cooperation and Development (OECD) league. This could be an indication that at the moment the United Kingdom is lagging behind their competitors, on a global scale. In reinforcing the rhetoric of global competition driving the higher education policies, the DfES (2003) states:

> Our competitors see—as we should—that the developing knowledge economy means the need for more, better trained people in the workforce. And higher education is becoming a global business. Our competitors are looking to sell higher education overseas, into the markets we have traditionally seen as ours. (p.13)

The neoconservative vision of a strong state is evident in the funding structure of higher education outlined in the White Paper 2003, although a shift towards state supervision (Scott, 1996, cited in Bauer et al., 1999) and an entrepreneurial element to universities income is also included in the White Paper 2003. This could be conceived to have been a section of the policy that reflected neoliberal ideas; namely creating conditions for universities to act like businesses, institutional leadership developed and encouraged, and high levels of accountability. The following excerpt from the White Paper 2003 was one of the most significant with its implications for students. It provides the rationale for universities to attempt to regain its freedom or autonomy to an extent, and also allows them to seek alternative funding streams.

> The Government is making an unprecedented investment in universities and will stand by them in future spending reviews. But to be really successful, universities must be free to take responsibility for their own strategic and financial future. Strong leadership and management, freed from excessive red tape, will help them not just to respond to change, but to drive it. And more financial freedom will allow them to fund their plans, and unleash their power to drive world-class research, innovative knowledge transfer, excellent teaching, high-quality, greater and more flexible provision, and fair access. (DfES, 2003, p.76)

The policy detail that is forwarded to bring about this can be summarized as follows:

Creation of a Leadership Foundation to improve leadership and management in the sector; David Vandelinde's task force to report on measures to reduce unnecessary red tape; support in building university endowments; set up of a task force to promote corporate giving—to be matched by creating a matched fund for endowment; ask new students to pay for the benefits they get from higher education; universities to have the freedom to set their own tuition fee (between £0 and £3,000) from 2006; no student or parent to pay any up-front fees as contributions to be paid back through the tax system once they are earning (Graduate Contribution Scheme), and; threshold of loan repayment to be raised from £10,000 to £15,000 a year (from 2005). (DfES, 2003, pp.76–77)

'NEW' LABOUR *MARK II*'S THIRD TERM

The success of this policy depended on the students' perception on whether or not investing in higher education will secure them a guaranteed rate of return; namely the acquisition of credentials to give them a positional advantage. Underpinning this policy was the government assumption that "graduates on average earn much more than those without degrees and are far more likely to be in employment" (DfES 2003, p.9). This policy was symbolic of the reforms of a competition state, raising a challenge to the dependency culture of the post-war settlement and attempting to change individual and group attitudes to entrepreneurship (Evans, 2005). Commenting on the adoption of competition state reforms by New Labour 'Mark II,' Watson (2006) states that:

> The government wanted a 'market' and it now has one, but not where planned. Fees are not only almost uniform, but have the significant merit of being deferred (with income-contingent payment after graduation). The serious competition will be over bursaries and other incentives, without much positive impact on widening participation. The most socially progressive institutions will feel obliged to re-cycle the greatest proportion of their additional fee income to needy students, while most of the relevant action will be about well-qualified students from clued-up families operating their own 'post-qualifications auctions.' This is the other form of PQA [post-qualifications admissions system]: "what can you offer me?" (p.5)

Watson (2006) depicts the initial stages of New Labour's third term of office as attempting to address three areas of unfinished business from the previous two terms in office: paying for HE; expansion and fairness; and purpose (what's it all for?). Reaffirming the dependence of New Labour 'Mark III' on neoliberal ideology to create and preserve an institutional framework appropriate to facilitating entrepreneurial freedoms, Ruth Kelly (in the first 'letter of direction' (January 31, 2006) from the Secretary of State to the Higher Education Funding Council for England (HEFCE)) stated:

> We expect the Council [the Higher Education Funding Council for England] to continue to use the various funding streams at its disposal to support excellence across the full range of activities which institutions undertake, whilst encouraging each institution to define and implement its distinctive mission. (Cited in Watson, 2006, p.7)

As the Dearing Report 'celebrated' its tenth anniversary, Gordon Brown replaced Tony Blair as Prime Minister in New Labour's third term of office. The chief minister of the Department for Education and Skills in the UK government was the Secretary of State for Education and Skills, this position was discontinued on June 28 2007 with the creation of the new posts of Secretary of State for Children, Schools and Families (Ed Balls) and Secretary of State for Innovation, Universities and Skills (John Denham). The Department for Innovation, Universities and Skills (DIUS) brings together functions from the former Department of Trade and Industry (DTI), including responsibilities for science and innovation, with further and higher education and skills, previously part of the Department for Education and Skills (DfES). In addition to this, the Department (DIUS) will work closely with the new Departments for Children, Schools and Families (DCSF) and Business, Enterprise and Regulatory Reform (BERR) as well as other key Departments—including Communities and Local Government (CLG) and the Department for Culture, Media and Sport (DCMS) to ensure the wider personal, community and cultural benefits of education are supported (DIUS, 2007a). The formalizing of the inexorable link between higher education and innovation again demonstrated New Labour's drive for entrepreneurship from universities. The additional emphasis on supporting the wider benefits of education to society through broadening the stakeholder influences from a range of government departments revisits the Third Way agenda, accepting the reality of the market and devising policies that would bring the *losers* along (Bottery, 2000).

In relation to the HE sector, the DIUS (2007b) indicated that they would work to: sustain and develop a world-class research base; maximize the exploitation of the research base to support innovation across all sectors of the economy, and; raise and widen participation in HE. The focus of widening participation, despite it being described by Watson (2006, p.12) as "the most troublesome item in talk about higher education; in the media, in politics and beyond," is a significant change from the diminished emphasis on redistribution, equity and social justice noted by Tomlinson (2001) in relation to the introduction of market forces in the 1980s. Three successive terms of office by New Labour still resulted in the expansion and fairness of HE being termed as 'unfinished business' (Watson, 2006).

In order to "ensure that all people with the potential and qualifications, no matter what their background, have the opportunity to participate and succeed in HE" (DIUS, 2007c), on July 5, 2007 the Prime Minister and Secretary of State for Innovation, Universities and Skills announced major changes to the system of student support in HE. These changes included increasing the number of students entitled to non-repayable maintenance grants by increasing the threshold for the entitlement of the maximum grant from £17,500 in 2006/07 to £25,000 for 2008/09, and also students from families with incomes of up to £60,000 will be entitled to a partial grant. The DIUS (2007c) intimated that a third of students from 2008/09 would receive a full grant (worth £2,825 a year) and a further third would receive a partial grant, meaning that two thirds of students would now be the recipients of some grant each year in comparison to just over a half in 2003. Firm guarantees of the amount of financial support for participation in HE would be given to all those 16 year olds who qualify for an Education Maintenance Allowance (EMA), more choice would be given to graduates over how to repay their student loans, and there would be an expansion of the Student Associate Scheme where high achieving undergraduates act as mentors for young people who might not otherwise go on to HE. In total, the government argued that 250,000 students from low, modest, and middle incomes would gain from the new proposals once fully implemented (DIUS, 2007c).

The rhetoric from the DIUS in 2007 seemed poised to continue to attempt to address questions about how to support students, representing a shift in emphasis from the debates surrounding institutional funding that were prominent in the White Paper (2003) and the subsequent Higher Education Bill (2004). Issues related to the tension between expansion and participation such as the 'dumbing-down' of HE (including entry standards, "Mickey Mouse" courses, vocationalization, grade inflation and so on)[15] (Watson, 2006), and also 'fairer' admissions processes, employer support of HE, and the role of HE and the public interest were all topics that required careful consideration in this political era.

A NEW TWIST TO THE ACADEMIC MARKET: STUDENTS AS CONSUMERS

In 2009, the Browne Review was commissioned, focusing on the effectiveness of the system in terms of widening participation and affordability to students and the taxpayer. The review reported in October 2010 and recommended the removal of the cap on tuition fees.[16] The coalition government's[17] response was to propose a cap of £9,000.[18] The Great Recession has enabled those who are committed to the marketization of public goods, such as education, to introduce policies under the guise of cost cutting public expenditure. This is particularly the case in England where a new experiment in the funding of higher education has been launched. In many ways England has been the champion of neo-liberal experiments in education. In the case of university funding we have seen a system that was 80% funded by the state being replaced largely by full cost fees for students.

The White Paper, *Higher Education: Students at the Heart of the System* (BIS, 2011) introduces a series of initiatives designed to fund higher education, while raising its teaching quality through placing students, as consumers at the heart of the system[19]. The justification for this extraordinary change in the funding of higher education is precisely in terms of the economic crisis:

> We inherited the largest budget deficit in post-war history, requiring spending cuts across government. By shifting public spending away from teaching grants and towards repayable tuition loans, we have ensured that higher education receives the funding it needs even as substantial savings are made to public expenditure. (Executive Summary, paragraph 4)

The major features of this new system are as follows:

- Higher education will be largely funded by student fees
- There will be loans to cover students' fees
- There will be market based on genuine price competition
- For profit providers will be allowed to expand within the system

It was argued in the report leading to the White Paper 2011 that:

> Students are best placed to make the judgement about what they want to get from participating in higher education. (Browne, 2010, p.29)

Hence it follows logically that when students can pay for their education they will be at the forefront of ensuring that they improve the quality of teaching and what is now called, the student experience.

It is important to stress that this is an experiment in which the consequences for both universities and students are difficult to predict. We should note that the structure of the 'market' is arcane. No markets are 'free' all are structured by rules, regulations and institutions but this market contains within its design a range of contradictory government aims including academic 'excellence,' equity with the aim of improving social mobility and cost reduction to the state. Hence there is a 'free' competition for top A-level students amongst the elite universities that can charge the maximum £9,000 but at the same time for those less prestigious universities that charge a lower fee and are more likely to attract working class students, there is also some room for competition, while the overall numbers of students that can be admitted to university is restricted.

In looking at the government's aims, then it is immediately clear that this is a market that will cement in a system that is already stratified by class. The majority of top A-level grades are gained from students from privileged backgrounds who will attend the universities who will compete for their 'custom.'

Naidoo and Jamieson (2006) argue that placing consumerism at the heart of the university system will lead to quite different experiences in the knowledge acquired, teaching and learning in different kinds of university. The key here is that the stratification that already exists by academic reputation will be bolstered by the market. Elite universities will continue to have the freedom to teach as they wish because what students are fundamentally paying for it the reputation of the credential. Below this universities of lower reputation which attract lower fees will engage in cost cutting measures like modularization, web-based learning and the dissemination of the kinds of knowledge required for routine work. In other words, when this position is placed against the White Paper's ideal of the student as consumer we see quite different possible outcomes from those trumpeted by the government.

Finally, if we return to the themes earlier in the chapter, it is worth noting that the government believes that this system will serve the national interest but markets are no respecters of national borders and there is no reason to believe that, what in effect, is a fully privatized system will serve English interests, rather than those of nations abroad or multinational organizations. If universities are to gain revenue from wherever they can, then they will serve the interests of those that fund them.

CONCLUSION

In conclusion, through illuminating the current moment in society, this chapter has mapped the key tensions associated with the assumption that a market economy delivers prosperity, democracy, and social justice. Lauder et al. (2006) three fundamental problems confronting individuals and societies were deployed–the control of technological and economic forces that threaten global catastrophe, the paradox of prosperity, and the opportunity trap–and illuminates that the 'euphoria' surrounding the end of *History* was indeed premature. Dramatic events, such as the terror attacks in New York, London, and Madrid and the repressive government actions serves to demonstrate the fragility of one of the benchmarks of Western capitalism; democracy. The existence of the 'paradox of prosperity' at both a national and global level is more evidence challenging the success of the market economy, whether it is child poverty rates, income inequalities, or the gap between the richest and poorest nations. The issue of the existence of the 'opportunity trap' and the scramble of individuals—referred to as contestants by Brown (2006)—chasing credentials, jobs, and rewards that only a few can attain further challenges the *success* of the market economy.

Our understanding of the current moment within higher education—whether it is paraphrased as our 'proto-fascist present' (Giroux, 2005a) or as the 'pernicious present' (Silk and Andrews, 2011)—can be seen to have evolved from the dominant global discourse surrounding a theory of political economic practices termed neoliberalism. It was demonstrated that neoliberalism can be viewed as a nebulous phenomenon, variegated in character, evolving over time that can be manipulated or reframed at a local level. The end result is a liberal capitalist order dominant in the 'locality' of the higher education system, with a concomitant increase in commercialization, vocationalization, privatization, marketization, and managerialism. The importance of an increased awareness in the rise in 'corporate power' (Giroux, 1999) in higher education and the adoption of the market economy with the trappings of capitalism (maximizing profits and minimizing costs) place an emphasis on a strong civic society to act as a countervailing power to hold the corporate power in check:

> This is not to suggest that capitalism is the enemy of democracy, but in the absence of a strong civil society and the imperatives of a strong democratic public sphere, the power of corporate culture when left on its own appears to respect few boundaries based on self-restraint and those non-commodified, broader human values that are central to a democratic civic culture. John Dewey was right in arguing that democracy requires work, but that work is not synonymous with democracy. (Giroux, 1999, p.14)

In the following chapter, we will illuminate the impact that neoliberalism has had on the core functions of universities and the academic community. It will also consider whether the role education has to play is in producing a strong civil society and be treated as a public good—what Giroux (1999) would describe as developing a 'vibrant democratic culture'—as opposed to a site for commercial enterprise.

3   What is the Role of Academia within the 'McUniversity'?

> According to many social theorists, the latter years of the second Millennium saw changes which have resulted in a tendency towards more individualized risk-taking. Labour markets have changed rapidly, making the 'job for life' a thing of the past; global communications have problematized pre-existing notions of time, place, and community; goods and services have become increasingly commodified, and consumption has increasingly replaced production as a prime concern. Taken all in all, increasingly abstract and globalized systems and institutions have left individuals isolated from relatively fixed local communities and structures, and have imposed upon them increasing demands to make continual lifestyle choices. (Stables, 2003, p. 11)

INTRODUCTION

The early twenty-first century has seen global social and economic change that has prompted re-conceptualization of our understandings of higher education in relation to the economy, society, labor markets and knowledge (see Ball, 2012; Barnett, 2000a; Burgan, 2006; Cannella, 2011; Delanty, 1998; Delanty, 2001; Frank and Gabler, 2006; Giroux, 2010; Lauder et al., 2006; Lincoln, 2011; Sagaria, 2007; Shavit et al., 2007; Slaughter and Rhoades, 2004). Framed with the logics of neoliberalism, a new 'governmentality' (Olssen and Peters, 2005) and 'audit culture' (Frith, 2001) that regulates higher education has impacted on the core functions of universities and the academic community. This chapter addresses these challenges. In addition, we draw upon Max Weber's notion of the 'iron cage' and George Ritzer's application of Weber to the ubiquitous 'Golden Arches.' Ritzer argues that bureaucratic and commercially rationalized efficiencies—termed McDonaldization—has crept out of the fast-food franchise and into all aspects of life, including the public university. In doing so, we will frame how McDonaldization—a metaphor that speaks to a set of principles of profit-driven instrumental rationality—has contributed to a particular understanding and way of doing 'science' within [Mc]universities.

TOWARDS ACADEMIC CAPITALISM IN THE NEW ECONOMY

Slaughter and Rhoades (2004) developed the theory of 'academic capitalism' to explain the process of university integration into the new economy.[1] It should be emphasized that university integration into the new economy is not merely a response to the wider world (Barnett, 2000a), or the result of academia being 'duped' (Dimitriadis, 2006). Universities have actively positioned themselves *in* the new economy and are driving the corporate dispositions that have resulted in the evolution of the 'entrepreneurial university' (Clark, 1998). The theory of academic capitalism is based on the analysis of the changing relations between higher education institutions and society in the 'new' global knowledge society:[2]

> The theory of academic capitalism moves beyond thinking of the student as consumer to considering the institution as marketer. When students choose colleges, institutions advertise education as a service and a life style. Colleges and universities compete vigorously to market their institutions to high-ability students able to consume high debt loads. Student consumers choose universities that they calculate are likely to bring a return on educational investment and increasingly choose majors linked to the *new economy*, such as business, communications, media arts . . . When students graduate, colleges and universities present them to employers as output/product, a contribution to the *new economy*, and simultaneously define students as alumni and potential donors. (Slaughter and Rhoades, 2004, pp.2–3, emphasis added)

In addition to the *new economy*—what Said (1983) referred to as the 'free' market forces—Dimitriadis (2006) also alludes to the inextricably linked influence of the multinational corporations:

> Universities are actively marketing sponsored products (e.g. negotiating exclusive licensing rights for Pepsi, McDonalds, or Apple computers etc.) to their captive students while aggressively capitalising on the intellectual work of their faculties (e.g. securing patents and copyrights from ongoing faculty research, etc.). (p.369)[3]

Slaughter and Rhoades (2004) emphasize how higher education institutions in the United States have embraced this new economy; "In the new economy, knowledge is a critical raw material to be mined and extracted from any unprotected site; patented, copyrighted, trademarked, or held as a trade secret; then sold in the marketplace for a profit" (p.4).

Certain 'for-profit' higher education corporations (such as the University of Phoenix) would use all the mechanisms outlined in order to protect its intellectual property. Slaughter and Rhoades (2004) cite the example of the Billionaire John Sperling who made his money through the University of Phoenix to demonstrate the trade in services characteristic of the new economy:

> University of Phoenix, Inc., became a subsidiary of a larger enterprise run by Sperling, the Apollo Group, which included the Institute for Professional Development, The College for Financial Planning Institutes

Corporation, and Western International University, Inc. (Apollo Group, 2002, cited in Slaughter and Rhoades, 2004, p. 3)

Sperling and Tucker (1997) emphasize that public and nonprofit private universities receive around 60% of their operating expenses from public subsidy. In addition to this, Sperling and Tucker are critical of public and nonprofit universities, stating that they have "capital-intensive input standards and operationally inefficient structures" (1997, p.52). Slaughter and Rhoades (2004) do however point out that 'for-profit' institutions are indirect recipients of substantial federal subsidy through the students participating in government sponsored financial aid programs that have evolved as a result of the government shifting resources from public welfare functions to production functions.

Presenting the higher education system in the United States as being divided between for profit and public universities is too simplistic. Further blurring of the distinction between 'for-profit' and 'non-profit' (public) institutions comes as a result of the nonprofit institutions of higher education using many of the same mechanisms as those demonstrated by their profit oriented competitors:

> . . . extended managerial capacity, part-time faculty, copyright, and information technology—to create profit centers. These profit centers do not accrue revenue for stockholders, but they do generate (non-taxed) external monies that are used to cross-subsidise other institutional activities, which often involve investment in infrastructure to integrate colleges and universities with the new economy. Like [the University of] Phoenix, public and nonprofit private higher education institutions rely heavily on public funding, expending taxpayer dollars in pursuit of external revenues from corporations. (Slaughter and Rhoades, 2004, p.4)

Although Slaughter and Rhoades (2004) were writing about the United States, the same increasing engagement in market and market-like activities are now evidenced in university life worldwide, England and contemporary Australia being two of the most notable examples (Dimitriadis, 2006; Kennedy-Wallace, 2000). In British universities the underlying problem is underinvestment, with successive governments demanding that universities teach more students without appropriate resourcing. In essence, this has resulted in a reduction in funding of 50 percent (Frith, 2001).[4] Indeed, Frith (2001) cites that in his department, which offers film and media studies, the Scottish Higher Education Funding Council (SHFCE) formula means that they make a financial loss on each student taken. This inevitably puts pressure on universities to undertake short-term policy-making decisions,[5] resulting in crisis management, an audit culture, and the need to secure funds by different means.[6] The theory of academic capitalism therefore positions educational institutions as places that are "less concerned with developing citizens who can thoughtfully deliberate the 'common good' in the public sphere than with producing workers ready to take their attendant positions in the economic system" (Dimitriadis, 2006, p.370).

IMPACT OF THE NEW ECONOMY ON ACADEMICS

Edward Said developed the idea of 'Orientalism,' a theory of the relationship of colonial knowledge to imperial power. Said transformed the humanities, "in that it pointed to a new way of understanding colonialism and the historical construction of the Orient as an object of western gaze, variously represented as alien, barbaric, uncivilized, sensual, or exotic" (Rizvi and Lingard, 2006, p.295). The importance of Said's contribution to post-colonialism as a theoretical perspective needs to be acknowledged. However, in contrast to the popularity of post-modernism he argued that:

> Whereas post-modernism in one of its programmatic statements (by Jean-Francois Lyotard) stresses the disappearance of the grand narratives of emancipation and enlightenment, the emphasis behind much of the work done by postcolonial artists and scholars is exactly the opposite: the grand narratives remain, even though their implementation and realization are at present in abeyance, deferred or circumvented. (Said, 2003, p.351)[7]

Rizvi and Lingard argue that for Said:

> . . . the idea of critical sense consisted of the ability to go beyond the special interests of the experts and be prepared to be self-reflexive of their relations to power. He [Said] thus drew a fundamental distinction between power elites and the critical sense that intellectuals are able to bring to political deliberations. (2006, p.300)

This critical sense that *humanistic* intellectuals bring to political deliberations requires them to be able to 'speak truth to power,' nevertheless some might think it problematic that to speak truth to power involves not only speaking to, but also imploring and reacting to power. Situating the role of the intellectual vis-à-vis power affirms that the intellectual must raise a challenge to market forces. It is the impact of the 'free' market forces and multinational corporations and its influence on the role of the academic that will be mapped out in the following discussion. Unfortunately, Said did not write anything specifically about education,[8] however Said's work on the nature of the intellectual is "important and particularly critical for navigating this moment of political, cultural, and economic retrenchment" (Dimitriadis, 2006, p.369).

The impact of the new economy has been described by Etzkowitz et al. (1998, p.1) who talk of an [academic] revolution that involves "the translation of research into products and into new enterprises." The revolution is dependent upon academia developing distinct collaborations and networks. Slaughter and Rhoades (2004) present these collaborations and networks as:

> . . . new circuits of knowledge, interstitial organisational emergence, networks that intermediate between public and private sector, extended managerial capacity—that link institutions as well as faculty, administrators, academic professionals and students to the new economy. New investment, marketing and consumption behaviours on the part of the university community also link them to the new economy. Together, these mechanisms and behaviours constitute an academic capitalist knowledge/learning regime. (p.15)

This academic capitalist knowledge regime[9] has had a number of consequences for academia. Academics now undertake research in collaboration with companies,[10],[11] and public and voluntary sector organizations, an activity that is termed 'co-production' research. Frith (2001, p.89) demonstrates the impact this has on academic staff by intimating that "so far this academic year I've spent far more time at meetings with potential commercial partners than I have at academic conferences . . . another consequence is the loss of any day-to-day sense of academic freedom." Lyotard's concept of 'performativity' is a useful concept for framing the commodification of teaching and research (Barnett, 2000b) and also the various ways in which universities meet the new performative criteria with the emphasis on measurable outputs (Olssen and Peters, 2005). The following excerpts from tenured full professors (cited in Slaughter et al., 2004, p.134) demonstrate the shifting boundaries in terms of academic's attitudes' towards private contract research and away from the previously highly coveted prize of federal (government) grants:

> When I was younger, I was very upset by the attitude of the chair of my department. He and the other thoroughbred academicians [said] that drug company money was dirty money and that's always been a notion in academia. That attitude has [since] changed. (Professor, Biochemistry)

> Ah, 20 years ago . . . [participating in a startup company][12] would have been thought, for an academic person, this would have been terrible . . . Some people still feel that way . . . Over the past 10–15 years, it's becoming much, much more common, but there are still people . . . older generation people who still think this is not a proper thing for an academic person to be doing, and that's inevitable there will be conflicts of interest somewhere along the line. (Professor, Endocrinology)

Despite the drive for collaborations and networks (the *new circuits of knowledge*), Dimitriadis (2006) sees the resultant move towards specialized knowledge in the service of funding "niches" as a hyper-professionalization of academics' work that is paradoxically driving academics to have greater individual responsibility, greater autonomy and a reduction in social responsibility:

> Our [academics] responsibilities are now increasingly diverted from broader public good towards narrow specialities and sub-specialities, along with their attendant journals, presses, conferences, honours, etc. . . . As smaller and smaller numbers of academics manoeuvre and succeed in smaller and smaller corners of the world, large amounts of intellectual labour (adjuncts, part-timers) are simply being written off. Survival for the neo-liberal subject is now an individual responsibility, not a social one. (p.370)

This hyper-professionalization of academics' work is curiously opposite to the call from Said (1994) for 'amateurism' in intellectual life. Said (1994) argues that intellectuals are not professionals denatured by their fawning service to power, but should remain principled to enable them to speak the truth to power. Said (1994) sees professionalism as an attitude that represents a specific threat to the intellectual, and by professionalism he means:

> . . . thinking of your work as an intellectual as something you do for a living, between the hours of nine and five with one eye on the clock, and another cocked at what is considered to be proper, professional behaviour—not rocking the boat, not straying outside the accepted paradigms or limits, making yourself marketable and above all presentable, hence uncontroversial and unpolitical and 'objective.' (p.55)

Giroux's (1995) notion of the educator [intellectual/academic] demonstrates support for Said's (1994) call for amateurism in intellectual life. Giroux (1995, p.140) rejects what he termed the "universal intellectual" and also the "specific intellectual," and presents the notion of the "border intellectual" who is not constrained by the accepted paradigms and limits of the professional intellectual. Importantly, Giroux (1995) maintains that border intellectuals *can* contribute to wider social issues:

> If the universal intellectual speaks for everyone, and the specific intellectual is wedded to serving the narrow interests of specific cultural and societal formations, the border intellectual travels within and across communities of difference working in collaboration with diverse groups and occupying many sites of resistance while simultaneously defying the specialised, parochial knowledge of the individual specialist, sage, or master ideologue . . . As border intellectuals, educators can

articulate and negotiate their differences as part of a broader struggle to secure social justice, economic equality, and human rights within and across regional, national, and global spheres. (p.140)

THE *END* OF KNOWLEDGE: CHALLENGE *OR* OPPORTUNITY?

Having alluded to the paradox of professionalism, of the academic/intellectual, the new circuits of knowledge forged through the university-industry-government partnerships emphasize a shift towards corporate principles of efficiency, accountability, and profit maximization, and away from social responsibility. Henry Giroux highlights this move towards the new partnerships, and reinforces the sentiments of Dimitriadis (2006) and Davies (2005) that in the new economy academics no longer have the same responsibility to the social:

> . . . the modeling of higher education after corporate principles and the partnerships they create with the business community do more than reorient the purpose and meaning of higher education; such reforms also instrumentalise the curricula and narrow what it means to extend knowledge to broader social concerns. (Giroux, 1999, p.19)

In the new circuits of knowledge, "knowledge no longer moves primarily within scientific/professional/scholarly networks" (Slaughter and Rhoades, 2004, p.22), and corporate 'outsiders' to the education profession now influence the production and dissemination of knowledge . . . something that Olssen and Peters (2005) see as the privatization of knowledge production that has resulted in an age of 'knowledge capitalism.' This age of knowledge capitalism is a historically decisive moment,[13] "in that knowledge is not only structured to be economically productive but itself becomes wholly a commodity under market conditions" (Halsey et al., 1997, p.23) and therefore a site of contestation. Indeed, David (2007) states that both knowledge and methodological approaches to notions of research for and on/in higher education are increasingly becoming contested. Peer review is the cornerstone of the academic profession, and is no longer conducted exclusively by university members. Slaughter and Rhoades (2004) highlight the increase in numbers of industrial scholars[14] sitting on the National Science Foundation (NSF) peer review programs as an indication of the shift as a result of the new circuits of knowledge created under an academic capitalist knowledge/learning regime. The consequences of the move away from public good knowledge/learning regime[15] is emphasized by Giroux (1999):

> Research guided only by the controlling yardstick of profit undermines the role of the university as a public sphere dedicated to addressing the most serious social problems a society faces. Moreover, the corporate

model of research instrumentalises knowledge and undermines forms of theorising, pedagogy, and meaning that define higher and public education as a public good rather than as a private good. (p.20)

The instrumentalization of knowledge that Giroux (1999) alludes to as redefining higher education away from a public good knowledge/learning regime, has led some commentators to suggest that we are witnessing 'the death of universities' (Evans, 2004–2005) and 'the end of knowledge' (Barnett and Griffin, 1997; Delanty, 1998) in a higher education system that is in 'ruins' (Readings, 1996) and in 'crisis' (Frith, 2001).[16] This move is captured in the following excerpt from a faculty member of a research-intensive institution who, for the last five years, has had significant research interactions with industry:

In my mind, money is money . . . So long as it lets me do the science, that's all I care about. I mean, I don't think that it is seen as a negative, so long as I have money to do the science. I mean, it's not like we are getting it from drug traffickers or something like that. (Assistant Professor, Biology, cited in Slaughter et al. 2004, p.151)

The reconciling of competing values by academics and the acceptance of an industrialized, commercial view of higher education results in a culture of pessimism and weariness amongst the academic community. This is a concern shared by numerous commentators (Bone and McNay, 2006; Burgan, 2007; Schuster and Finkelstein, 2006; Slaughter and Leslie, 1997).

The 'end of knowledge' thesis argues substantively, ideologically, and procedurally that the knowledge function of the university is at an end. Despite citing academic capitalism, the demise of contemplative knowledge, the need for knowledge to be cashable in some way in knowledge competences (Lyotard, 1984), the commodification of knowledge, an increase in the accountability of universities to the state, and the drive for transferable vocational skills, Barnett (2004a) refuses to accept the 'end of the university' thesis:

The forms of knowledge that the academic community has favoured may now be threatened; the monopoly over high status knowledge production that the university has enjoyed may be at an end. However the university is not at an end. New, even more challenging, roles are opening up for it, roles that still enable us to see continuities with its earlier self-understandings built around personal growth, societal enlightenment and the promotion of critical forms of understanding. (p.411)

The shifting of the forms of knowledges[17] evident in the 'corporate' university that is under the influence of private sector companies—whose main business is the production of knowledge-based products (Kennedy-Wallace,

2000) results in the function of universities being presented as existing along a continuum. At one end of the continuum, universities adopt the role as skills training centers, and at the other, universities become the research and development arms of the companies with educational functions attached as an appendage. Barnett (2000a) states that in essence the companies are looking to develop two sets of capacities: the knowledges and skills required developing new products; the knowledges and skills required for more effective and efficient management of those processes. Barnett (2000a) indicates that the very infrastructure of corporate universities is influenced directly as a result of this shifting of knowledges:

> Characteristically . . . there would be two 'faculties' in such [corporate] 'universities': a science and technological faculty built around certain sciences and technologies (for instance, biological sciences; electronic sciences; computational sciences) and a management studies faculty. Both 'faculties' would be organised with the particular needs of the company concerned in mind, the knowledges and skills being developed being framed in terms of that 'mission.' (p.412)

The result of this is that universities—especially the 'old' universities—are feeling a challenge to their market share as a consequence of potential applicants to higher education going directly into industry, thus gaining paid employment *and* access to a corporate university. In addition to this, the challenge also exists over the production of knowledge and over their educational function through the knowledge organizations controlling knowledges that previously have been in the public domain,[18] and by the way that invitations to tender for research projects, is no longer exclusively made to universities but increasingly an entirely open process including the private sector (Barnett, 2000a).

Essentially, Slaughter and Rhoades (2004) support Barnett's (2000a) less pessimistic outlook for higher education, and indicate that:

> The academic capitalist knowledge/learning regime is ascendant. It is *displacing*, but not *replacing*, others such as the public good knowledge regime or the liberal learning regime. Although other knowledge regimes persist, the trend line in emphasis and investment is the academic capitalist knowledge/learning regime, as evidenced in public policy, in relations among market, state, and higher education organisations, and in the employment structure and work practices of the academy. (p.305, emphasis added).

The importance of 'displacing,' but not 'replacing' other knowledge regimes indicate that although the current trend is towards the academic capitalist regime, this does not preclude the other regimes. Indeed, Slaughter and Rhoades (2004, p.305) argue that there are "possibilities of networks for socially productive purposes." This positive viewpoint is also shared by David (2007, p.687, emphasis added), who 'celebrates' the ways in which the new forms of academic capitalism "allow for a *diverse* and potentially inclusive form of higher education."[19] This diversification of higher education knowledges is a move that Kincheloe and Steinberg (2006) would support, as it can nurture an institutional culture and a political will that allows for a challenge to the epistemological naïveté demonstrated in the education system, and ultimately be the catalyst towards the development of a critical education based on appreciation of difference. Indeed, Giroux (1995, p.130) states that "the university has long been linked to a notion of national identity that is largely defined and committed to transmitting traditional, Western culture."[20] With diversity a possible outcome of the new forms of academic capitalism, this must in turn inform the work of critical pedagogues, cultural studies practitioners, and antiglobalization activists who have most consciously addressed issues of democracy, diversity, and social justice in the education system. Hytten (2006) states that recently:

> Critical educators have turned their attention to challenging the negative effects of globalisation . . . they worry that market-driven imperatives are increasingly directing educational decision making and that the needs of individuals have been overshadowed, and even sacrificed, in a narrow minded pursuit of economic profits. (p.223)

With the objectives of critical pedagogy to empower the powerless and to transform social inequalities and injustices (McLaren, 2003) and, cultural studies considering the relationship among culture, knowledge, and power (Giroux, 1995), the critical educators need to accept the possibilities and opportunities for socially productive purposes presented by the new forms of academic capitalism. Darder and Mirón (2006) also state that the implementation of a critical pedagogy founded on Paulo Freire's (1972) groundbreaking work, *Pedagogy of the Oppressed*, can within educational institutions see students excel both in their academic and civic participation. It should be remembered that "just as Marx reminded us that capitalism might actually be an improvement over feudalism, we may need to take seriously the possibility that some of the institutions behind new managerial impulses may also constitute an improvement over previous visions of university life" (Apple, 2005, p. 23).

The managerial impulses in higher education, has led to a blurring of the boundary between vocational and academic education in ways that reinforce the power of market forces (Frith, 2001). What some commentators might document as declining standards (Leathwood and Hutchings, 2003; Williams, 1997) by the development of new departments and degrees,[21] others would perceive it as an opportunity to reflect new issues of pedagogic and research concern. Interestingly, Margaret Hodge (former Secretary of State for Lifelong Learning and Higher Education) sees the blurring of these boundaries as not representing a dumbing down of higher education because these students will not be going to study 'Greats at Oxford.' Thus, Hodge (2002) portrays the 'widening participation' and 'vocationalization' issues as separate to an academic education, and therefore the increase in vocational courses, foundation degrees, and the development of sub-degree qualifications do not represent a decline in educational standards.[22]

Education is increasingly becoming understood in terms of its *use* for students and employers, with both vocational and non-vocational programs requiring a justification in utilitarian terms. Frith (2001) states that this leads to:

> . . . an ever more philistine functionalism. If universities have always had to justify themselves generally by reference to what they do for the economy, now this has to be done on a course by course basis. Any proposal for a new degree, or even a new class, has to begin with a statement of its 'market,' the competition from other universities, its 'transferable skills,' its value to employers. The academic case for a new degree is made last and considered least. (p.92)

As the university has been a site of considerable conflict over who can and can't go (Apple, 2005),[23] the blurring of the boundary between vocational and academic education affords increasing opportunities to those students once excluded by an academic regime.[24] For example, in Britain, there has been a threefold increase in the number of universities since the 1960s,[25] and a growth in consumers from 400,000 in the early 1960s to over 2,000,000 in the year 2000 (Greenaway and Haynes, 2003). Additionally, the public accountability resulting from the new managerial impulses can impact positively on the universities hiring practices:

> The intense struggles over the university's gendered and raced hiring practices, ones in which it has taken decades even to begin to address the cultural and social imbalances in serious ways, stand as eloquent witness to the continuing nature of the problems that need to be faced. Because of this, some forms of public accountability—to ask universities to provide evidence that they are taking seriously their social responsibilities concerning hiring practices for example—were and continue to be partial victories. (Apple, 2005, p.23)

MCDONALDIZATION: THE MCUNIVERSITY AND MCKINESIOLOGY

Max Weber developed the notion of the 'iron cage' to capture the increased organizational bureaucratization and productive rationalization of human existence within modernizing capitalist societies. According to Weber

(1958), the 'iron cage' of capitalism traps individuals in highly complex and rule-based organizational structures (they are bureaucratized), in which evermore aspects of their existence become productivity and goal-oriented (they are rationalized). Updating this notion, George Ritzer's 'iron cage' is, of course, the ubiquitous 'Golden Arches,' and, in succinct terms:

> McDonaldization . . . is the process by which the principles of the fast-food restaurant are coming to dominate more and more sectors of American society as well as of the rest of the world. (2004, p.12)

In Ritzer's formulation, McDonaldization is a metaphor that speaks to the organizing and rationalizing of the institutionalized production and delivery of products and services, according to a set of principles of profit-driven instrumental rationality (which Ritzer identified as being the institutional cornerstone of the fast food industry). These principles are based on: *efficiency* (the streamlining of production processes, and the simplification of products and services); *calculability* (the belief that things should be assessed by quantitative [objective] as opposed to qualitative [subjective] measures); *control* (increased influence of rules and regulations, and non-human technologies over workers/consumers); and, *predictability* (the creation of institutionally standardized products and services).

As Ritzer, and numerous others have identified, the 'Golden Arches' of bureaucratic and commercially rationalized efficiencies has crept out of the fast-food franchise and into all aspects of life, including *the public university*. Fully entrenched within academe are a series of discourses, power relations and ways of knowing framed around the rationalization of rationality (Clegg, 2002) which are manifest in the all too familiar 'metrics' that dominate the discourses and lived experiences of our everyday lives within our McDonaldized institutions:

Efficiency: Cutting costs/downsizing/becoming leaner and meaner/ doing more with less/temporary contract instructors increasingly replacing tenure track positions/McJobs/Small central/main campuses, proliferating satellite campuses

Calculability: Various metrics used to measure the "valued" outcomes of universities/ FTE/cost to the university per credit hour, department by department set against the cost paid by students/ Retention rates, and the importance of retaining paying students, and perceived negative effect on institution/Educational or economic utility, and the relationship between them.

Control: The McJob system allows for more control over curriculum/system-wide rules and regulations. Post-tenure review (an initiative which recently failed)

Predictability: Creation of inter-institutionally standardized products and services (curricula)

However, the element of McDonaldization we are most concerned within this chapter, is its contributive association with the rise to prominence of a particular understanding and way of doing 'science' within universities and therefore its influence on the production of [sports coaching] knowledge. The McDonaldizing rational productivity ethos of liberal capitalist society found its epistemic corroboration in the positivist objectivism that underpins the scientific method, as conventionally understood. Both are constituents, and simultaneously constitutors, of a particular understanding of modernity, centered around linear evolutionary assumptions pertaining to the (assumed) inexorable progress of human civilization through the advancement of empirically grounded—often a euphemism for quantitatively driven and objectively reasoned—science. Hence, the scientific hegemony presently in place within the contemporary university speaks less about the veracity of the scientific method *per se*, as it does about the political economy of the McDonaldized university, and the broader political, economic, cultural, and technological context in which the process of McDonaldization exists and operates (Daniels et al., 2000; Nandy, 1988; Rutherford, 2005).

Giroux (2003) proposes higher education is increasingly being redefined in market terms as corporate culture subsumes democratic culture, and, critical learning is replaced by an instrumental logic that celebrates the imperatives of the bottom line, downsizing, and outsourcing.[26] In this formulation, academics become obsessed with grant writing, fund raising, and capital improvements, and, higher education:

> Increasingly devalues its role as a democratic public sphere committed to the broader values of an engaged and critical citizenry. Private gain now cancels the public good, and knowledge that does not immediately translate into jobs or profits is considered ornamental. In this context, pedagogy is depoliticized and academic culture becomes the medium for sorting students and placing them into an iniquitous social order that celebrates commercial power at the expense of broader civil and public values. (pp.22–23)

In this regard, 'knowledge' production is to some extent 'privatized' (Olssen and Peters, 2005; Slaughter and Rhoades, 2004) whereby "knowledge is not only structured to be economically productive but itself becomes wholly a commodity under market conditions" (Halsey et al., 1997, p.23). Within this rationalized McUniversity, research—as detailed earlier—is guided only by the "controlling yardstick of profit undermines the role of the university as a public sphere dedicated to addressing the most serious social problems a society faces" (Giroux (1999, p.20). Such instrumentalized knowledge is declared *a priori* superior and undermines forms of theorizing, pedagogy, and meaning that define higher and public education as a public good (Giroux, 2003). As such, dominant pedagogic practices within the corporate university becomes reduced to the status of training future students for the (corporatized, and increasingly militarized) workplace, and any knowledge that might challenge anti-democratic forms of power or that questions dominant social practices, values, power relations, and, morals, is dismissed by administrators, students and their parents, as *irrelevant* to gaining a foothold in the job market (Giroux, 2003). This is, perhaps the strongest possible counter to academics like Bauman who argue that scholarship must "never stop criticizing the levels of justice already achieved and seeking more justice and better justice" (Bauman, 2002, p.54).

Science then, as a 'reason of state' (Nandy, 1988), is not an epistemological accident: it is quintessentially reductionist and related to the needs of a particular form of economic organization based on exploitation, profit maximization and capital accumulation (Shiva, 1988). As distinct as possible then from the historically stated mission of 'higher' education, and completely at odds with providing students with the skills and information necessary to think critically about the knowledge they gain, colleges and universities have become, or are increasingly perceived—and perceive themselves—as training grounds for corporate (and military) existence. This is clearly a dangerous turn—not least given science can inflict violence in the name national security and development (Nandy, 1988)—and one that all but removes the *ethical referent* from the meaning and purpose of higher education (Giroux, 2003). Indeed—as previously mentioned–this instrumentalization of knowledge has led some commentators to suggest that we are witnessing 'the death of universities' (Evans, 2004–2005) and 'the end of knowledge' (Barnett and Griffin, 1997; Delanty, 1998) in a higher education system that is in 'ruins' (Readings, 1996) or in 'crisis' (Frith, 2001). Said (1983, p.4) for example, suggests this as another space in which citizens "have been left to the hands of 'free' market forces and multinational corporations." Resultantly, and given that the McUniversity is, if nothing else, a pragmatic environment, it has responded to the corporate and "governmental manipulation of science" by reinforcing the primacy of "high-quality science" (Lather, 2006, pp.35, 34). The actions of public and private funding bodies have made it apparent that the nearer one approaches the "gold standard" of randomized experimental design, the more one is likely to receive funding for doing "objective and good science," and the larger that funding is likely to be (Lather, 2006, p.32).

A pervasive grant culture within the McUniversity has thus skewed the epistemological hierarchy, such that research areas are valued for their funding potential and records, more than their intellectual impact and relevance. Such are the laws of the neo-liberal academic jungle: an academic and economic order in which primacy is afforded to rationally conceived, empirically grounded and objective research, with critical, interpretive, and reflexive forms of intellectualizing coming under increasing pressure due to their inability to generate "big grants" (Denzin and Giardina, 2006). Indeed, over the past decade or so, there has been a backlash against various forms of subjective, interpretive, and constructivist thought which is as much economic in its derivation, as it is epistemologically constraining and exclusive in its effects.

Within this context, Kinesiology (and other like-focused departments or units)[27] could be said to be within a condition of perpetual epistemic crisis. The epistemological hierarchy (privileging particular ways of knowing over others) presently operating within the broader university, and placing many areas of the social sciences and humanities under threat of extinction, has certainly been materialized within kinesiology departments, whose comprehensive interdisciplinarity have long been compromised by the political and economic weight of an increasingly hegemonic scientism (Whitson and Macintosh, 1990). This should come as little surprise. As Kuhn (1970) suggested, particular regimes of power are underpinned by specific regimes of truth, and vice versa. The rational productivity ethos of liberal capitalist society finds its epistemic corroboration in the positivist objectivism that underpins the scientific method, as conventionally understood. Both are constituents, and simultaneously constitutors, of a particular understanding of modernity, centered around linear evolutionary assumptions pertaining to the inevitable progress of human civilization, through the advancement of empirically grounded; often a euphemism for quantitatively driven and objectively-reasoned science. Hence, the scientific hegemony presently in place within kinesiology speaks less about the veracity of the scientific method per se, as it does about the political economy of the corporate university, and the broader political, economic, cultural, and technological context in which the process of corporatization exists and operates (Daniels et al., 2000).

Our discussion of the McUniversity offers a neo-Weberian contextualization of the broader forces and processes of capitalist-inspired economic rationalization that have transformed: American society; the American public university; and, are impacting the field of kinesiology (specifically within the American setting) leading to the materialization of what could be termed McKinesiology. The term McKinesiology is meant as a provocative pejorative, as it seeks to capture the partisan version of kinesiology that we are in danger of creating (if indeed, we have not already done so). Further, and in addition to the irrationalities of rationality alluded to above, we propose that a McDonaldized Kinesiology is infused with one of the most significant irrationalities of higher education rationality: namely, an epistemological empirical calculability and its correlative, constrictive curricular efficiency.

The neophyte, and therefore self-consciously vulnerable, discipline of kinesiology has been efficiently co-opted into the self-legitimizing hegemony of evidenced-based natural science. Although unfortunate, it is wholly understandable why those commanding the precarious kinesiology amalgam should privilege the epistemic order (science) that is most readily rewarded, and thereby valued, by managerialist administrators. However, in doing so, economic considerations now come to augment the normalized scientism evident within the kinesiology community; a stance that asserts that the (natural) scientific method takes primacy over all others, regardless of the focus of empirical inquiry. This "first positivist assumption" by Westkott, and rests on the claim (long since discredited) that "the methods appropriate for studying the natural world are equally appropriate for the study of human experience" (Lather, 2006, p.33). Yet, the ways of knowing associated with the active body/human movement are not the exclusive domain of the quantitative data-driven logical positivist. Let us not forget, the active body is as much a social, cultural, philosophical, and historical entity, as it is a genetic, physiological, and psychological vessel, and needs to be engaged as such through rigorous ethnographic, autoethnographic, textual and discursive socio-historic treatment. The aim of qualitative inquiry being to generate otherwise inaccessible interpretations and understandings of the active body/human movement: such social and cultural phenomena simply cannot be imagined, let alone approached, using a logical positivists predilection for identifying and testing the existence of objective rationalities.

McKinesiology's self-evident epistemological hierarchy—what we can term an epistemological violence (Shiva, 1988; see also Kincheloe and McLaren, 2005) that privileges specific 'scientific' ways of knowing—has structurally and intellectually constrained the kinesiological project, in terms of realizing its aims of developing a truly integrative and interdisciplinary approach to the study of physical activity. This has resulted in the triumph of a depthless, bland, and wholly unsatisfying, politicized McKinesiological sciences, stripped of much that made kinesiology a potentially distinctive and significant integrative intellectual project. As a consequence, today's McKinesiology departments tend either to be exclusively bio-science focused, or unapologetically bio-science centric (the social sciences and humanities being grudgingly tolerated, but habitually under-funded and under-supported).

Clearly, the ways of knowing/truths associated with the active body/human movement are not the exclusive domain of the positivistic adherence to the quantitative data-driven generation of models and predictions. As much a social, cultural, philosophical, and historical entity—as it is a genetic, physiological, and psychological vessel—there are important, interpretive engagements (materialized in ethnographic, autoethnographic, textual and discursive, socio-historic methodologies) whose aim is to generate otherwise inaccessible interpretations and understandings of the active body/human movement. Such social and cultural dimensions of corporeality simply cannot be imagined, let alone understood, using a logical positivists predilection for identifying and testing the existence of objective rationalities. Nonetheless, within some circles—not least of which being within the corridors of McKinesiology—the myth of the natural body persists, and is effectively reinforced through the institutional (overt and covert) promotion of the *natural* bio-science dimensions of kinesiology.

CONCLUSION

This chapter has problematized the impact on academia of university integration into the new economy and the adoption of an academic capitalist knowledge/learning regime. This integration—or McDonaldization—has 'forced' academia to promote a permeable interface through developing distinct collaborations and networks with knowledge businesses—the *new circuits of knowledge*—with academics now undertaking research with an emphasis on collaboration with companies, and public and voluntary sector organizations. The commodification and instrumentalization of knowledge, as best represented through the recent White Paper *'Higher education: students at the heart of the system'* (BIS, 2011) in England poses fundamental challenges to academics. Some perceive this as the 'end of the university' as it has been advocated by Humboldt and Newman. However, others have argued that it does in fact afford the opportunity for the academic community to engage in practices that *can* contribute to wider social issues (Giroux, 1995). In light of abandoning university knowledge as a pure, objective reading of the world, Barnett (2000a) calls for universities to adopt a new critical function, developing a new epistemology for the university within the context of neoliberal influences. In embracing this opportunity for a new critical function, scholars can feel empowered in seeking a challenge to existing taken-for-granted knowledge in established fields of research; such as the position afforded to current scholars working within McKinesiological sciences undertaking research in the 'field' of sports coaching research.

4 Conjunctural History of the Sports Coaching Present

Question: How many people would willingly sit in front of their television sets for five weeks to watch 64 games in which 11 overpaid athletes try to move an inflated leather ball across a 24-foot line, while another 11 try to move the same ball across another line 100 yards away?

Answer: 37 billion, including 1.7 billion—a quarter of the world's total population—for the final 90 minutes alone.[1] (Cashmore, 2000, p.1)

INTRODUCTION

This chapter aims to *locate* the 'theme field' of sports coaching research within the critical interrogation of sport. "It is impossible to fully understand contemporary society and culture without acknowledging the place of sport" (Jarvie, 2006, p.2) and indeed the importance that is placed on sport by nation states and global associations *must* be mapped to fully appreciate the conjunctural history of the sports coaching present. This chapter will emphasize that sport is not impervious to the characteristics of the 'pernicious present' (Silk and Andrews, 2011), whether that is neoliberal ideology, politics, or the forces of globalization.

In the UK, the leisure industry—of which sport is the fastest growing sector—accounts for over a quarter of all consumer spending (Davies, 2002), with sport-related employment estimated as accounting for 1.8% of all employment in England in 2003 (Sport England, 2007) and 2.2% of all jobs in the UK (Carter, 2005). It is also estimated that over six million people receive sports coaching in the UK, with approximately 1.2 million people involved in the practice of sports coaching (Bush et al., 2012). Approximately 80% of these involved in the practice of sports coaching contribute their time on a voluntary basis (SkillsActive, 2011); yet the 240,000 coaches in paid employment represent a significant part of the sport-related workforce.

The commercial impact of sport is also difficult to overlook when we are confronted with headlines such as 'Premier league wages break the £1 billion barrier' (The Telegraph, 2008) or that the Sydney 2000 Olympic Games attracted more than US $600 million in sponsorship and was viewed on television by more than 3.7 billion people (Jarvie, 2006).[2] In addition to these commercial factors, sport's social power makes it a "potentially potent force in the modern world, for good or bad" (Jarvie, 2006, p.2). The United Nations declared 2005 to be the Year of Sport and Physical Education (Coalter, 2007), corporations, charities, governments and other agencies deploy sport through the world in any number of (pseudo-)development initiatives related to say gender based violence or sexual health, and with more and more children participating in organized sport around the world (De Knopp et al., 1996) there is an argument (albeit with very little hard evidence) that sport—and the sports coach—can be the vehicle for addressing a wide range of social issues.

This chapter will initially look at the influences of political ideology on sports policy and then unpick the role that sport has on a global scale. The genealogy of sports coaching as an academic endeavor is considered and then the current sports coaching research landscape is presented and then critiqued.

SPORT POLICY

Houlihan (2004) describes the role of the state in determining the pattern, momentum and direction of the engagement between national and global sport as substantial and central "due to the dependence of almost all national sport systems on state funding and administrative support" (p.67). As a consequence of this, the policy objectives that the government seeks to achieve through sport are an integral component shaping the current sporting moment and the sporting space that we inhabit. The idea that sport is not a part of politics or has nothing to do with politics—the myth of autonomy[3]—has been marginalized as utopian ideology (Maguire et al., 2002). Indeed, Green and Houlihan (2006) argue that over the last 40 years or so, governments in many developed countries have taken an increasing interest in sport. Chapters 2 and 3 demonstrated how neoliberal ideology has influenced policy formation in the field of higher education and then subsequently how this has impacted on the role of academia, and as sports policy occupies a contested space on the edge of mainstream government policies, an understanding of the policy processes can crucially be gained through an appreciation of the ideology shaping them (Bramham, 2004).

The major political ideologies of conservatism, liberalism, and social reformism each define their preferred association between nation state, civil society and markets in a different manner, and as a consequence would present different prescriptions for public policy. Numerous writers have unpicked what sports policies would look like if driven directly by a political ideology (For example: Bramham and Henry, 1985; Bramham and Henry, 1991; Henry, 2001; Riordan, 1978; Riordan and Krüger, 1999; Sam and Jackson, 2004; Wilson, 1988; Whannel, 1983)[4] and in addition to this there is a burgeoning range of literature giving detailed histories of the development of sports policy in the United Kingdom (For example: Haywood et al., 1995; Houlihan, 1991; Houlihan and White, 2002; Bloyce and Smith, 2010; Collins, 2010; Morgan, 2012).

Demonstrating how a political ideology is manifested in public policy is highly visible with the transition to the Labour government in May 1997. The dominant core policy paradigm shaping the early years of the Blair government was social reformism, with "its concern to promote moral, urban and economic regeneration reflected in its commitment to address social exclusion and its support for economic modernization and creative excellence" (Houlihan and White, 2002, p.81). Coalter (2007) supports Houlihan and White's (2002) assertion about social reformism, and further adds to the discussion the dimension of the new importance of sport in social policy that has then resulted in an emphasis on measurement, evaluation and effectiveness.[5]

> In recent years sport has achieved an increasingly high profile as part of New Labour's social inclusion agenda, based on assumptions about its potential contribution to areas such as social and economic regeneration, crime reduction, health improvement and educational achievement. However these new health opportunities (welcomed by many in sport) have been accompanied by a potential threat–evidence-based policy-making. This reflects an increased emphasis on outcomes and effectiveness and an aspiration to base policy and practice on robust evidence to ensure the delivery of the government's policy goals. (p.1)

As many of the branches of central government have a vested interest in the value of sport,[6] co-operation between different branches of government was seen as the way to break down the traditional culture of departmentalism to allow for a comprehensive policy response to a complex and multi-dimensional problem; a process that Houlihan and White (2002) term 'joined up government.' Priority was given to bringing the three most important departments together that were concerned with sport policy, the Department of Culture, Media and Sports (DCMS), the Department for Education and Employment (DfEE) and the Department of Environment, Transport and the Regions (DETR). In addition to this, the Sports Councils, the regional assemblies (Northern Ireland, Scotland and Wales) and regional consortiums in England "added a further dimension to the infrastructure of the policy process" (Houlihan and White, 2002, p.81). The DCMS (2000) strategy 'A *Sporting Future for All*' is a reflection on the 'joined up' policy process, using schools at the heart of the policy as the vehicle for development of participation in sport and also talent identification and elite achievement (Houlihan and White, 2002). To ensure the fulfillment of the 'evidence-based policy-making loop,' evidence needs to be accumulated to inform sports policy, provision, and practice in a range of areas:

In sports policy several research reviews were commissioned by government and public organizations to examine the evidence for sport's claimed wider impacts and to identify 'good practice' models as a basis for policy. However . . . the overall conclusion of these reviews was that there was a general lack of robust research-based evidence on the outcomes of sports participation." (Coalter, 2007, pp.25–26)[7,8]

It is important to emphasize that, as previously mentioned, Coalter (2007) sees evidence-based policy-making as a threat due to the lack of robust research evidence on which policies are derived. Indeed, he reflects on the disappointment of his commissioning clients (Sport England and UK Sport) to the ambiguous and inconclusive conclusions drawn from all reviews produced (with John Taylor) to the on-line research database the *Value of Sport Monitor.*' Coalter (2007, p.1) describes the findings at best "equivalent to the Scottish legal verdict of 'not proven.' There are no 'killer facts' and few 'best buys'".

In response to the successful London 2012 Olympic bid, the DCMS (2008b) launched the *'Playing to Win: A New Era for Sport'* strategy. This strategy sought to change the culture of sport in England and centralized playing to win. The plan was to get the best out of the £250 million for community sport and to maximize the number of people taking part in sport—put oxymoronically in the strategy as taking part "simply for the love of sport" (DCMS, 2008, p.2)—in order to expand the pool of talented athletes. The rhetoric was around breaking records, winning medals and winning tournaments for this country. The establishment of the Conservative/Liberal Democrat coalition in 2010 ushered in a new sports strategy. *'Creating a Sporting Habit for Life'* (DCMS, 2012) once again promises to transform our sporting culture, but this time through increasing the number of young people developing sport as a habit for life. Over a five-year period, Sport England will invest at least £1 billion of lottery and Exchequer funding to break down the barriers preventing young people from continuing their interest in sport into their adult life. It is interesting to note—and emphasizing Coalter's (2007) concerns about the robustness of research evidence on which policies are derived—that this strategy centralizes links between schools and community sports clubs in 'traditional' team sports such as football, cricket, and rugby,[9] and therefore is based on a very narrow understanding of sport that ignores the myriad of possibilities for engaging young people in physical activity.

The vested interest that central government has in relation to sport is posited by Bramham (2008) who concisely differentiates intrinsic and extrinsic *objectives* obtained from sport:

Sport may be valued intrinsically for its own sake because it develops personal skills, competition, individual self-esteem and fun for participants. Sport can also produce wider externalities, by making a valuable contribution to other government policy with respect to national prestige, to foreign policy and international diplomacy, to tourism and city regeneration, to local community development, to health, as well as helping to redress social divisions around class, 'race,' gender and disability. (p.10) [10]

Successive Conservative and Labour governments set up quangos such as the Arts Council, the Sports Council and agencies to distribute National Lottery funds. Bramham (2008) suggests that this 'arm's length' approach to policy has been both politically and ideologically expedient by providing institutional continuity and allowing governments to provide subsidy and appoint key personnel without being held directly accountable in Parliament for decisions and outcomes. He emphasizes that this is in no way a reflection of governments dismissing the power of sports wider externalities:

> This is in no way to suggest that sports policy is an ideologically battle-free zone. Sports policy cannot avoid moral panics in the media about national elite sports performance, alcohol and drug abuse, football hooliganism, racism and sexism, childhood obesity and so on. The sports policy universe is inevitably drawn into each government's political ideology and political agenda. (p.19)

It is the capability of the 'sports policy universe' to help contribute to wider government policy goals that in essence facilitates a certain permanence for sports policies no matter what the ideological script the transient government is working from at a particular moment in time. It should be remembered however that linking sport policy to the wider government agenda can be critiqued. Bloom et al. (2005, preface) concludes that "policy makers lack the evidence required to make informed policy decisions and to connect sport issues to other policy priorities" and indeed not only is there a lack of systematic, robust measurement of outcomes, but also a deficiency in the understanding of "the mechanisms and processes via which they are achieved (especially in 'real life' situations)" (Coalter et al., 2000, p.85). Coalter (2007) indicates that in sport policy making there is a marked difference between the theoretical logic of evidence-based policy making and what happens in reality. Coalter (2007, p.26) uses Weiss's (1997b) vivid phrase to highlight that "sports policy and practice has been, and continues to be not 'aim, steady fire,' but 'fire, steady, aim'!"

Whether we unpick New Labour's social inclusion policy shaping *'A Sporting Future for All'* (DCMS, 2000) or the Conservative / Liberal Democrat coalition's lifelong participation rhetoric shaping *'Creating a Sporting Habit for Life'* (DCMS, 2012), such rhetoric needs to be understood in relation to the underlying constant to the transient interventionist and instrumentalist strategies of a particular government's political ideologies; namely neoliberalism. Chapters 2 and 3 mapped the neoliberal influences on higher education and also on the role of the academic, and indeed we intimated earlier in this chapter at the parallels between the new importance of sport in social policy—and the concomitant rise in the emphasis on measurement, evaluation and effectiveness—and the 'audit culture' permeating education (Apple, 2005). Green and Houlihan (2006) draw upon neo-Foucauldian writings on "governmentality" to explain the nature of the relationship between governments and national sporting organizations (NSOs). Green and Houlihan (2006) conclude that although effective 'responsibilization' of NSOs remains a clear ambition, the government in the United Kingdom show themselves to be very willing to apply disciplinary forms of practice to ensure compliance from NSOs in relation to government rationalities. To ensure compliance in the sport policy universe—and once again analogously with the evolution of higher education policy—there is evidence of "the 'govenmentalisation of the state,' referring to the tendency for state power to be exercised and realized through a heterogeneous array of regulatory practices and technologies" (MacKinnon, 2000, p.297). This disciplinary practice—as legitimized through UK Sport's modernization and autonomization of NSOs—has seen the recipients of services provided by NSOs now constituted as customers or stakeholders (Green and Houlihan, 2006). Once again, this is essentially mirroring what we see in the higher education context.

We posit that we could go further, and what we are witnessing is the McDonaldization of the sports policy universe. As we discussed in Chapter 3, in Ritzer's formulation, McDonaldization is a metaphor that speaks to the organizing and rationalizing of the institutionalized production and delivery of products and services, according to a set of principles—efficiency, calculability, control, and predictability—of profit-driven instrumental rationality. Through the disciplinary practices of the state, an institutional framework exists in sports policy that embraces an ever increasing investment by advanced capitalist countries in elite sport framed by the logics of neoliberalism—governmentality, audit culture, modernization, rationalization, autonomization—and therefore, in essence, what we are witnessing is an elitist agenda through the evolution of the 'McSportsPolicy.'

Unlike emerging states—such as the Balkans, where international sporting success is often linked to a long, dormant insignia (flag, emblem, anthem etc.) or isolated or (relatively) newly formed states, like Australia, using sport as a cornerstone of national identity—the United Kingdom does not appear to have a strong rationale for elite sport investment. The notion that elite sport success promotes participation among citizens, leads to international prestige, and creates a feel-good factor—leading to a healthier nation, reduction in crime levels, and a wide pool of participants from which future champions can be selected; what Grix and Carmichael (2011) term the 'virtuous cycle' of sport—are examples of where there is a lack of robust research evidence to measure the outcomes. Indeed, Green (2006) advocates that "the storyline that elite sporting success motivates the generality of the population to participate and compete is what might be termed a *'usual suspect'* in any discussions of the ways in which funding for elite development is allocated" (p.233, emphasis added). However, we feel that this has now reached a point where the elite agenda could be described as 'evangelical' (Coalter, 2010; Grix and Carmichael, 2011) and is the dominant discourse being maintained through the government's disciplinary practice. Grix and Carmichael (2011) suggest that this disciplinary practice behind sports policy formulation in the United Kingdom—policies that centralize the elite sporting agenda—is a discursively constructed discourse that ensures the privileging of the 'virtuous cycle' of sport; a discourse that is driven solely by a political and ideological choice.

GLOBALIZATION, THE NATION STATE AND SPORT: A GLOBAL ROLE FOR SPORT?

To fully explicate the current moment, it is essential that consideration of sport is not limited to the national level, and that reflection on the global role for sport is considered in tandem with it. The term 'global sport' and the associated processes of globalization are common within discussions of contemporary sport (Jarvie, 2006). Indeed, Jarvie (2006) usefully differentiates these discussions as operating at two levels, the globalization of sport itself and also the contribution that sport makes to other globalization processes. The *success* of the market economy and the vindication of Western capitalism that occurred in the late 1980s/early 1990s were critiqued in the context of individuals and societies in Chapter 2 to frame the current moment and the time and space that we inhabit. To help articulate the conjunctural history of the sports present, Houlihan (2004) cites that the same chain of events were responsible for the concept of *globalization* to be applied to the sporting context:

> The stimulus for the *enthusiastic embrace* of the concept of globalisation in the early 1990s was due less to the spread of particular cultural practices, or the recognition of the global commercial interests in major sporting events such as the Olympics and the soccer World Cup, and more to the collapse of communism and the end of global political and economic bipolarity. (p.53, emphasis added)

The use of the term 'enthusiastic embrace' in relation to globalization confirms Houlihan's (2004) belief that globalization is assuming paradigmatic status, or has become "the new grand narrative of the social sciences" (Hirst and Thompson, 1999, p.xiii). There are numerous critiques of this position (For example: Baker et al., 1999; Bauman, 2000; Dearlove, 2000; Maguire, 1999; Michie and Grieve-Smith, 1999; Weiss, 1997a) and what is of importance here is that the critiques challenge the undifferentiated identity of the global and juxtapose that the global and national (nation state) need not present competing principles of organization but can indeed be complementary to one another. Interestingly, these thoughts are synonymous with the call for the *production of locality* (Hardt and Negri, 2000) or the concept of *glocalization* (Giulianotti and Robertson, 2004) that emphasizes the need for the local (nation state) to work symbiotically with, and not subordinate to, global influences in sport.[11]

It is therefore important to ensure that the utility of the concept [globalization] that is applied to the field of sport is examined "as there is a risk that it will become degraded and exhausted through indiscriminate use and constant challenge from its critics, and consequently move to the 'back-burner' in social science" (Houlihan, 2004, p.53). Interestingly Jarvie (2006) concedes that the term globalization has been poorly defined, meaning different things to different people, and that there is no single globalization theory upon which an understanding of contemporary sport can be built.[12] However, Houlihan (2004) uses the debate about the utility of the concept of globalization to "sharpen our understanding of the development of sport as it continues to move beyond the confines of national policy systems, and particularly the part played by the state in the process" (p.53).

Coakley (2001) intimates that Government involvement in sports is frequently motivated by a quest for "recognition and prestige . . . on local, national and even global levels" (p.389). Although it is not the purpose of this chapter to unpick government rationales for their use of sport,[13] in defining the sporting moment, distinction needs to be made between how and why a nation state *uses* sport on a global platform and also how global associations of governments (for example the United Nations) *use* sport. Bramham (2008) presents the transcending of sports policy beyond nation state boundaries:

> In a globalised world in which transnational economic, environmental, security and cultural forces reign supreme, even transcending nation state boundaries, sports policies continue to offer national governments the illusory temptation that ideologically based interventions can make a difference. Whether in bidding for mega-events, changing mass participation rates in sport, or using activities to regulate disorderly youth, sports policy remains, and has even grown in political salience in the twenty-first century. (p.22)

The hosting of one of sports mega-events in the UK[14]—the 2012 Olympic Games and Paralympic Games—is a prime example of how a government utilizes sport for wider policy objectives.[15] The DCMS (2008a, p.3) strategy document '*Before, during and after: making the most of the London 2012 Games*' sets out an action plan containing five 'promises' in relation to hosting the Games: to make the UK a world-leading sporting nation; to transform the heart of East London; to inspire a generation of young people; to make the Olympic Park a blueprint for sustainable living; to demonstrate the UK is a creative, inclusive and welcoming place to live in, visit and for business.[16] Interestingly only one of the promises relates to sport and even this promise can be critiqued for being 'diluted' with broader social objectives. The promise to "make the UK a world-leading sporting nation" has as one of its headline ambitions "elite achievement: aim for 4th in the Olympic medal table in 2012" with "UK Sport's World Class Performance Program" as the key program responsible for delivery of this (DCMS, 2000, pp.10–12). Houlihan and White (2002, p.109) suggest that "the government demonstrated an awareness of the tendency of NGBs [National Governing Bodies of sports] to adopt an overly narrow focus on elite achievement" and consequently NGBs were tasked with diverting resources towards social objectives. NGBs needed to "have a clear strategy for participation *and* excellence; and commit themselves to putting social inclusion and fairness at the heart of everything that they do" (DCMS, 2000, p.22, emphasis added).

"Sports 'mega-events' are important elements in the orientation of nations to international or global society" (Horne and Manzenreiter, 2006, p.1) and this concept of an international or global society reflects concerns that Houlihan (2004) and other academics[17] share about the erosion of hard-edged national identity.[18]

> Under conditions of globalised sport the concept of hard-edged, clearly defined and recognised national identity would give way to a more fluid, ambiguous and malleable concept, according to which athletes and club teams would reflect multiple or nested identities that would, arguably, be more sympathetic to commercial strategies of global media and business. (p.68)

Nation States have colluded in the dilution of national identity by issuing naturalization or work permits to foreign athletes, however Houlihan (2004) intimates that there are signs of a reaction[19] from national and international federations and also a number of member states in the EU (including Britain and France) "which perceive a threat to the development of national talent and the integrity of domestic sport systems" (p.68). Indeed, Houlihan (2004) suggests that with:

> The continuing significance of the state in shaping domestic engagement with international sport and the evidence of a strengthening capacity of the states, both individually and collectively . . . it is more accurate to talk of internationalised, rather than globalised, sport. (p.69)

Introducing the concept of an *internationalized* rather than globalized sport due to the individual and collective strengthening of the states is an important link to how global associations of governments *use* sport.

Not only is sport attributed a role in the search for solutions to social issues in the UK,[20] "even greater and much more ambitious claims are being made for sport on a global scale, as sport is increasingly regarded as an important component of development strategies" (Coalter, 2007, p.68) for promoting education, health, the economy, gender equality and peace. Although it is not the purpose of this chapter to unpick the global role for sport,[21] the emphasis placed on the developmental power of sport by the global association of governments (the United Nations) cannot be overlooked in the context of this text in defining the current sport space that we inhabit. Louise Fréchette (the UN Deputy Secretary-General, emphasis added) speaking at the opening address of the World Sport's Forum in March 2000, stated that:

> The power of sports is far more than symbolic. You are engines of *economic* growth. You are a force for gender equality. You can bring youth and others in from the margins, strengthening the social fabric. You can promote communication and help heal the divisions between peoples, communities and entire nations. You can set an example of fair play. Last but not least, you can advocate a strong and effective United Nations. There may not be any miracle finishes or perfect performances. But if we are even half as motivated and dedicated as the typical athlete, the *sporting world*, the *business community* and the United Nations can prove to be quite a winning team.

In Fréchette's (2000) opening address, the economic rationale for sport can be seen to have primacy over the developmental agenda. However, in explicating how sport is integral in the work for peace and to achieving the Millennium Development Goals (United Nations, 2005a)[22] the United Nations omits the economic rationale to emphasize the wide-ranging developmental role that sport can have:

> It [sport] is about inclusion and citizenship. Sport brings individuals and communities together, highlighting commonalities and bridging cultural or ethnic divides. Sport provides a forum to learn skills such as discipline, confidence and leadership and it teaches core principles such as tolerance, cooperation and respect. Sport teaches the value of effort and how to manage victory, as well as defeat. When these positive aspects of sport are emphasized, sport becomes a powerful vehicle through which the United Nations can work towards achieving its goals. (United Nations, 2005c, p.v)

Jarvie (2006) does however present a cautionary note to the role of global sport, describing global sport as nothing more than neoliberalism and equates to market forces controlling sport. Indeed, contradictorily to the positive portrayal of sports global mega-events by governments, Andrews (2004) intimates that this aura is fallacious:

> Politics, corruption and commercialisation have been an ever-present aspect of the modern Olympic movement since its inception with the Athens games of 1896. Nevertheless, even in the *hypercommercial* world of late twentieth-century sport, the Olympic Games somehow managed to maintain an aura—however spurious and symbolic—of sporting purity and unity seemingly unsullied by the world around it. (p.17, emphasis added)

In direct opposition to sport as the *vehicle* through which the United Nations can achieve its goals, Jarvie (2006) cites global sport and globalization as:

> . . . being the *vehicle* of global exploitation which has produced sports goods on the back of cheap labour, helped maintain global poverty levels and maintained different levels of inequality in sport, particularly in terms of access of women and ethnic minority groups to positions of power in global sport. (p.95, emphasis added)

Thus, there is a need for sport to seek to replace the traditional, Western power bases to allow for any strategies aimed at producing change to go beyond the dualism that portrays globalization as good or bad and towards considering the multiple levels in a unitary and totalizing manner.[23]

THE RISE OF SPORTS COACHING AS AN ACADEMIC ENDEAVOUR

Having critically interrogated 'sport' on a national and global level, it is now essential to explicate the rise of sports coaching as an academic endeavor, framed by the current 'moment.' In the practice of sports coaching there is an inexorable link between knowledge and competence. A designated level of competence and acquired knowledge is assumed if an individual obtains a 'sports coaching' related qualification. In research conducted by Pullo (1992) on strength and conditioning coaches, three of the characteristics in the profile of an 'effective' coach were formal coaching/sport related qualifications, including degree (and higher degree) level study. Jones (2005a) alludes to the recent recognition of sports coaching (i.e. improving the sporting performance of others) as a bone fide area of academic study, alongside the more established subject areas of sport psychology and exercise physiology. The latest undergraduate and postgraduate admissions data for the UK indicates that, not only has coaching become established alongside the more traditional subject areas, it is eclipsing them in terms of provision at Higher Education (HE) institutions.

An undergraduate course search (UCAS, 2008a) reveals that, of the 1,783 undergraduate (excluding foundation degree) sport courses with entry in 2008, 210 (11.8%) concentrate on sports coaching, while the closely-linked specialism of sport education accounts for 69 (3.9%) programs. The more established areas of sport psychology and sport/exercise physiology are the basis of 104 (5.8%) and 40 (2.2%) programs respectively. It should be noted that the umbrella term 'sport science' (incorporating aspects of sociology, physiology, psychology and biomechanics) accounts for 800 (44.9%) programs. These data when compared with comparable data from 2006[24] highlight the dynamic fluidity of undergraduate sports programs. The emerging trend is a reduction in the umbrella program of 'sports science,' from 1054 (62.7%) programs in 2006 (Bush, 2007), 800 (44.9%) programs commencing in 2008, down to 765 (43.8%)[25] programs commencing in 2009 (UCAS, 2008b), and a concomitant increase in sports coaching undergraduate programs from 192 (11.0%) to 217 (12.4%) programs commencing in 2009 (UCAS, 2008b). With overall sport undergraduate provision remaining constant, the dramatic reduction in 'sports science' programs (from 62.7% of the undergraduate sports provision in 2006 to 43.8% in 2009) has also allowed for an eclectic mix of 'sports' related undergraduate programs to proliferate to fill the void.[26]

Similar positive results are found when looking at postgraduate study in sport. A postgraduate course search (The Guardian, 2008) indicated that 54 institutions offered postgraduate qualifications in a sport-related field, of which 11 (20.4%) of the institutions offered sports coaching programs. Coaching is not only flourishing as an academic subject at both undergraduate and postgraduate level, but is also emerging as a popular option in the more vocational HE qualifications (foundation degrees). Of the 224 foundation degrees in sport (including 'Sports Studies' and 'Sports Science'),[27] 62 (27.7%) include 'coaching' or 'coach' in the program title (UCAS, 2008c).

The expansion of coaching as an academic area of study is mirrored by its increased appearance in government policy. The prospect of hosting the Olympic and Paralympic Games in 2012 has provided a driving force for the recruitment and support of current and future coaches, which is seen as critical in ensuring a sporting legacy to reach beyond the 2012 Games (sports coach UK, 2006). Sports coach UK has been tasked with the development of a UK Action Plan for Coaching[28] in conjunction with national governing bodies of sport (NGBs) and the key funding agencies (UK Sport; the Department for Culture, Media and Sport; Home Country Sports Councils; the Department for Education and Skills; the British Olympic Association; Youth Sport Trust and SkillsActive). The 'UK Coaching Framework: A 3-7-11 Action Plan' incorporates a range of initiatives, including a fast-track scheme for the production of 60 elite British coaches by 2012, the UK Coaching Certificate (UKCC) to endorse coach education programs against agreed criteria, and the establishment of 3000 Community Sports Coaches (CSCs) and a network of 45 Coach Development Officers (CDOs). The Coaching Task Force report published in July 2002 resulted in the Government committing £28 million over a three-year period to coaching (DCMS, 2006a), and £60 million ring fenced between 2004 and 2008 to implement the UK Action Plan for Coaching (DCMS, 2006b). The Government having also confirmed the allocation of £300 million to the athlete preparations for London 2012 (DCMS, 2006c), a significant investment is secured for coaching for the foreseeable future.

THE CURRENT SPORTS COACHING 'RESEARCH' LANDSCAPE

According to Gilbert and Trudel (2004a, p.388) "the development of any profession relies on research, training programs and innovations in practice. These endeavors, however, depend on knowledge of the current state of the field." Throughout the infancy of sports coaching research, debate surrounded the notion that coaching was essentially either a scientific or artistic activity, or even a blend of the two. The perception of coaching as a science implies that specific acquired knowledge can be prescribed in order to bring about incremental performance improvements. In comparison to coaching as a science, coaching as an art form results in performance improvement without rational, instrumental application of knowledge but through applying knowledge to a dynamic, complex environment in a less prescriptive, more creative and mystical manner. The perspective of coaching being a composite of science and art is supported by a number of coach educators (see Lyle, 1986; Potrac et al., 2000), although there are proponents for coaching being mainly scientific (see Balyi, 1992; Bompa, 1996; Bompa, 1999a; Bompa 1999b), or artistic (see Dick, 1989). Whichever perspective is adopted, there are important implications for the knowledge that underpins each. Woodman (1993, pp.1–2) highlights the major areas of science that are impacting on coaching, "anatomy, physiology, biochemistry, biomechanics, growth and development, statistics, tests and measurements, motor learning, psychology, sports medicine, nutrition, pedagogy, sociology, and information and communication technology". The complex nature of the art of coaching, according to Woodman (1993, p.4), emphasizes the requirement for the coach to develop knowledge of a different kind:

> The coach, like the artist, must have creative flair and technical mastery over the material and tools used. In his analogy the athlete is the instrument and the material, but, being an adaptive and reasoning being, is very complex to work with. Dick (1989) states that the coach must clearly understand the purpose of each practice and its relevance

to the total scheme of preparation, while at the same time understand the growing, changing person of the athlete and the role of sport in his or her life.

Whether one predominantly supports a science or an art base to the profession, coaches must increase their knowledge in all aspects to be 'fully effective.' If we accept this holistic view of sports coaching and concede that a coach requires facets of both perspectives, then the debate *between* the two perspectives is now redundant:

> Lyle (1986) concludes that coaching is neither an art nor a science but a little of both. Lyle says that sports performance is not an exact science and that the individuality of the coach, decision-making based on experience, and the vagaries of the psychological aspects of performance point to human factors as a key part of the process. (Woodman, 1993, p.5)

In reality, this is what we see 'on the ground,' with coaches blending relevant components derived from both perspectives. As the science/art debate subsided in the late 1980s, there was a need for a new characterization of research perspectives on coaching.

Presenting an overview of sports coaching and coach education research is a tremendous challenge considering the amount of coaching literature (Trudel and Gilbert, 2006), and despite a burgeoning body of coaching literature few attempts have been made to summarize the information (Hastie, 1992). In Gilbert and Trudel's (2004a) 'Analysis of Coaching Science Research Published from 1970–2001' the published research on 'coaching science' (the 'theme field') was conceptually defined as a composition of 'theory fields' (e.g. sport psychology, sport pedagogy, sport biomechanics, sport sociology) linked to a 'mother science' (e.g. psychology, pedagogy, sociology). Ultimately the coaching research was organized into four research categories (coach behaviors, coach thoughts, coach characteristics, and coach career development) that were drawn from 54 coaching themes. Interestingly, Gilbert and Trudel's (2004a) data demonstrates that 'coaching scientists' traditionally have been most interested in what coaches do, representing 50.7% of all articles coded from 1970–2001 and 55.7% of articles coded in the most recent time period of analysis (1998–2001). This is supported by Douge and Hastie (1993) who intimated that coaching research tended to be a one-dimensional evaluation of coach behaviors.

Current scholarly activity can be viewed as underpinned by four approaches to sports coaching (Jones, 2005a). These are (1) psychological (see Bloom et al., 2003; Brewer and Jones, 2002; d'Arripe-Longueville et al., 1998; Gilbert and Trudel, 2004b), (2) modeling (see Côté et al., 1995; Cross and Lyle, 1999; Lyle, 2002; Sherman et al., 1997), (3) sociological (see Cassidy et al., 2004; Jones, 2000; Jones et al., 2004; Jones et al., 2003;

Lombardo, 1987; Potrac et al., 2002) and (4) pedagogical (see Jones, 2005b; Jones and Wallace, 2005; Kidman, 2001; Potrac et al., 2000). It should be noted that these four approaches are not independent of each other; many of the authors who are identified as aligning with a particular approach might argue that to place their work in a particular category is an over-simplification, and that in a number of cases sports coaching research blurs the allocated boundaries. A presentation of the concepts central to each of the four approaches follows.

According to Jones (2005a), the parent discipline of coaching is psychology. Proponents of a psychological approach to coaching relate to the idea that 'it is all in the mind' and focus on areas such as decision making, skill acquisition, coach–athlete interactions, the role of the coach, self-esteem and cognition. Scholars working in this area see the development of sports coaching research as being parallel to the progress in psychological understanding. Historically, sport coaching was aligned with widely accepted and established behavioral and cognitive principles, before being enhanced by a branch of psychology that added the human dimension, namely humanistic psychology. This 1950s development within psychology has remained a domineering influence over contemporary sports coaching research. This was demonstrated by Lyle (2002) embracing the humanistic approach as a 'benchmark' for behavior in sports coaching. Recent developments in the field of psychology continue to inform contemporary sports coaching research, which has largely remained faithful to the psychological approach.

The modeling approach to coaching is based on the premise that 'coach effectiveness' or 'coaching success' can be achieved through the identification, analysis and control of variables that affect athlete performance, and the application of a sequential process. This sequential view of coaching conveniently allows for modification of the process to achieve success. The modeling perspective is highlighted by Kidman and Hanrahan (2004); "if coaches are not achieving success (however it is defined), they need to look at changing what they are doing, that is, changing the process" (p.16). Jones (2005a) describes the existence of two forms of research within this approach to sports coaching, 'models of' the coaching process that are based on empirical research investigating effective coaching practice, and 'models for' the coaching process as *idealistic representations* that develop from the identification of a set of assumptions about the process.[29] Douge and Hastie (1993) identify that there is a clear research gap that requires context specific work to be undertaken, and that the modeling approach does not consider effectively the different needs that individuals have at different stages of their development that would require a diversification in the coaching environments (Martindale et al., 2005). Indeed, Trudel (2006) concedes that to 'model' coaching is a complex task as it would need to consider the influences of both the coach and athlete's personal characteristics, and also the specific contextual factors of the coaching environment.

The precursor to a sociological approach to coaching according to Jones (2005a) was a perceived dissatisfaction with the presentation of coaching as a sequential process, which was felt to be an oversimplification of a much more complex procedure. Jones et al. (2004) indicate that "a professional coach is much more than a subject matter specialist and a systematic method applier" (p.2). The sociological approach is concerned with looking at issues largely ignored by the psychological and modeling approaches to sports coaching, often the elements defined as 'intuition,' 'wisdom,' or the 'art of coaching.' Key issues dealt with under the sociological approach are the acquisition; maintenance and advancement of social power; the constructionist nature of coaching knowledge; the social role of the coach; coaches' philosophies; coaches' agency; coaches' interactions; the coaching environment and the pedagogic setting. In essence, scholarly activity within this approach aims to question the practices presented in other research perspectives (and often taken for granted) that portray an "oddly inhuman account of this most human of jobs" (Connell, 1985, p.4).

A pedagogical approach to sports coaching encroaches into the territory of the sociological approach in the area of the learning [coaching] environment, referred to in this context as the 'pedagogic setting.' The pedagogic approach is based on the premise that coaching is fundamentally a teaching activity, with the goal being athlete learning. In addition to the identifiable links to the sociological approach, the roots of the scholarly activity defined as a pedagogical approach to sports coaching are also linked to sports coaching's parent discipline, psychology. The behaviorist nature of the pedagogic approach to sports coaching defines the topics that are open to investigation; they must be observable and measurable. Deviation from the psychological approach to sports coaching occurs as the development of an individual's cognitive and meta-cognitive strategies, and other internal processes, are not considered. Jones (2005a) suggests that this approach to sports coaching has provided useful information, but its one-dimensional view cannot be generalized across contexts. Despite its limitations, recently there has been an emergence of scholarly activity that has used educational theory to reconceptualize sports coaching as a critical pedagogical process (see Jones, 2005b; Jones and Wallace, 2005).

Authors would concede that a blurring of the boundaries between the four approaches to sports coaching does exist, opening up the possibility of scholarly activity being increasingly reflective of the more complex nature of coaching and utilizing a broader range of theory fields. For example, drawing on ideas from social psychology and using a combination of the assumptions made in both the sociological and psychological approaches to sports coaching, Bowes and Jones (2006) used relational schemas and complexity theory to put forward an alternative theoretical framework for a more realistic conception of coaching. What Bowes and Jones (2006) seek to do is to familiarize coaches and coach educators with the reality that coaching is in essence a complex, interactive process, and that the understanding of different concepts of coaching will ultimately make coaches better prepared to cope with the demands placed upon them. In emphasizing the need for coach education to take a fuller account of the interactive, social nature of coaching, Bowes and Jones (2006) demonstrate the importance of moving beyond more traditional coach education models towards a presentation of coaching as a dynamic process that takes place within the social arena and not in isolation.

The previous discussion using Jones' (2005a) characterization of research into sports coaching, explicitly covers three of Gilbert and Trudel's (2004a) research categories–coach behaviors, coach thoughts, and coach characteristics—however coach career development, that would be subsumed into the 'modeling' approach is a research category that is emerging as one of key importance[30] and therefore in need of further discussion. Lyle (2008) highlights that "government proposals for the professionalization of coaching have a clear developmental context, and the discourse is directed to community sport and high performance sport. (p.214)"[31] In addition to this, Lyle (2008) presents sport coaching as a key component of sport provision:

> Part of sport participation is dependent to a greater or lesser extent on sport leadership, teaching, instruction or coaching. In so far as sports development is a process that is intended to lead to increased sport participation, more sustained participation or improved standards of performance, sport coaching (as a collective term) becomes an extremely important element of provision. However, sports coaching is a contested term in the sense that there are quite distinct forms of coaching that can be associated with sport participation domains and contexts. (p.215)

Critically, Lyle (2008) indicates support for the necessity of both domain-specificity and context-specificity in sport coaching. Lyle (2008) uses examples from each end of the 'participation continuum' to emphasize the need for this:

> Sports coaching education/certification has traditionally neglected the pedagogical delivery skills, and this may render such coaches less suitable for the initiation-level demands in school-based interventions . . . As a picture gradually emerges of coaching roles with specialised functions and expertise being associated with specific domains, there is also potential for the 'wrong' forms of coaching to be adopted. This is generally thought to describe the deployment of (usually) higher level sports-specific coaches whose emphasis on technical development and preparation for competition is assumed to be less suitable for the less committed beginner, for whom sport is often a means to achieving other benefits. (p.222)

Unfortunately policy formation influencing the practice of sports coaching can be seen to respond in line with the drive for evidence-based policy-making in the wider context of sport policy without consideration that there is a marked difference between the theoretical logic of evidence-based policy making and what happens in reality. This is what Coalter (2007) would highlight as one of the methodological weaknesses associated with research evidence informing policy and practice, and that this "reflects the *mythopoeic status* of sport and the assumption of inevitably positive outcomes, with little need for monitoring and evaluation [in a sports coaching context]—sport works" (p.1). This is evident in 'The UK Coaching Framework: A 3–7-11 Action Plan' in which sports coaching levels have become aligned with LTAD [Long Term Athlete Development] stages, and indeed the language of Balyi's work now dominates such that coaching development in now termed 'Long Term Coaching Development' [LTCD].[32] Although there are those that support the premise of LTAD being used as a framework for coach education (Van Neutegem, 2006; Way and O'Leary, 2006) Lyle (2008) critiques the policy on the basis that the alignment created between LTAD stages and levels of coaching are achieved through the coach's role function and not the coaching domain. Indeed, Trudel (2006) disagrees with LTADs use for coaches' development as LTAD is based on physiological growth and development theories of adolescents (the 'what' and 'when' of coaching) whereas coach education should be based on adult learning theories (the 'how' to coach). There are now calls for research into the training and development of coaches (Lyle, 2007; Nash and Collins, 2006) with the next step looking at it from a lifelong learner perspective (Côté, 2006; Gilbert, Côté and Mallett, 2006).

INFLUENCE OF SPORTS COACHING RESEARCH

Having demonstrated that that the major policy shaping the professionalization of the sport coaching profession—'The UK Coaching Framework: A 3–7-11 Action Plan'—is based on an adherence to the governments propensity for evidence-based policy formation and a problematic research base, it is necessary to critique the practice of sport coaching research in order to be able to argue for a reconceptualization of the 'theme field.'

Coaching research has had very limited influence on the way that coaches are trained or the content of policies and large-scale programs (Abraham and Collins, 1998; Lyle, 2002) signifying a theory-practice gap.[33] Trudel and Gilbert (2006) suggest that producers of coaching research typically publish their results in scientific journals written for other scientists with little or no consideration on applying the findings to coach education, the practice of coaching, or coaching practitioners. The tension between practitioners and researchers is not unique to the 'theme field' of sports coaching,[34] and can be attributed to different goals between different stakeholders in the research process: "the professional wants new solutions to operational problems while the researcher seeks new knowledge" (Bates, 2002b, p.404). This propensity to align the research to an academic audience might also lead to the researchers asking the 'wrong' types of research questions.[35]

> Are the research questions driven by basic research agendas, which may or may not have application for coaching, or by practical issues in coach training and coaching? This raises two issues for immediate consideration: what are the main research questions that have been posed in coaching research, and who are the main authors of this research? (Trudel and Gilbert, 2006, p.524)

In answer to the questions posed, 80% of the main research questions investigated in coaching research have been oriented towards a quantitative epistemology. However, it must be highlighted that the adoption of a qualitative research methodology is on the steady increase (from 1970–77 [0%] to 1998–2001 [28.2%]) (Gilbert and Trudel, 2004a). Extrapolating from Gilbert and Trudel's (2004a) data to present day,[36] a conservative estimate of 45% of coaching research adopting a qualitative approach could be postulated. Within the confines of methodological orientation, it is not surprising to see that questionnaires were by far the most common method of data collection (69%), however recent increases in qualitative methodology have resulted in a concomitant increase in the use of interviews and a relative decline in questionnaire use (Gilbert and Trudel, 2004a). Indeed, not only is there an increase in the use of interviews as the method of data collection (See Jones et al., 2004), it must be emphasized that contemporary coaching research can be seen to embrace an eclectic range of qualitative methods such as autoethnography (See Haleem et al., 2004; Jones, 2006; Purdy et al., 2008), narratives (See Denison, 2007; Tsang, 2000), poetic representations (See Sparkes et al., 2003) and fictional dialogue (See Jones, 2007). Methodological concerns can also be expressed regarding the reliance on a single method of data collection (only 14.4% of articles combined two or more methods in the same study), the focus on one type of research participant–the head coach—[37]leading to a one-dimensional portrait of coaching, a scarcity of portraits of the coaching process from a female[38] or other so-called 'minority' groups,[39] a predominance of team sports as the medium for study,[40] and an over emphasis on school (college/university) based sport coaching. It is these methodological concerns that a reconceptualized field of sports coaching must address.

Interestingly, in relation to Trudel and Gilbert's (2006) second question—who are the main authors of this research? An issue that was highlighted from Gilbert and Trudel's (2004a) analysis is that there is a wide range of contributors to coaching research, and between 1970 and 2001 only six authors had contributed at least ten or more journal publications: Pastore (n = 21); Chelladurai (n = 13); Salmela (n = 13); Trudel (n = 13); Gould (n

= 12), Solomon (n = 10). In addition to this, seventeen authors have all authored or co-authored at least six articles in the database. These seventeen scholars frequently collaborate on research publications. However, in Gilbert and Trudel's (2004a) analysis these seventeen authors collectively represent only 2% of the published articles. This leads to the issue that few scholars have had a programmatic research line in coaching (Kahan, 1999) which has left the vast majority of sport coaching research at the formative stage and thus limiting its development and application as a field of research (Trudel and Gilbert, 2006). The effect of this on an academic's career progression is that:

> Because coaching science is at the stage of a topic (theme field) and not a theory field, it is not likely that university departments will hire coaching science specialists in the theory fields . . . If by chance, those who are hired have interests in investigating a theme field such as coaching science, then research on coaching science will continue to be generated (Gilbert and Trudel, 2004a, p.395)

Even within the confinement of this context, Trudel (2006) identifies a range of academics that have managed to undertake and disseminate research in the theme field of sport coaching research. The work of Gould and his colleagues (Diffenbach, Moffett, Guinan, Greenleaf, Chung) in the United States and also the work of Salmela and colleagues in Canada are similarly defined as instrumental in line with Gilbert and Trudel's (2004a) analysis, however importantly other academics are creating a programmatic research line in sport coaching and therefore facilitating it's development as a field of research on the journey to establishing a theory field:

> While in Canada we must consider the work of . . . Côté and colleagues [Baker; Abernathy; Baria; Russell; Sedgwick; Dowd]. In England we have to mention Lyle, Jones and colleagues [Armour; Potrac], as well as Jowett and colleagues [Cockerill]. Finally, in France, the work of d'Arripe-Longueville and colleagues [Fournier], and the study of Saury and Durand are often referenced. A search in any sport research database using the names of these authors will provide reading for hours. (Trudel, 2006, p.127)

Essentially it is these scholars—'the elders' (Mitchell, 1992) or 'the gatekeepers of Good Science" (Murray et al., 2007)—that are controlling the "invisible networks of prestige" (Mitchell, 1992, p.426) determining what research is accepted for publication in professional journals and ultimately prescribing what is the knowledge base for the theory field of sport coaching. In addition to this Trudel and Gilbert (2006) allude to the focus of 'the elders' being narrowly defined by one or two categories within the coaching database:

Thus although scholars from different fields have contributed to coaching research, if there is no effort made to work together and combine the different perspectives we will lose an opportunity to create a holistic understanding of the coaching process, and a better understanding of its complexity.[41] (p.525)

CONCLUSION

This chapter has explicated the central space that sport inhabits in contemporary society. Not only is sport valued intrinsically for its own sake in developing skills, self-esteem, enjoyment, tolerance, discipline and fun for its participants, sport is seen as an important vehicle by nation states and global associations to contribute to a corporate, economic strategy and external, wider social roles. The marginalized utopian ideology that sport is not a part of politics or has nothing to do with politics—the myth of autonomy (Maguire et al., 2002)—is critiqued from the position that political ideology can be seen to manifest in public policy through sport. The process of 'joined up government' (Houlihan and White, 2002) evident with the Labour government has led to embracing the assumption that sport possesses the potential to contribute to the public policy drive of a social inclusion agenda. The wider role for sport nationally includes social and economic regeneration, crime reduction, health improvement and educational achievement, and additionally gender and ethnicity equality and peace on a global scale, although Coalter (2007) questions whether there is robust research evidence on which to base these policies.

Even with the debate surrounding the robustness of the evidence-based sports policy universe, there is no question that sport is *valued* for both intrinsic and extrinsic reasons and more and more children are participating in organized sport around the world (De Knopp et al., 1996). With more sport participants and a wider social role for sport, then more emphasis needs to be placed on the environment in which this participation takes place, and indeed "one major factor that influences all performers [at all levels] throughout their sporting careers is the quality and appropriateness of the coaching environment" (Martindale et al., 2005, p.353). There has been a considerable increase in sports coaching as an academic endeavor at foundation degree, undergraduate, and postgraduate level that has mirrored the rise in government policy. In order to bridge the theory-practice gap for coaching practitioners, stakeholders in the coaching process (athletes, parents, officials, etc.) and policy makers, there is need for the reconceptualization of the 'theme field' of sports coaching research to establish itself a programmatic research line that is sympathetic to the wider externalities presented by sport. This would require overcoming the invisible networks of prestige afforded to the 'elders' or 'gatekeepers' of sports coaching research and also prevail over the methodological *crisis* that posits a one-dimensional portrait of sports coaching (Gilbert and Trudel, 2004a). The result would be research that not only reflects the current sports coaching moment but also meets the desire to create a holistic understanding of the sports coaching process, and a fuller understanding of its complexity (Jones et al., 2002; Trudel and Gilbert, 2006) and of the potential influences and impacts that meaningful sports coaching knowledge can, and should, have.

5 A Brief Genealogy of Cultural Studies and Sport, Physical Cultural Studies, and the McUniversity

The greatest enemy of scientific progress is orthodoxy. (Brignell, 2000, p.209.)

INTRODUCTION

According to Ben Carrington (2001), cultural studies have achieved something of a hegemonic position within contemporary intellectual life. Certainly, cultural studies have long occupied an important place within the international sociology of sport/sport studies community, just as it does within other realms of transdisciplinary inquiry. Of particular concern however, especially within the sporting context, has been the widespread and oftentimes superficial appropriation of cultural studies epithets by sport-focused scholars. In seeking to counter the obfuscatory and apolitical trend discernible with some cultural studies of sport-work, we fully recognize the cultural studies outlined herein is but one, of numerous, likeminded intellectual trajectories. We equally acknowledge that our predilection for what is a largely British—in origin, if not subsequent development and dissemination—understanding of cultural studies is a product of our own cultural and geographic histories, and linguistic inadequacies. Nonetheless, the (British) cultural studies approach briefly outlined herein does display mutually reinforcing affinities within intellectual movements derived from other socio-historic settings, including France, Italy, the U.S., Africa, and Latin America (Miller, 2001b). Thus, we consider it to be an on-going and generative understanding of cultural studies, increasingly complicated by unfolding transnational linkages and appropriations.

CONTEXTUAL CULTURAL STUDIES AND SPORT

Cultural studies' most globally recognizable form derives from the work that emanated from the Center for Contemporary Cultural Studies (CCCS) at the University of Birmingham, particularly between the years 1964 to 1979 (Lee, 2003). During this time, figures such as Richard Hoggart,

Stuart Hall, John Clarke, Chas Critcher, Angela McRobbie, Dick Hebdige, and Paul Willis, engaged and advanced the post-war intellectual project initiated by E.P. Thompson (*The Making of the English Working Class*), Raymond Williams (*Culture and Society* and *The Long Revolution*), Hoggart himself (*The Uses of Literacy*) trained on rescuing the everyday cultures of the industrializing and industrialized working classes from the condescensions of entrenched academic disinterest. As such, the CCCS became a vanguard of the near-mythologized—if not universally welcomed (Rojek and Turner, 2000)—cultural turn, that has significantly revised the sensibilities, preoccupations, and products of intellectual life within the United Kingdom and beyond (Hall, 2007). There are, of course, myriad constitutive facets responsible for this turn to the cultural realm, not least of which being the conclusive disruption of institutionalized hierarchies that had long positioned *high/elite* culture as a legitimate realm of academic inquiry, and *low/popular* culture as the target for widespread academic disdain and disregard. In the decades immediately following the end of World War II—a time of great social and cultural upheaval within British society—such hierarchies began to be undermined, through the outpourings of Thomson, Williams, Hoggart et al., who identified the popular realm as a key site through which power and power relations were enacted, expressed, and experienced.

Given its preoccupation with the structure and experience of popular cultural formations and expressions, it should come as no surprise that sport featured regularly within early CCCS work. Indeed, Hoggart fully recognized sport as a popular practice inextricably linked to the material conditions and experiences of working class existence. The Uses of Literacy was one of the first cultural analyses to implicate popular institutions, including sport, in the production of "individual's private, everyday life—family roles, gender relations, language patterns, the community's 'common sense'" (Turner, 1990, p. 48). Subsequently, studies by Critcher (1971, 1974), Watson (1973), Willis (1974), Clarke (1973, 1975), Peters (1976), Critcher et al. (1977), Ingham (1978), and Green and Jenkins (1982), demonstrated cultural studies' recognition of sport as an important, and diverse, site of critical analysis. During the 1970s and 1980s, a number of researchers more institutionally anchored within the sociology of sport and sport studies communities also developed, and/or encouraged, cultural studies-informed research focused on sport. In terms of their influence, uppermost among these was arguably Jennifer Hargreaves (1982b, 1984; 1986b) and John Hargreaves (1982a; 1986a; 1987). Nonetheless, numerous others also made significant contributions, including: Susan Birrell (1989, 1990); Peter Donnelly (1983, 1988); Richard Gruneau (1983, 1988); Robert Hollands (1984, 1988); Alan Ingham (1984; 1985); Alan Tomlinson (1989; 1984); Garry Whannel (1986, 1992); and, David Whitson (1984, 1986). These, and other, cultural studies-informed sport scholars laid the foundations for what became, and to a large extent remains, an important school of thought, position, and/or sensibility within sport studies (c.f. Carrington, 2010; Carrington and MacDonald, 2009; Cole, 2007; Giardina, 2005; J.W. Howell and Ingham, 2001; King, 2006; Mary G. McDonald, 2008; M.G. McDonald and Toglia, 2010; Miller, 2001a, 2009; Newman and Giardina, 2011).

Despite the influence of the aforementioned works, the sometimes trite and superficial appropriation of cultural studies within the sport studies community, is a manifestation of what Gottdiener (2000, p.7) referred to as the reductive forcing of "complex conceptions into simple catchwords," and the resultant trivialization of the approach to all and sundry. As a result, cultural studies is oftentimes reduced to being an empty metaphor; a vacuous and bland descriptor of any study focused on sport as a cultural form. As with cultural studies more generally, it would be remiss to characterize cultural studies of sport exponents as being linked by a single theoretical or methodological position. Both exemplify a perpetual and generative "unity- in-difference" (Clarke, 1991, p.17), through which multiple theoretical influences, research methods, and sites of analysis operate, oftentimes in contention with each other. However, and as the phrase implies, there is a unity within cultural studies which links its seemingly disparate elements, and which needs to be re-invoked for fear of compromising its very *raison d'être*. Paraphrasing Miller (2001b), there is a need for vigilance in terms of outlining precisely what cultural studies is, and indeed what it isn't. Or, in Grossberg's terms, in order to preserve the integrity of the cultural studies project, it is important to recognize "that not everything is cultural studies, that the field is not entirely open" (Grossberg, 1997b, p.344).

Recognizing the need to establish parameters—however protean—it is our enduring assertion that a cultural studies approach to sport is not, and can never be, simply about the examination of sport as a form of (popular) culture. Rather, it requires a deep-rooted, and unapologetic, political commitment to sport as a cultural form inexplicably tied–in, expected and unexpected, corroborative and combative, empowering and disempowering ways–to the enactment, expression, and experiencing of wider power relations. Hence, it is our committed belief that sport matters as a focus of critical intellectual inquiry: the cultural studies of sport being "a vital component of the struggle to change the world and to make the world more humane, and that cultural studies, as a particular project, a particular sort of intellectual practice, has something valuable to contribute" (Grossberg, 2006, p. 2).

From its very inception, cultural studies was a politically-inspired intellectual movement that congealed as a response to the contingencies of a specific historical context. A series of "long term shifts taking place in British society" (Hall, 1980b, p. 15) came to a head during the 1950s, creating new forms and expressions of material affluence, and an ensuing widespread panic among many intellectuals fearing the sweeping Americanization of Britain as a consumer society (Moran, 2006). Among many of the British left, the intensification of British consumer culture was linked to the perceived break-up of traditional culture, especially traditional class cultures, which seemingly disrupted what were established class-based political affiliations and allegiances. Hence, the origins of cultural studies were "firmly anchored in a strategy of political struggle . . . its priorities were those of an elaboration of the cultural problems facing the left" (Davies, 1990, p.2); not least of these being attempting to understand why, in the wake of the emergence of the Welfare State and the relative commodity affluence of the mid-late 1950s, large sections of the British working class voted Conservative and thereby aligned themselves with a political ideology which did not appear to represent traditional working-class values. With the passing of the decades, and the simultaneous global diffusion of the cultural studies project, the social problems facing cultural studies exponents have understandably altered. Nonetheless, and despite changing spatial and temporal contingencies, a constant and defining characteristic of the cultural studies' praxis, is its status as a "project that reshapes itself in and attempts to respond to new conjunctures as problem-spaces" (Grossberg, 2010, p.1). In a fundamental sense, therefore, cultural studies of sport can be considered a critical and contextually-driven intellectual project prefigured on furthering the understanding of the politics of contemporary sport culture: sport culture being understood in Williams' (1981) terms, as an important signifying system through which humans make sense of the contextual complexities world they live in, and produce meanings by which power and power relations become communicated, experienced, explored, reproduced, and/or contested.

At the definitional core of our understanding of the cultural studies of sport is the intellectual practice and praxis of "radical contextualism" (Grossberg, 2010), within which "context is everything and everything is context": an understanding of cultural studies "as a contextual theory of contexts as the lived milieux of power" (Grossberg, 1997b, pp.7–8). Stuart Hall's (1996b) "Marxism without guarantees" provides the conceptual framework for this contextual approach to sport culture. He engaged culture as a continually contested terrain: a "sort of constant battlefield" between the constraining influence of the social structure and the creative impulses of human agents (Hall, 1981b, p.233). In doing so, Hall advanced "a different conception of 'determinancy'" (Hall, 1996b, p.44) to that circumvented by both the economically deterministic perils of vulgar Marxism (which asserted a necessary correspondence between the various elements of society and the overbearing economic realm) and the romanticism of cultural humanism (which asserted a necessarily no correspondence between the various elements of society, thus providing the human agent and cultural practices with a romanticized level of autonomy). As its name implies, within his "Marxism without guarantees" there exists "no guarantee . . . there is no necessary correspondence . . . there is no necessary non-correspondence" between one level of a social formation and another, between the social structure and the human agent, or between a cultural practice such as sport and the varied forces acting within a social structure (Hall, 1985, p.94).

> Hall's neo-Gramscian approach keys on the uniqueness of the spatial and/or temporal moment in question. Nevertheless, according to this thinking: while there are no necessary correspondences (relations), there are always real (effective) correspondences. The meaning, effects, and politics of particular social events, texts, practices, and structures (what we in fact mean by their "identity") are never guaranteed, either causally (by their origins, however deferred) or through inscription (as if they were self-determined) . . . The specificity of any conjuncture, at whatever level of abstraction, is always produced, determinate. (Grossberg, 1997b, pp.220–221)

Hall's contextualism is thus prefigured on the uniqueness of any historical moment, which has to be reconstructed in terms of the levels and trajectories of determination that help to constitute the context and the experience thereof. So, determinate relations do exist, they just cannot be guaranteed in advance:

> Understanding "determinancy" in terms of setting of limits, the establishment of parameters, the defining of the space of operations, the concrete conditions of existence, the "givenness" of social practices, rather than in terms of the absolute predictability of particular outcomes, is the only basis of a "Marxism without final guarantees." It establishes the open horizon of Marxist theorizing—determinancy without guaranteed closures. (Hall, 1996b, p.45)

In advancing this understanding, Hall returns cultural studies to the Marx of the *Grundrisse. He* asserted an understanding that acknowledges that cultural forms (practices, products, institutions, organizations, etc.) represent and comprise "a rich aggregate of many determinations and relations" (Marx, as cited in McLellan, 1977, p.351) but reminded us that the nature and direction of these correspondences cannot be guaranteed in advance:

> They are, in a dialectic sense, contingent on the specificities of the conjuncture which they help to constitute. In other words, a cultural entity cannot "be defined independently of its existence within the context. An event or practice . . . does not exist apart from the forces of the context that constitute it as what it is." (Grossberg, 1997b, p.255)

In many ways, epistemological and ontological glue of Hall's understanding lies within the notion of the articulation. According to Hall:

> . . . an articulation is the form of the connection that, under certain
> conditions, can make a unity of two different elements. It is the linkage
> which is not necessary, determined, absolute and essential for all time.
> You have to ask, under what circumstances can a connection be forged
> or made? (1996a, p.141)

Unearthing the socially and historically contingent matrix of social, economic, political, and technological articulations represents the primary
method of contextual cultural studies. Moreover, it is the theory and
method of articulation that "transforms cultural studies from a model of
communication (production-text-consumption; encoding-decoding) to a
theory of contexts" (Grossberg, 1997b, p.347).

Cultural studies' conjunctural theory-method engages society as a concrete, historically produced, fractured totality made up of different types
of social relations, practices, and experiences. Each form of cultural practice has its own relatively autonomous field of effects. Yet, the meaning
and effects of any concrete practice—its conjunctural identity—are always
over-determined by the network of relations with which it is articulated
(Hall, 1996a, 1996b). Identifying the conjuncturally contingent points of
articulation involves "drawing lines or connections which are the productive links between points, events or practices . . . within a multidimensional
and multi- directional field. These lines map out reality in terms of the productive relations between events" (Grossberg, 1992, p.50). This production
of contexts should not infer that the method involves inserting a cultural
practice into a pre-existing context, out of which it generates its identity
and effects. For, it is important to stress that context is "not something out
there, within which practices occur or which influence the development of
practices. Rather, identities, practices, and effects generally, constitute the
very context within which they are practices, identities or effects" (Slack,
1996, p.125). Articulation, then, involves a method reconstructing a cultural practice's conjunctural relations, identity, and effects to produce a
contextually specific map of the social formation. Clearly, this has important ramifications for the place of theory within cultural studies of sport
practice. For, according to this contextual cultural studies approach, theories are not mobilized uncritically and in toto, thereby letting the researcher
off the interpretation hook by "providing answers which are always known
in advance" (Grossberg, 1992, p.50). The search for an "exact theoretical
fit" is futile (Slack, 1996, p.113). Rather, as Hall outlined:

> I want to suggest a different metaphor for theoretical work: the meta-
> phor of struggle, of wrestling with the angels. The only theory worth
> having is that which you have to fight off, not that which you speak
> with profound fluency (1992, p.280)

Differently put, contextual cultural studies of sport requires a critical
engagement with theory; a grappling with theory to see what is useful and

appropriate within a particular sporting context, and discarding/reworking that which is not.

To operate within a contextual cultural studies strategy means recognizing that sport forms (practices, products, institutions, etc.) can only be understood by the way that they are articulated into a particular set of complex social, economic, political, and technological relationships that compose the social context, recognizing that "there are no necessary correspondences in history, but history is always the production of such connections or correspondences" (Grossberg, 1992, p.53). Moreover, whereas cultural practices, such as sport, are produced from specific social and historic contexts, they are also actively engaged in the ongoing constitution of the conditions out of which they emerge. The structure, identity, and effect of any sport form is thus:

> . . . given, in part, by the social field into which it is incorporated, the practices with which it articulates and is made to resonate. What matters is not the intrinsic or historically fixed objects of culture, but the state of play in cultural relations. (Hall, 1981b, p.235)

The method implicit within Hall's articulated conjuncturalism is about reconstructing a context within which a sporting practice, product, or institution becomes understandable. It is and aggressively non-reductionist (the multiplicity of forces and effects deny the possibility of reducing causality to one factor, i.e., the economic), yet contingently determinate (it acknowledges the notion of determinacy but stresses its multidirectionality, fluidity, and uncertainty), theory-method, which implores the researcher to actively create context by "forging connections between practices and effects" (Grossberg, 1992, p.54). Often, this forging of connections necessitates interpreting (theorizing) the relationship between the sporting phenomenon under scrutiny and prevailing determinate forces.

Instead of engaging sport as a foundational, originary, or essential category, it is important that an explicitly contingent understanding of sport should emerge as an outgrowth of contextually grounded and sensitive research practice. According to this approach, sport is engaged and interpreted as a fluid, dynamic category, whose definition and composition is contingent on the specificities of the context (both synchronic and diachronic) in question: Sport has meant, and continues to mean, different things in different cultural and temporal contexts. The structure and influence of sport in any given conjuncture is a product of intersecting, multidirectional lines of articulation between the forces and practices (including sport) that compose the social context. The very uniqueness of the historical moment, or conjuncture, means there is a condition of no necessary correspondence, or indeed non-correspondence, between sport and particular forces (i.e., the economic): Forces do determine the givenness of sporting practices, their determinacy just cannot be guaranteed in advance. So, sport-oriented research demands a truly contextual sensibility premised on, and seeking to excavate and theorize, the contingent relations, structure, and effects of sport forms: a sport without guarantees.

TOWARD A *PHYSICAL* CULTURAL STUDIES (PCS) SENSIBILITY

Although cultural studies has come to occupy an established—if by no means inalienable—position within the sociology of sport community, its presence and influence has perhaps encouraged some critical scholars to question the value of the term sport, as a descriptor of their intellectual focus and practice. Doubtless propelled by the broader turn to cultural theory and method—and its concomitant refocusing on the body as a social and cultural construction— the range of sociology of sport research has expanded to incorporate a broad range of empirical domains. In addition to *sport*, sociology of sport schol- ars are now drawn to a range of empirical sites, including but by no means restricted to: exercise, fitness, health, dance, movement, leisure, recreation, daily living, and work-related activities. The empirical focus of the field now runs the whole gamut of physical culture. Hence, rather than an "expres- sive totality" coalescing around sport, the sociology of sport is, in actuality, characterized by a "unity-in-difference" (Clarke, 1991, p.17): the unifying element being a commitment toward understanding various expressions or iterations of the physical. Not that sport should be ignored or shunned, as it is by some elements of the academic community: doubtless fearful of its populist and anti-intellectual associations. Neither should it be the exclusive curricular or research focus. Rather, sport has to be considered one, of many, constituent elements within the broader domain of physical culture.

In recent years, there has been a marked physical culturalization (the process of becoming more attuned to and focused on physical culture as a field of inquiry) of the sociology of sport (and, indeed, other elements of the sport studies community). The physical cultural turn can be evidenced within research emanating from a number of disciplinary homes (Atkin- son, 2010; Brown, 2006; Duncan, 2007; Hargreaves and Vertinsky, 2007; Hughson, 2008; Kirk, 1999; Markula and Silk, 2011; Peabody, 2009; Pronger, 1998; Rich, 2011; Thorpe, 2009; Zweiniger-Bargielowska, 2006). However, this physical culturalization is perhaps most apparent in the on- going dialogue pertaining to the possibilities for, and preoccupations of, a Physical Cultural Studies (henceforth, PCS) (Andrews, 2008; Atkinson, 2011; Giardina and Newman, 2011a; Giardina and Newman, 2011b; Silk and Andrews, 2011). Despite its seeming contemporaneity, the roots of PCS can be traced back to Alan Ingham's radical prescription for the future of kinesiology, as outlined in his chapter "Toward a Department of Physical Cultural Studies and an End to Tribal Warfare" (Ingham, 1997). Therein, Ingham implored researchers to venture beyond the relatively narrow (if admittedly ill-defined) sporting domain. For Ingham, and numerous others who presently exist and operate under the increasingly nebulous sociology of sport label, there are numerous ways of being physically active which demand critical attention. For them, limiting their scope of inquiry to sport is as inappropriate, as it is artificial.

The palpable intellectual migration from sport to physical culture realized by various PCS scholars, nevertheless represents the corollary of numerous inter-related trends, not least of which was a tangible yearning by many to mobilize alternative objects and modes of inquiry. This desire was oftentimes prompted by the restrictive and disenabling parochialisms of some branches of the sociology of sport, for which sport (in the narrow sense of the term) was the-be and end-all. Differently put, the roots of PCS can be discerned from the exercise, fitness, recreation, movement, health, or dance-related research of numerous scholars, whose non-sport foci and endeavors placed them on the periphery—at the very least the empirical periphery—of the sociology of sport community. Concurrently, and unencumbered by such sub-disciplinary baggage and expectations, physical culture (in all its myriad forms: sport, exercise, fitness, recreation, movement, health, and dance) drew increased attention from those navigating the cultural turn within sociology from the 1980s onwards. Within such a moment, the structures, practices, representations, and experiences of physical activity certainly proved natural extensions for the emergent fields of sociology of the body/embodied sociology, body studies, and for researchers drawn from diverse intellectual constituencies, yet for whom the body had become inescapable (i.e., Gender Studies, Queer Studies, Race and Ethnic Studies, Media Studies, and Urban Studies). In this way, it is possible to consider physical culturalization—particularly as manifest with the emergence of a Physical Cultural Studies—as a phenomenon occurring both within, and outside, the sociology of sport.

In prefatory terms, PCS is a critical, transdisciplinary, multi-method project focused on generating contextually-based understandings of the corporeal practices, discourses, and subjectivities through which active bodies become organized, represented, and experienced in relation to the operations of social power. Empirically, PCS thus identifies the body—and even more specifically the active body–as the central focus of its intellectual labor. Physically active bodies—the institutional and discursive formations which both and enable and constrain them, and the subjectivities they inhabit, perform, and embody—may appear natural (an authentic expression of some biological essence). Yet, this masks the sociocultural constitution of the body, which has to be understood in relationship to its biological constitution. In problematizing—and thereby countering—the scientific knowledges and naturalizing truths that have commandeered the body as an object of inquiry, PCS is a project motivated by the need to better understand the sociocultural organization, representation, and experience of active embodiment.

Without question, PCS is not an established, commonly accepted, or even widely recognized intellectual formation. Rather, PCS encompasses a loosely constituted, disparately located (both intellectually and spatially), yet noticeably emergent community of scholars whose diversely-focused and enacted work is united through a common commitment toward engaging varied dimensions or expressions of active physicality. While routinely identified as sociologists of sport, these researchers are clearly not restricted by an adherence to an exclusive and limiting understanding of sport as their empirical focus, nor by an overbearing obligation to the theoretical and methodological precepts of sociology as their superordinate disciplinary configuration. Not that all, or indeed any of them, would necessary characterize their work as PCS: that is perhaps an act of unsanctioned ascription made in an attempt to discursively constitute the preoccupations and boundaries of PCS as a field of inquiry at this moment in time. Nonetheless, we have identified three characteristic dimensions, or sensibilities, evident within PCS scholarship.

THE THREE CHARACTERISTICS OF PCS SCHOLARSHIP

First, PCS recognizes the ontological complexity and interrelatedness of physical culture. As previously indicated, there are numerous ways of *being physically active*. Pace Frow and Morris (2000) the empirical field of physical culture can be considered an ontologically mixed entity. Ingham (1997) identified the exercise, health, movement, recreation, and sport-related dimensions of physical culture (to which one could probably add the pedagogic, work, and ADL: Activities of Daily Living). Each of these spheres possesses a "relative autonomy" (Hall, 1981a) in relation to each other, in as much as they incorporate (quite literally) different motivations for, and practices of, organizing and regulating human movement. However, it needs to be reiterated that the boundaries marking the various facets of physical culture are necessarily fluid, dynamic, and thereby always likely to encourage processes of contamination; something which makes sectoral delineation, at best, contingent, suggestive, and approximate, but nonetheless necessary for the purposes of empirical analysis.

It should also be noted that physical culture's ontological complexity is compounded by the fact that each of its various dimensions can be engaged or experienced in multiple ways. For each of them, the active body is something that can either be experienced (by the instrumental subject) or observed (as a representational object). Hence, PCS encompasses a breadth of empirical sites and experiences[1]. In order to illustrate this diversity, we would draw attention to the following studies which although they may not have identified themselves as such, are boundary marking exemplars of the PCS project: "Pink Ribbons, Inc.: Breast cancer and the politics of philanthropy" (King, 2006); "Skatepark as Neoliberal Playground: Urban Governance, Recreation Space, and the Cultivation of Personal Responsibility" (Howell, 2008); "From social problem to personal issue: The language of lifestyle" (Howell and Ingham, 2001); "Ballin' Indo-Pak style: Pleasures, desires, and expressive practices of "South Asian American" masculinity" (Thangaraj, 2010); "How to look good (nearly) naked: The performative regulation of the swimmer's body" (Scott, 2010); "Teaching the Politics of Obesity: Insights into Neoliberal Embodiment and Contemporary Biopolitics" (Guthman, 2009); "Chronic everyday life: Rhythmanalysing street performance" (Simpson, 2008); "Cyborg and Supercrip: The Paralympics Technology and the (Dis)empowerment of Disabled Athletes" (Howe, 2011); "Sport, Spectacle, and NASCAR Nation: Consumption and the Cultural Politics of Neoliberalism" (Newman and Giardina, 2011); "Girl, Interrupted: Interpreting Semenya's Body, Gender Verification Testing, and Public Discourse" (Vannini and Fornssler, 2011); "Hanging out and hanging about: Insider/outsider research in the sport of boxing" (Woodward, 2008); ""Healthism" and looking good: Body ideals and body practices in Norway" (Rysst, 2010); "Islam, Hijab and Young Shia Muslim Canadian Women's Discursive Constructions of Physical Activity" (Jiwani and Rail, 2010); and, "McDonald's at the Gym? A Tale of Two Curves®" (O'Toole, 2008). Clearly, the ontological complexity of physical culture (ranging as it does from the production and consumption of embodied performance through the production and consumption of mediated representations of various forms of embodiment) encourages a methodological dynamism that requires the PCS researcher to become proficient within a range of qualitative and interpretive approaches.

Second, the PCS project is profoundly and radically contextual, in that it is concerned with excavating how active bodies become organized, represented, and experienced in relation to the operations of social power. As such, PCS can be characterized as a critical sensibility and approach toward interpreting physical culture's role in the construction and experience of the "lived milieux of power" (Grossberg, 1997b, p.8). To operate within a contextual Physical Cultural Studies strategy means recognizing that physical cultural forms (practices, discourses, and subjectivities etc.) can only be understood by the way in which they are *articulated* into a particular set of complex social, economic, political, and technological relationships that comprise the social context; recognizing that "There are no necessary correspondences in history, but history is always the production of such connections or correspondences" (Grossberg, 1992, p.53). Determinate relations do exist, they just cannot be guaranteed in advance: hence, a *Physical Culture without Guarantees.*

The various dimensions of physical culture can never be substantial (possessing some fixed, immutable essential form), rather, they are unavoidably relational, and always in process: its contemporaneous iteration providing a persuasive–if illusionary–semblance of fixity within what is, in actuality, an ever-changing world. In the broadest sense, with its domineering presence within contemporary life, physical culture represents a "pressure point of complex modern societies" (Frow and Morris, 2000, p.325). It is a *site* or *point of intersection, and of negotiation of radically different kinds of determination and semiosis*; a place where social forces, discourses, institutions, and processes congregate, congeal, and are contested in a manner which contributes to the shaping of human relations, experiences, and subjectivities, in particular, contextually contingent ways.

Physical culture thus incorporates numerous 'events': the moments of "practice that crystallizes diverse temporal and social trajectories" (Frow, 2000, p.325) through which individuals negotiate their subjective—and for our interests embodied—identities and experiences. Power operates multidimensionally and multidirectionally, therefore the role of critical contextual analysis is not to involve oneself in some teleological determinism, based on a priori assumptions about the effectivity and direction of power, but rather to discern the state of conjunctural power relations, directions, and effects: the "state of play in cultural relations" (Hall, 1981b, p.235). Hence, the practice/method of Physical Cultural Studies involves identifying an "event," almost in an abstract sense, that represents a potential important focus of critical inquiry (in as much as it is implicated in hierarchical, iniquitous, unjust power relations and effects). Thus follows a process of connecting/articulating this "event" to the multiple material, institutional, and discursive determinations which suture the event—in a dialectic sense—into the conjuncture of which it is a constituent element. The commitment to, and practice of, articulation thus involves: "starting with the particular, the detail, the scrap of ordinary or banal existence, and then working to unpack the density of relations and of intersecting social domains that inform it" (Frow and Morris, 2000, p.327). Such a dialectic method and approach also presumes that while physical cultural *events* (the moments of practice), are produced from specific social and historic contexts, they are also actively engaged in the ongoing constitution of the conditions out of which they emerge.

Third, a PCS sensibility assumes that societies are fundamentally divided along hierarchically ordered lines of differentiation (i.e. those based on class, ethnic, gender, ability, generational, national, racial, and/or sexual norms), as realized through the operations of power and power relations within the social formation:

> *Power* operates at every level of human life; it is neither an abstract universal structure nor a subjective experience. It is both limiting and productive: producing differences, shaping relations, structuring identities and hierarchies, but also enabling practices and empowering social subjects . . . At the level of social life, power involves the historical production of "economies"—the social production, distribution, and consumption—of different forms of value (e.g. capital, money, meanings, information, representations, identities, desires, emotions, pleasures). It is the specific articulation of social subjects into these circuits of value, circuits which organize social possibilities and differences,

that constructs the structured inequalities of social power. (Grossberg, 1997c, p.241)

PCS contends that the various dimensions of physical cultural represent moments at which such social divisions are imposed, experienced, and at times contested. A Physical Cultural Studies is thus driven by the need to understand the complexities, experiences, and injustices of the physical cultural context it confronts (particularly in relation to the relations, operations, and effects of power). Hence, at its most fundamental level, Physical Cultural Studies seeks to "construct a political history of the *(physical cultural)* present" (Grossberg, 2006, p.2, italics added), through which it becomes possible to construct politically expedient physical cultural possibilities out of the historical circumstances it confronts.

PCS is motivated by an unequivocal "commitment to progressive social change" (Miller, 2001b, p.1), and thereby struggles to produce the type of knowledge through which it would be in a position to intervene into the broader social world, and *make a difference*. One often overlooked consequence of this, it that PCS' relationship with theory is necessary, yet ambivalent and certainly unpredictable. As within the cultural studies project itself, the mobilization of social and cultural theorizing is "never about finding 'the right theory,' or demonstrating one's theoretical acumen, or playing some theoretical chess game of one-up-manship. It is about understanding what is going on, and therefore, it is about finding out whatever theoretical positions will enable that project" (Wright, 2001, p.134). PCS rests on a form of "performative pedagogy"(Giroux, 2001, p.7) in which empirical theorizing becomes the basis for "intervening into contexts and power . . . in order to enable people to act more strategically in ways that may change their context for the better" (Grossberg, 1996, p.143).

PCS is thus political in the sense of identifying, and analyzing—and thereby seeking to intervene into–the operation and experience of power and power relations (sometimes liberatory, oftentimes repressive, frequently both), through the examination of the contested and complex realm of physical culture. In what we might term a pernicious present, we need to be prepared to confront the injustices of a particular society or public sphere, unembarrassed by the label political, and unafraid to consummate a relationship with emancipatory consciousness (Kincheloe and McLaren, 2005). We need an approach concerned with issues of power and justice and the ways the economy, class, race, gender, ideologies, discourses, education, religion, and other social institutions and cultural dynamics interact to create an unjust social system and produce work targeted toward the present conjuncture (e.g., neocolonialism and neoimperialism) that can empower individuals by confronting injustices and promoting social change. In short, the project of PCS needs to be a pragmatics of hope in an age of cynical reason (Kincheloe and McLaren, 2005). This is an approach that is ensconced in the need to reclaim education as a public good and recognize that academic labor is a social endeavor. Therefore, theoretical work is not an end in itself. PCS must be meaningful through connecting private troubles and public concerns, extending its critical, performative, and utopian impulses to address urgent social issues in the interests of promoting social change (Giroux, 2001).

CONCLUSION AND PCS IN THE MCUNIVERSITY

Cultural studies holds special intellectual promise to the study of sports coaching for a multiplicity of reasons. Sports' coaching, as a cultural site, is imbued with power relations; therefore our research should be underscored by a pragmatics of hope (Kincheloe and McLaren, 2005) that can understand, critique and expose such power relations as they constitute the empirical core of our field. Moving beyond interdisciplinarity towards active and aggressive anti-disciplinarity—however uncomfortable this might be to some in the academic community—affords sports coaching scholars the freedom to draw from whatever fields are necessary to produce the knowledge required for a particular project (Nelson et al., 1992). This chapter has provided a brief genealogy of cultural studies from the early CCCS work through to the appropriation of cultural studies within the sports studies community. Recent years have witnessed a marked physical culturalization of the sociology of sport with the physical turn being evidenced within research from a number of disciplinary homes. It is this physical culturalization that is most apparent in the on-going dialogue pertaining to the possibilities for, and preoccupations of, a Physical Cultural Studies. It is PCS, with its migration from sport to physical culture, the ontological complexity of this physical culture, its radical contextualism, and, commitment to progressive social change that provides a new theoretical lens through which to view a reconceptualization of sports coaching research. PCS has largely overlooked sports coaching as a site of inquiry; something which this book seeks to address.

An important part of PCS practice—indeed, one could argue its only way of ensuring its survival—is to be constantly vigilant in terms of its position within, and relationship to, the changing role, structure, and mission of the contemporary university. In numerous respects, the interpretive and progressive objectives underpinning the PCS project stands in contradistinction to the entrepreneurial scientism that has come to dominate what has been dubbed the corporate university (Giroux, 2009; Rutherford, 2005). As a social institution, the public university is arguably more intransigent, and less dynamic in its ability to change than some others, but it is nonetheless an institution that is dialectically linked to the broader forces (political, economic, social, cultural, and technological) and context in which it is located. As such, any type of knowledge generation and dissemination takes place within the context of larger social forces.

It is our contention that PCS represents a strategic *contextual, inter-ventionist, multimethodological, and interdisciplinary* counterpoint to the methodological fundamentalism (Lincoln and Cannella, 2004b) that aggressively pushes evidence-based progress, policies, and programs, gen-erates a nation of researchers locked into a governmental policy, produces research that "serves policy," and privileges the randomized experiment, as the only real "science" that "counts" (Atkinson in Lather, 2006; Denzin and Giardina, 2006; House, 2006). In Chapter 6, we detail the ontologi-cal, epistemological, and, methodological boundaries framing the putative intellectual project that we call the *Physical Pedagogical Bricolage* (PPB).

6 An Evolving Criticality in Sports Coaching Research

> At this moment in history, a concatenation of forces led by the conservative cultural logics of neo-liberalism seeks to shape a definition of inquiry that precludes multiple paradigms, epistemologies, and theoretical perspectives from the policy arena. (Lincoln, 2005, p.179)

INTRODUCTION

This is not meant to be a defensive attack on science *qua* science, merely an observation or interpretations as to why particular ways of knowing have become privileged over others within particular social and historical contexts. Whether we choose to realize it or not, it is the context in which [sports coaching] has been, and is being, disciplined and institutionalized that has had the most profound impact on the nature of the field. As Kuhn (1970) suggested, particular regimes of power are underpinned by specific regimes of truth and visa versa. The rational productivity of liberal capitalist society finds its epistemic corroboration in the positivist objectivism that underpins the scientific method, as conventionally understood (Andrews, 2008, p.48).

Within this chapter we offer what is hopefully both a suggestive (as opposed to definitive) and generative (as opposed to suppressive) signposting of the ontological, epistemological, and, methodological boundaries framing the putative intellectual project that is the *Physical Pedagogical Bricolage* (PPB)—a project formed in, and to some degree against, the neo-liberal, corporate 'logics' of McHigher Education. Ground in a commitment toward engaging varied dimensions or expressions of *active physicality* and the theoretical contingencies of physical cultural studies (Silk and Andrews, 2011; see also Newman and Giardina, 2011; Thorpe et al., 2011; Friedman and Van Ingen, 2011; Rich, 2011) as discussed in the previous chapter, we outline a contextually-based understanding of, and methodological approach to, the corporeal practices, discourses, and subjectivities through which sports coaching is organized, represented, and experienced in relation to the operations of social power. As was clear in the last chapter, the approach we outline is one that *requires* a motivation towards progressive social change; in so doing, we sketch out the epistemological, axiological and methodological contingencies of the PPB and how we may produce the type of knowledge that is able to intervene into the broader social world and *make a difference*.

As we argued in Chapter 4, Gilbert and Trudel (2004a) suggested that 45% of contemporary sports coaching research adopts a qualitative approach (and this figure has likely risen since their research), indicating an increase in the acceptability of a plurality of research perspectives. The danger is that these divergent perspectives become weighed down within what are somewhat redundant—although at the same time, rather concerning given the increasing dismissal of research that fails to live up to the 'gold-standard' as defined by those who beat the 'evidence' drum—so-called 'paradigm wars' (Hinings and Greenwood, 2002) than as raising questions with which the theme field of sports coaching has to be concerned. We are less concerned then with fighting any redundant wars about what matters, what counts, and who gets to define this (we hope we have all grown up and learnt from such debates that have defined the field over years) than with explicating the inconvenient truth that is at the core of the *crisis* facing the theme field of sports coaching. This sad, and inconvenient truth is that "the instantiation of an epistemological hierarchy that privileges positivist over postpositivist, quantitative over qualitative, and predictive over interpretive ways of knowing" (Andrews, 2008, p.45) remains as an omnipresent, assumptive and deeply divisive 'truth' that frames the production of knowledge in sports coaching research. That is, despite gains in other perspectives in the field of sports coaching, the majority of research privileges scientifically-based research (SBR) or as it alternatively referred to, evidence-based research (EBR). We of course vehemently oppose this position and the subsequent marginalization, trivialization and disrespect for scholarship that counters such an approach. The field of sports coaching therefore needs to be concerned with, and address how this has "turn[ed] social enquiry into the handmaiden of a technocratic, globalizing managerialism" (Denzin et al., 2006, p.772), reflecting an acquiescence to the neoliberal regime and a necessity to pursue quantitative methodologies.[1] As such, this chapter confronts the "invisible networks of prestige" (Mitchell, 1992, p.426) that define and shape the knowledge base for the theme field of sport coaching—and to be clear, these are not necessarily the output of the most robust research programs, as it is those that are best located, resourced and publicized that are taken to be the most robust (Clegg, 2002). Rather, in this chapter we refute those who control these invisible networks and the ways in which such networks become adopted into the *evidence*-based based sports policy universe by the most powerful patrons; the resultant power allows them to "play the incommensurability card by constituting those who do not agree with their 'paradigm' as, at best, marginal—not people like us—or, at worst, belonging to a dangerously separate or lunatic fringe" (Clegg, 2002, p.435).

Our position then in this chapter is that there can no longer be any pretense to epistemological orthodoxy (Clegg, 2002); rather, we are calling for a field of study (sports coaching) that is interdisciplinary, transdisciplinary and counterdisciplinary in nature[2] (Kincheloe and Maclaren, 2005). To this end, we are referring to an evolving criticality in the theme field of sports coaching that is devoid of discrete schools of analysis—what Denzin and Lincoln (2000) have referred to as bricolage. Thus, following the notion that sports coaching scholarship can be located "in a transformative praxis that leads to the alleviation of suffering and the overcoming of oppression" (Kincheloe and McLaren, 2005, p.321), this chapter builds upon the notion of a *Physical Culture Without Guarantees* (Chapter 5), and unpicks what it means to adopt a physical cultural sensibility and the impact this has on the ontological complexity, epistemological position, axiological praxis, methodological toolbox, and representational considerations for scholarly activity in a reconceptualized theme field of sports coaching. Preceding this discussion, we begin by outlining what we feel is a dangerous and highly pervasive and persuasive threat to sports coaching research: allowing for research to be held to the political, economic, and epistemological orthodoxies of the evidence-based movement (EBM) in sports coaching research and beyond.

EVIDENCE-BASED SPORTS COACHING (EBSC)

Given the amalgam of neo-liberal, neo-scientist and neo-conservative forces that frame higher education—safeguarding science and medicine at the expense of arts, humanities and the social sciences—the very existence and continuance of a critical, social science orientation towards sport, coaching and culture is imperiled perhaps more than ever. In this moment, and not surprisingly, the epistemological corroborator of these forces is once again championed; there has been an aggressive push towards 'science' defined by evidence-based programs, policies, and practices (EBR) as the sole and legitimate avenue for academic survival. Heralded as the 'gold' standard of academic research, and forged through university-industry-government partnerships, the evidence-based research mantra emphasizes a shift towards corporate principles of efficiency, accountability and profit maximization. Sports coaching research is far from outside of such political and economic arrangements; a creeping EBR-based epistemological orthodoxy is seeping into the critical study of sports coaching, threatening to neuter the political, critical and practical production of knowledge and the potentialities of our field. In Chapter 4, we alluded to the inexorable link between 'evidence' and policy making in the 'sports policy universe' and the translation of this into the field of sports coaching research. The extent of the evangelical status of 'evidence' in the field of sports coaching research—termed evidence-based sports coaching (EBSC)—is emphasized by the opening line on Sports coach UK (2008, p.1, emphasis added) research section: "Research provides the underpinning *evidence* for decision making, policy and practice for coaching, coach development and education". This positioning manifests in the 'gold standard' for [sports coaching] research being ascribed to research that is 'scientific' or 'evidence'-based (St. Pierre and Roulston, 2006). To be clear, the politics of evidence—which Morse (2006, p.79) describes as "the politics of ignorance, stigma, and conflicting agendas"—extends to academic and governmental levels and acts as an impediment to research in the social sciences, thus constricting qualitative inquiry and knowledge production in sports coaching (Morse, 2006). Invoking and paraphrasing Morse (2006), this oppressive movement is impeding how, when, and to whom qualitative enquiry is taught, contracted, funded, conducted, published, read, and implemented.

The pervasive epistemological and methodological fundamentalism, or the legacy "Bush science" which privileges evidenced-based "scientific" practice, policies, programs, and, by inference, progress (Giroux, 2005a), is clearly felt within academe in the UK and within the disciplines that inform sports coaching research. Of course this methodological fundamentalism—which singularly positions the randomized experience as that which "counts" within social research (Freshwater and Rolfe, 2004; House, 2005)—is closely articulated to a pernicious and regressive form of neo-conservative moral fundamentalism. According to this line of thought: *the* source of truth is the Bible; there is authority located in the past; true believers have access to truth which others do not; access to this truth means they are 'correct'; contradictory evidence becomes dismissed; persuasion is somewhat granted by arguments consistent with their beliefs; people who disagree do not have their insights; there is an avoidance of non-believers; beliefs are promulgated via decree, law or policy, pressure or coercion; and, other viewpoints are curtailed by restriction of contrary ideas and those who espouse them (Giroux, 2005a; House, 2003; see also Denzin et al., 2006). President Barack Obama has critiqued the ideological stance of the Bush Administration's, highlighting the 'stacking' of scientific advisory boards and the suppression of research that conflicted with their political agenda (Obama and Biden, 2008). However, Obama's policy declarations do little to decry the legitimacy of 'high-science,' pushing instead to double investment in 'key' science agencies and through restoring integrity to U.S. science policy through a concerted quest for 'objective' evidence-based scientific research (Obama and Biden, 2008; Bhattacharje, 2008). In this regard, and while it appears there will be some movement from a covertly politicized epistemology, evidence still appears as incontestable, as if it speaks the truth, and is pure in the sense of being free from the inherent messiness of human language, human values, or indeed anything even recognizably human (Murray et al., 2007).

The actions of public and private funding bodies—and the musings from Obama seem equally, if not more fervently, alacritous—have made it apparent that the nearer one approaches the *gold standard* of randomized experimental design, the more one is likely to receive funding for doing "objective and *good* science," and the larger that funding is likely to be (Lather, 2006, p.32, emphasis added; see also Denzin and Lincoln, 2005c on the National Research Council; House, 2005 and Smith and Hodkinson (2005) on educational research in the US and UK). As government sponsored funding for research in US and UK higher education settings has significantly dropped in recent years, so the pressure on faculty to secure such funding has increased. Indeed, the contemporary university is, if nothing else, a pragmatic environment, and has responded to this corporate and "governmental manipulation of science" by reinforcing the primacy of "high-quality science" (Lather, 2006, p.35). Such are the laws of the neoliberal academic jungle: an academic and economic order in which primacy is afforded to rationally conceived, objective knowledge, with critical and reflexive forms of intellectualizing coming under increasing pressure (Denzin and Giardina, 2006). Evidently, over the past decade or so, there has been a concerted backlash against various forms of subjective, interpretive, and constructivist thought which is as much economic in its derivation, as it is epistemological in its effects. Academic freedom meets fiscal constraint, resulting in widespread intellectual compliance to the corporate scientific norm; with little, or no, guarantee that *science* and *scientific thought*, as classically understood, is actually being advanced. We would locate the field of sports coaching, and its growing preoccupation with EBR, within this regressive epistemological moment. While unfortunate in our view, it is wholly understandable why some would privilege the epistemic order (science) that is most readily rewarded, and thereby valued, by managerialist administrators, journal editors, gatekeepers and so on. However, in doing so, economic considerations now come to augment the normalized scientism evident within the our loose amalgam of a community; a stance that asserts that the (natural) scientific method takes primacy over all others, regardless of the focus of empirical inquiry.

Not surprisingly then, given the forces shaping scholars, the championing of the evidence-based research mantra—itself the epistemological corroborator of neo-liberal empire—is evident among certain sections of the sport coaching research community. From countless iterations within conference presentations, journal articles, EBR is readily engaged by the sports coaching researchers whose epistemological underpinnings draw upon positivist and objectivist assumptions pertaining to the *discovery* of sporting truth (singular). For, despite the interpretive and subjectivist turn within sports coaching—in case you had not noticed, there has been one—residues of mid-twentieth century positivism endure. This *conciliatory strategy,* involves modifying research and teaching practices according to the rationally bureaucratic dictates of the corporate university, thereby producing scholarship whose commercial value within the academic marketplace (i.e. its grant-funding potential) takes precedence over its intellectual worth (if, indeed, it possesses any; it is only the academic neophyte who believes in a necessary relationship between funding awards and intellectual prescience).

Perhaps, as many appear to advocate, the widespread adoption of this conciliation to positivist hegemony is the only means to ensure the survival of the field? However, and no matter how precarious, we stand in opposition to such a position, given it strikes at the very core of our approach, one that understands sport and sports coaching as a key site in which social forces, discourses, institutions, and processes congregate, congeal, and are contested in a manner which contributes to the shaping of human relations, subjectivities, and experiences in particular, contextually contingent ways. In essence, and as countless others have expressed, sport is, a site of power relations, and, championing evidence-based research (EBR), is, nothing short of collusion with, and explicit support for, existing regimes of power. To condone—better put, to pander to—EBR, compromises, if not neuters, everything that we, as critical intellectuals strive for and believe in; it is a powerful virus of sorts that speaks against our ontological, axiological, epistemological, methodological and political approaches, acting as mere handmaiden (if you allow us the play on the gendered language of science) to the very forces to which we suggest sports coaching research should be looking to respond to, oppose, and, critique. It is, in the words of Zygmunt Bauman (1999), the latest rendition of a society that has stopped questioning itself, a force that legitimates and essentially concretizes a form of 'science' that serves industry, the economy and existing power blocs, yet ignores, for the most part, the most pressing social problems of our time, producing a politics that offers nothing but more of the same (Giroux, 2001). We vehemently counter the EBR orthodoxy within this discussion, although are at pains to point out that this is not a defensive attack on science *qua* science. Rather, we seek to illuminate the contemporary politics of science, and provide a more transparent and informed understanding of the political and economic pressures and processes responsible for the production, legitimation (and, indeed, de-legitimation) of particular forms of knowledge. For, as Kuhn (1970) famously noted, specific regimes of power are underpinned by specific regimes of truth, and *vice versa*.

EVALUATING EVIDENCE

> *What is there, then, that can be esteemed true? Perhaps this only, that there is absolutely nothing certain.* (Descartes, 1637 [1949])

The evangelical status of 'evidence' in academe rests on a "dangerously naïve commonsense view on truth" (Murray et al., 2008, p.273), wherein 'seeing is believing.' Of course, such a view fails to recognize the political workings of power that silently operate behind the mask of objectivity, inscribe rigid norms and standards that ensure political dominance, and, set the agenda with regard to what questions about 'truth' can be asked and by whom. Based in the doctrines of logical positivism, and following

Murray et al. (2008, p.273), "this view betrays an almost unshakeable faith in the human capacity for unbiased or objective observation and analysis." As we alluded to above, in this formulation, science becomes supplanted by ideology shaped by the commercial and moral logics of neo-liberalism, even as it basks in the dubious (post-Bush) glow of its spurious value-free objectivity (Lincoln, 2005; see also Fukuyama, 2006; Grossberg, 2005; Giroux, 2005a; Harvey, 2003; Lakoff, 2006). Paradoxically, philosophers and critical theorists would argue that 'seeing' and 'believing' make strange allies. Indeed, Murray et al. (2007) argue that to see is, in some sense, to interpret that which is seen. These interpretations are not always conscious, but will determine how something will appear to us as either true or false. Consideration therefore must be given to "the ways in which evidence is manipulated and contextualized under the aegis of efficiency, in the name of political expediency or in the name of scientific progress, and sometimes all three at once" (Murray et al., 2008, p.274). This manipulation of evidence of course raises questions about the value-free objectivity that proponents of EBR so fervently seek:

> 'Evidence', we learn, is far from neutral; 'truth' and 'evidence' are always overdetermined by the social, historical and political contexts that lend them their currency and power. These inform our methodologies, and we know that these methodologies, in turn, directly and indirectly shape the object of inquiry. (Murray et al., 2007, p.515)

Murray et al. (2007; 2008) intimate that in the extreme 'evidence' becomes 'fixed,' and is made to fit procrustean policies, and subsequently propose that our ways of seeing as informed by an episteme: the accepted and dominant manner of gaining and organizing knowledge within a given historical period. An episteme then, as a strategic apparatus, provides the conditions and possibilities for something to appear as true or false, good or evil (Murray et al., 2007). Dominant epistemes become expressed in part through various discourses, disciplines, and institutions. Furthermore, the discursive effects are intricate and far reaching and are powerful given their mechanisms mask the ways they operate (Murray et al., 2007). A telling and all too 'real' example of ways in which an episteme organizes knowledge, framing the way we see and experience the world, was the manipulation and distortion of 'evidence' that the Bush (and Blair) administration 'sold' to the public with regard to the unilateral intervention and occupation of Iraq to the world. Here, supposedly neutral evidence was given the *appearance* of being 'objective,' 'reliable,' and 'generalizable.' Indeed, according to Denzin et al. (2006), "under the Bush regime, a fact or piece of evidence is true if it meets three criteria: (a) it has the appearance of being factual; (b) it is patriotic; and (c) it supports a political action that advances the White House's far-right neoconservative agenda" (p.775). Thus, in this sense, an episteme drives specific actions, allows for "knowledge development in certain domains, and, fosters regulatory mechanisms. EBR thus supports and bolsters such 'truth' and provides a framework to measure the 'epistemic compliance" of science (Murray et al., 2008, p.274). As a result, any evidence that contradicts the (political) agenda is deemed flawed and/ or biased; and is systematically ranked lower in value as a form of evidence (Murray et al., 2007). Indeed, researchers who do not deploy EBR are subject to critique given they "fail to think or to act with intellectual integrity; they forsake scientific rigor and honest inquiry for the simple gratifications of ideology, greed, routinization and efficiency" (Murray et al., 2008, p.512). Of course, and following Goldenberg (2006), the irony here is that EBR does not necessarily *increase* objectivity, serving instead to *obscure* the subjective elements that are central to all forms of human inquiry (Goldenberg, 2006): a point seemingly lost on Bush, Obama and others who value the gold standard of 'evidence.'

Using the Socratic dictum concerning wisdom,[3] when the 'scientist' knows that he or she has arrived at this rational standoff, Murray et al. (2007) use this moment, and the concomitant rupture in one's epistemological world-view, to 'open the door' to another way of thinking or acting: "Rather than continuing down the road to nowhere, wisdom calls for detours, new and different paths, a new vista on the same problem, a working—and thinking— through the *aporia* (p.513)."[4] There is a need for cross-pollination between academic disciplines and between theory and practice, and as real innovation often comes from the margins or boundaries of a discipline, sometimes a relative 'outsider' is best positioned to offer a new 'lens,' resulting in new terms of understanding or a new methodological approach:

> . . . the outsider is not limited by the theoretico-practical terms that govern the insider's regime of knowledge; the outsider brings a different lexicon, novel explanatory terms and a fresh *modus operandi*. The outsider puts her or his theory into practice. As Deleuze famously remarks, here theory 'is exactly like a box of tools'; the outsider (whom he [Deleuze] also calls the 'nomad') sets to work to build something new, trespassing upon our familiar terrain and transgressing our traditional topologies. (Murray et al., 2007, p.513)

The outsider can be perceived as a threatening interloper, leading the critical examination of the evidence-based movement to be a target of a strong, disparaging reaction (Murray et al., 2007). However, there are those that subscribe to the view that evidence-based practices do not *increase* objectivity but *obscures* the subjective elements that are central to all forms of human inquiry (Goldenberg, 2006). Ideally, "Critical, interpretive qualitative research creates the power for positive, ethical, communitarian change, and the new practitioners entering this field deeply desire to use the power of the university to make such a change" (Denzin et al., 2006, p.779). Morse (2006) emphasizes the challenge this poses to qualitative researchers:

As researchers, we are tired of conducting underfunded research that seemingly goes nowhere. Yet, forcing ourselves into a quantitative system does not appear to be the answer. Although we know that our research is significant and addresses problems that may otherwise be declared not researchable, our seemingly insurmountable problem is to convince those who control research funding, curricula, and the publication of texts and mainstream journals that our work is significant. (p.90)

EBR forms a central component of the "new circuits of knowledge" (Slaughter and Rhoades, 2004, p.215) forged through the university-industry-government partnerships, emphasizing a shift towards corporate principles of efficiency, accountability and profit maximization, and away from social responsibility and broader social concerns (Davies, 2005; Dimitriadis, 2006; Giroux, 1999). As we suggested in Chapters 2 and 3, with Giroux (2003), higher education is increasingly being redefined in market terms as corporate culture subsumes democratic culture, and, critical learning is replaced by an instrumental logic that celebrates the imperatives of the bottom line, downsizing, and outsourcing. In this formulation, academics become obsessed with grant writing, fund raising, and capital improvements, and, higher education:

> increasingly devalues its role as a democratic public sphere committed to the broader values of an engaged and critical citizenry. Private gain now cancels the public good, and knowledge that does not immediately translate into jobs or profits is considered ornamental. In this context, pedagogy is depoliticized and academic culture becomes the medium for sorting students and placing them into an iniquitous social order that celebrates commercial power at the expense of broader civil and public values. (Giroux, 2003, p.22–23)

In this regard, 'knowledge' production is to some extent 'privatized' (Olssen and Peters, 2005; Slaughter and Rhoades, 2004) whereby "knowledge is not only structured to be economically productive but itself becomes wholly a commodity under market conditions" (Halsey et al., 1997, p.23). Peer review, for example, the cornerstone of the academic profession, is no longer conducted exclusively by university members; this in and of itself is not necessarily a negative move, perhaps what is of concern are that this process does not take place in line with participants and communities we could potentially serve, but with 'outsiders' from corporate and governance spheres. For example, Slaughter and Rhoades (2004) highlight the increase in numbers of 'industrial scholars' sitting on the National Science Foundation (NSF) peer-review programs as an indication of the shift as a result of the new circuits of knowledge created under an academic capitalist knowledge/learning regime. The consequences of the move away from the 'public good knowledge/learning regime' (see Merton, 1942) is emphasized by Giroux (1999):

> Research guided only by the controlling yardstick of profit undermines the role of the university as a public sphere dedicated to addressing the most serious social problems a society faces. Moreover, the corporate model of research instrumentalizes knowledge and undermines forms of theorizing, pedagogy, and meaning that define higher and public education as a public good rather than as a private good. (p.20)

Furthermore, pedagogic practices within the corporate university becomes reduced to the status of training future students for the workplace, and any knowledge that might challenge anti-democratic forms of power or that questions dominant social practices, values, power relations, and, morals, is dismissed by students and their parents as *irrelevant* to gaining a foothold in the job market (Giroux, 2003).

As distinct as possible then from the historically stated mission of 'higher' education, and completely at odds with providing students with the skills and information necessary to think critically about the knowledge they gain, colleges and universities have become, or are increasingly perceived— and perceive themselves—as training grounds for the corporate world. This is clearly a dangerous turn, and one that all but removes the *ethical referent* from the meaning and purpose of higher education (Giroux, 2003). Thus, fully entrenched within academe—even in disciplines such as sociology, where one might look for a politics of hope—are a series of discourses, power relations and ways of knowing that address the rationalization of rationality without a moral dimension and sees "truth" as outside of social practices (Clegg, 2002). As discussed in Chapter 3, this instrumentalization of knowledge has led some commentators to suggest that we are witnessing 'the death of universities' (Evans, 2004/5) and 'the end of knowledge' (Barnett and Griffin, 1997; Delanty, 1998) in a higher education system that is in 'ruins' (Readings, 1996) or in 'crisis' (Frith, 2001). More than 25 years ago, Said (1983) suggested the University has become yet another space in which citizens "have been left to the hands of 'free' market forces and multinational corporations" (p.4). Today this situation has reached crisis point; EBR echoes with an all too familiar unquestioning air in which any ontological or epistemological position that may counter it is usually viewed with suspicion at best and outright hostility at worst, and, predictably marginalized. Thus, the training that most doctoral students receive, and particularly the orientation provided in most research design courses, results in the vast majority of students gaining an implicit and explicit understanding of, and comfort with, *foundational* (see Smith and Hodkinson, 2005; Amis and Silk, 2008) beliefs of how to 'do' *rigorous* research.

Thus, within the field of sports coaching, there is a need to ensure that 'nomadic' researchers within academic institutions are empowered to challenge the 'elders' or 'gatekeepers' that remain faithful largely to EBSC research and indeed those who unproblematically or naively embrace a highly politicized research agenda. The challenge is also to ensure that this empowerment takes place in tandem with a change in the 'political economy of evidence' (Larner, 2004). The 'political economy of evidence' explicates that it "is not a question of evidence *or* no evidence, but who controls the definition of evidence and which kind is acceptable to whom" (Larner, 2004, p.20). It needs to be emphasized that it is qualitative researchers that address the confusing and chaotic—but still important— problems that are too difficult to tackle quantitatively (Morse, 2006). It is also the qualitative researchers that "sit on the fringes of research, but remember that it is on the fringes where the greatest advances are often made" (Morse, 2006, p.90).

THE EPISTEMOLOGICAL, POLITICAL, AND AXIOLOGICAL PRAXIS OF THE PHYSICAL PEDAGOGIC BRICOLAGE (PPB)

In the following section, we address what we believe to be critical (and self-reflexive) discussion pertaining to the epistemological, political, and axiological contingencies of Sports Coaching Research. As addressed in the previous chapter, we have suggested that sports coaching research is, at its core, concerned with excavating how active bodies become organized, represented, and experienced in relation to the operations of social power and is radically contextual in its approach and intent. This requires that sports coaching research recognizes that coaching practices, discourses, subjectivities, coach-athlete relationships and so on can only be understood by the way in which they are *articulated* into a particular set of complex social, economic, political, and technological relationships that comprise the social context. For example, it would be impossible to understand the power that operates on the young female gymnast body if research were to isolate the role of the coach. This would decontextualize understand-ing of the power that operates on that body; for example, how is this body understood in relation to mediated constitutions of normalized bodies, discursive and material construction of nutrition and eating disorders, the highly gendered (and classed and consumerized) discourses of 'appropriate' female athletic subjectivity and so on. Equally, we could not adequately understand the young male English coaching student spending a summer abroad in Zambia coaching young girls football without thinking through the various power relations related to, for example, post-coloniality, racial hierarchies, gender-based violence, sexual health politics, international development, genocide, war, and peace.

Sports coaching then, as a multifarious set of research sites, can never be substantial (possessing some fixed, immutable essence), rather, it is always unavoidably relational, and always in process: its contemporaneous iteration providing a persuasive—if illusionary—semblance of fixity within what is, in actuality, an ever-changing world. Yet, in the broadest sense, the omnifarious planes of physicality within the field of sports coaching represent a "pressure point of complex modern societies. These planes are 'sites' or 'point(s)' of intersection, and of negotiation of radically different kinds of determination and semiosis" (Frow and Morris, 2000, p.352); a place where social forces, discourses, institutions, and processes congregate, congeal, and are contested in a manner which contributes to the shaping of human relations, subjectivities, and experiences in particular, contextually contingent ways. In the more specific sense, the *physical* comprises a litany of "events," the moments of "practice that crystallizes diverse temporal and social trajectories" (Frow and Morris, 2000, p.352) through which individuals negotiate their subjective identities. Following Frow and Morris (2000), the physical is a complex multi-layered site replete with numerous types of events can and do "happen"—the product and producer of numerous overlapping systems and discourses (economic, political, aesthetic, demographic, regulatory, spatial) that creates a bewilderingly complex, and dynamic, coherent, social totality.

Building on an understanding of meaningful and socially impactful sports coaching research that can be located "in a transformative praxis that leads to the alleviation of suffering and the overcoming of oppression" (Kincheloe and McLaren, 2005, p.321), we envision the sports coaching researcher as one who operates not as "an anonymous functionary or careful bureaucrat" (Said, 1994, p.13); rather, as one who can make a difference and even take sides (cf. Amis and Silk, 2008; Becker, 1967; Denzin, 2002) and contributes to an intellectual life that has the possibilities of dissent against the status quo. We are thus suggesting that we need to reconceptualize the ontological core of the field around a sensibility that assumes that "societies are fundamentally divided along hierarchically ordered lines of differentiation (i.e., those based on class, ethnic, gender, ability, generational, national, racial, and/or sexual norms), as realized through the *operations of power* and *power relations* within the social formation" (Andrews, 2008, p.57, emphasis added). This is a sports coaching research horizon driven by the need to understand the complexities, experiences, and injustices that coaches, athletes, children, parents, physiotherapists, social workers, medical staff, strength and fitness advisors, teachers, and the many other (yet unimagined) constituents of the field, face on a daily basis. Further, these are researchers who, when confronting such issues, should not be afraid to tackle them head on. That is, as a field, we need to be motivated by a "commitment to progressive social change" (Miller, 2001b, p.1), with an explicit aim to produce the type of knowledge "through which [we are] in a position to intervene into the broader social world and *make a difference*" (Andrews, 2008, p.57). In some respects, and following Giroux (2001), and at the core of sports coaching is a *performative pedagogy* that locates the importance of understanding theory as the basis for "intervening into contexts and power . . . in order to enable people to act more strategically in ways that may change their context for the better" (Grossberg, 1996, p.143).

Although the borders or boundaries of a reconceptualized 'field' of sports coaching research are going to be fluid and malleable, it is of fundamental importance to identify the sites of critical engagement if the intellectual project is to achieve its emancipatory, intellectual, political, and, moral ends. *Sport* is a vague and imprecise noun (Andrews, 2008), and to alleviate criticism of the conceptual weakness presented by this signifier; it seems prudent to embrace the evolution of *sport* to physical culture (Ingham, 1997; cf. Andrews, 2002; 2008; Silk and Andrews, 2011). As discussed in Chapter 5, the broader domain of physical culture encompasses various dimensions of physicality; including, but not restricted to sport, exercise, fitness, dance, wellness, health, movement practices, 'Activities of Daily Living' (ADL), recreation, work, and the pedagogic. Each of these 'spheres' incorporates different motivations for, and practices of, organizing and regulating human movement and for each of them the *active body* is something that can be experienced (by the instrumental subject) or observed (as a representational object) (Andrews, 2008). In adopting this sensibility, we begin to create a progressive space with the opportunity for the very essence of the reconceptualized 'field' of sports coaching; with its multiple iterations of experiencing, communicating, instructing, teaching, and learning. As a consequence of the impreciseness of the noun 'sport' and also the richer description of the act of 'coaching' afforded by encompassing the motivations and practices of organizing and regulating, experiencing and observing, teaching and learning, and, communicating and instructing the active body, it seems critical for the reconceptualized 'field' to move away from the limiting and somewhat misleading terms 'sport' and 'coaching.' To invoke and paraphrase Silk and Andrews (2011), there is a need for the reconceptualized 'field' to embrace the conceptual underpinnings that understand a physicality focused on bodily movement and activity. Drawing on the discussion in the previous chapter, and following Ingham (1997) and Andrews and colleagues (Andrews, 2006; Andrews, 2008; Silk and Andrews, 2011), we mobilize the nomenclature 'physical' given it more accurately portrays the various dimensions of physicality that congeal to form the complex and diverse cultural space for inquiry. Further, the term 'pedagogic' more fully explicates the organizing and regulating of the teaching, learning, education and instructional approach undertaken in the cultural space. What is proposed then is for the reconceptualized 'field' to replace the limiting and misleading ascribed moniker, 'sports coaching'; instead, and perhaps more accurately, ascribing to parameters of what we term the '*Physical Pedagogic Bricolage*' (PPB). The immediate impact of ascribing PPB to the 'field' is that it opens up the reconceptualized 'field' to spheres of inquiry that might have been discarded or not seen as relevant by practitioners under 'sports coaching' research. One of the many implications of such a shift is the need to move beyond the intimation that the ontological core of research field is based around improving the sporting *performance* of others (Jones, 2005b). This misnomer has characterized the field since its conception, pace the work of Kidman and Hanrahan (2004) who suggest that "one of the primary roles of a coach is to help athletes improve their *performance*," (p.145, emphasis added) or Borrie and Knowles (2003) who refer to the process of coaching as helping a player/athlete learn and improve a particular skill. Rather, our conception of PPB is one that encompasses broader spheres of enquiry that have traditionally been discarded by the 'field,' the very essence of PPB—with its multiple iterations of experiencing, communicating, instructing, teaching, and learning—necessitates a radical reconceptualization of 'performance' as we understand it.

Given the fluid and emergent nature of PPB—the boundaries of which will be formed, created, contested, and will likely shift by those who contribute to what we see as an exciting and emergent sphere—it is beyond our remit to 'prescribe' specific ways of seeing, doing, and, acting. Indeed, this would be against the very essence of our anti-positivist convictions and approach to the field of research. Yet, by way of initiating dialogue, and indeed, by way of invitation to those currently perceived as external to the field, we briefly consider spheres of enquiry that may well sit comfortably within the PPB that to this point may have been 'discarded' or left to scholars in other fields of enquiry. For within the sphere of physical pedagogic bricolage, might we not expect the 'coach' to engage older populations in various forms of physical activity to, say, tackle obesity? Might the practitioner attempt to illuminate the under-representation of particular ethnic identities in recreational programs, or to encourage sedentary students to take up physical activity during key stages when drop out occurs (e.g. entry to University)? May we not consider potential 'events' (Frow and Morris, 2000) of interrogation the multiplicituous cultural politics (gendered, sexualized classed, raced) of dance? Should we not expect those engaged in the lives of children to understand the far from proven political rhetoric about supposed societal benefits (e.g. crime reduction) of engaging youth in regular exercise regimes, amongst many others? What should we make of the often unquestioned role of sport, and thus sport coaches, in the field of international development and peace studies? Should we not attempt to understand the everyday lives of coaches (and perhaps, athletes) and the multiple identities—parent, taxi driver, scientist, cook, social worker, activist, administrator, travel agent, community worker, police officer, health visitor, policy maker, politician, peace worker, health educator, nutritionist, and, coach—they inhabit? Should we not question how sports coaching may well be another form of governance of young, supposedly deviant bodies, as Nikolas Rose (2000b) might put it, how sports coaching may well be a device in the conduct of conduct? Might we not expect condescending voices against the high-performance, elite orientation of physical education policy or decry the loss of sport for all initiatives? Should our voices of critique not get louder and louder (Bauman, 2000) against the marginalization of academic programs in 'sport coaching' within the corporatized university, or, perhaps against the conformity of such programs towards governmental agendas (something we accept is extremely difficult in our present moment)? Why do we not explore, within, and against, our present institutional constraints, the potential collaborations and potentialities with 'colleagues' in health, social policy, management, and other yet unimagined allegiances? Or, and we fear that we are partly describing ourselves here, do we find too much comfort and solace within the well-trodden corridors of our own sacrosanct safe-havens? Or, should we not be 'crossing borders' (Giroux, 2001), forging allegiances with artists, activists, architects, and, yes, even our esteemed colleagues in sports science, as we continue to shape a meaningful, impactful, physical pedagogic bricolage that is responsive to, and formative of, our present social order? No matter our preference or our academic motivation, this is a physical pedagogic bricolage that excavates and theorizes this, articulating an ontologically complex project grounded in a moral-sacred epistemology that places moral order and ethics as a central concern of the research process (Christians, 2000; Christians, 2005; Denzin, 2002; Denzin, 2005). In the subsequent paragraphs, we aim to unpack the PPB, offering a suggestive pathway for how we might conceive of, and create, such a reconceptualized field.

We are suggesting then that sports coaching research should not just be concerned with the improvement of performance, it should equally be attuned to confront the injustices of a particular society or public sphere, unembarrassed by the label political, and, unafraid to consummate a relationship with emancipatory consciousness (Kincheloe and McLaren, 2005) if we expose or uncover various forms of social justice. We need an approach concerned with issues of power and justice and the ways the economy, class, race, gender, ideologies, discourses, education, religion, and other social institutions and cultural dynamics interact to create an unjust social system and produce work targeted towards the present conjuncture (e.g., the neoliberal governance of the body) that can empower individuals by confronting injustices and promoting social change. In short, sports' coaching, as a cultural site, is imbued with power relations; our research should be underscored by a pragmatics of hope (Kincheloe and McLaren, 2005) that can understand, critique and expose such power relations as they constitute the empirical core of our field. This is an approach that is ensconced in the need to reclaim education as a public good and recognizes that academic labor is a social endeavor—an approach that points to a meaningful, productive and impactful sports coaching field *beyond* a high-performance agenda. Therefore, theoretical work is not an end in itself; sports coaching research must be *meaningful* through connecting private troubles and public concerns, extending its critical, performative, and utopian impulses to address urgent social issues in the interests of promoting social change (Giroux, 2001).

Given the position advocated before, we believe there exists a number of epistemological currents that run through the project of PCS. As described in the opening section of this chapter, we are in a moment in which, at one and the same time, it appears necessary to confront the methodological fundamentalism (see House, 2005; Murray et al., 2008; Silk et al., 2010) that threatens to promote 'evidence'-based research as the only type of research that 'counts.' It thus becomes even more important to grasp hold of a utopian research agenda that criticizes the existing order of things, recognizes how sports' coaching is imbued with power relations, and that uses the terrain of culture and education to actually intervene in the world. This involves a struggle to change the current configurations of power and the allocation of resources in society, and, to push for politically motivated research that has an explicit concern with ending inequality (see Denzin, 2005; Giroux 2004a; Giroux, 2005a). We are thus talking about sports coaching research as a moral allegorical and therapeutic project avowed in its commitment to a project of social justice that can help us imagine a radical progressive democracy. It is, in short, a project that can, and should, "take sides" (Denzin, 2002; p.487; Denzin, 2005) as researchers align themselves with particular groups, categories, or, actors in such a way as to serve that group's interests. Such explicit demonstrations of partisanship have permeated social research for at least 40 years: feminist researchers have explicitly pronounced their goal as the emancipation of women, anti-racist researchers are committed to the struggle against white racism, and, disability researchers formulate their goal as empowering the disabled to emancipate themselves from the conditions imposed upon them by an able-bodied society (Hammersley, 2000). Such partisanship suggests that the death knell of value neutral research has sounded. Indeed, in a landmark article in the journal *Social Problems* in 1967, Howard Becker proposed that all sociologists are inevitably partisan, and that there could be no objective viewpoints and that sociologists should explicitly pronounce "whose side we are on" (Becker, 1967, p.239). Yet, we are proposing a somewhat different take on taking sides. Becker held that political positions should *emerge* from findings that in turn emanate from the application of robust scientific methods and quality criteria. Thus Becker's "political radicalism . . . is a *by-product* of a sound scientific approach" (Hammersley, 2000, p.80, emphasis added). This emphasis on scientific method with political considerations clearly secondary is at odds with an advocacy position that *centralizes* and *internalizes* the moral, ethical, and, political value of scholarship (see Amis and Silk, 2008).

Internalizing and centralizing morality, ethics, and the political is likely to encumber rethinking the civic and political responsibilities of academics. Giroux (2001) proposes that cultural workers and intellectuals engage in intertextual negotiations across different sites of production to assume their roles as engaged critics and cultural theorists. In essence, Giroux (2001) is advocating "border crossing" that will allow for:

> intellectual work to become both theoretical and performative . . .
> marked by forms of invention, specificity, persuasion, and critique as
> well as an ongoing recognition of the border as partial, fluid, and open
> to the incessant tensions and contradictions that inform the artists/edu-
> cators own location, ideology, and authority in relation to particular
> communities and forms of social engagement. (p.6)

In many ways, Giroux's position draws on Said's notion of intellectual amateurism in which we are physically and metaphorically exiled from our offices to connect with the political realities of society and in which we are encouraged to maintain critical distance from official or institutional bodies so that we can speak truth to power (Rizvi and Lingard, 2006; Said, 1994). Giroux's (2001; 2004a) border crossing advocates a view of intellectual work that re-theorizes the role of cultural workers and engaged artists in keeping justice and ethical considerations alive in progressive discourses and in revitalizing a broader set of social, political, and pedagogical considerations within a radical cultural politics. Drawing on the tradition of political work indebted to Williams and Hall, and continued through, among others, Mouffe, Fraser, and Grossberg, Giroux (2001) is calling for critical educators and cultural scholars to break down the artificial barriers, the separate spaces, and the different audiences that are supported through the infrastructure of disciplinary and institutional borders that "atomize, insulate and prevent diverse cultural workers from collaborating across such boundaries" (p.7). In this formulation, pedagogy becomes central to cultural politics and socially engaged citizenship; intellectual activity thus becomes a public exercise that includes how knowledge, values, identities, and social practices are produced and disseminated across a wide range of cultural sites and locations (Giroux, 2001). This means conversations with those in the street, the artists, the performers, the architects, the media, as well as opening spaces within our classrooms, within our texts, our academic journals, and our conferences for discussion of personal injuries and private terrors that we can translate into public considerations and struggles (Giroux, 2001). We are not suggesting we all abandon our offices and inhabit the spaces we probably know we should be in, but we are suggesting that such *border crossings* should be held alongside the classroom, the journal, the book chapter, and the conference presentation as key spaces in which intervention and understanding can take place within the PPB.

Reconceptualizing the role and place of the 'academic' is likely to rub against many of the 'standards' to which our work is held. Take for example your peers. How will they 'count' the oppositional art work created with the local artist, the poesis produced, the play performed at the community hall, or, for that matter, the public talk given at a residents meeting? Equally, how will the Institutional Review Board—an institution ground in a liberal Enlightenment philosophy built on value free social science that shies away from political and moral and which proffer research with a disinterested position—cope with any form on non-utilitarian ethics (Christians, 2005)? Following Christians (2005), such a constricted understanding of ethics in 'science' does not seem at all adequate for intervention in sports coaching research; we need to understand 'science' and 'education' as a regime of power that helps to maintain the social order by normalizing subjects into categories designed by political authorities. Rather, an alternative ethical approach is required that does not search for neutral principles to which all parties can appeal, does not see people as receptacles for data, as outsiders excluded from the research process, and, that breaks down the role of researcher as expert. Such a reciprocal or social ethical approach erases any distinction between epistemology, aesthetics, and ethics and is located within a feminist communitarian model that rests on a complex view of moral judgments as integrating into an organic whole various perspectives—everyday experience, beliefs about the good, and feelings of approval and shame—in terms of human relations and social structures (Christians, 2005; Denzin, 2005). In practical terms, this is an ethical approach that is based on interpretive sufficiency rather than experimentalism, instrumental sufficiency (technical, exterior, statistically precise), participate in a community's ongoing process of moral articulation, a representational adequacy free from racial, class, gender stereotyping, an effort to enable people to come to terms with their everyday experiences themselves, and, the generation of social criticism, leads to resistance and empowers to action those who are interacting (Christians, 2005).

This is an ethical approach to the PPB that relies on an ethics of care, puts community prior to persons, identifies subtle forms of oppression and imbalance, is the opposite of an individualist utilitarianism in that it is compassionate and respectful of the mosaic of particular communities and ethnic identities, and, teaches us to address questions about whose interests are regarded as worthy of debate (Christians, 2005). Advocating an alternate form of ethical practice is of course likely to meet resistance and struggle, especially as ethical approval is a central component in external funding applications. Yet, the epistemological currents sweeping through what we have defined as the PPB point towards what Denzin (2005) terms an interpretive sufficiency in which ethics is *measured* with regard to a politics of resistance, hope, and freedom and in which the researcher's responsibility is towards those studied. In this way, epistemology becomes both dialogical and aesthetic, it involves a give and take and ongoing moral dialogue between persons, it enacts an ethic of personal and community responsibility (Collins, 1991), and, politically, the aesthetic embodies an ethic of empowerment which enables social criticism and engenders resistance (Christians, 2000).

Indigenous scholars have lead the way to embracing an ethics of truth grounded in love, care, hope, and forgiveness, and in doing so, have attacked Western epistemologies and methodologies and called for the decolonization of scientific practices (see Smith, 2006). Such an approach has disrupted traditional ways of knowing and has highlighted the need to develop methodologies that privilege indigenous knowledges, voices, and experiences (Denzin et al., 2006). Ironically, as non-indigenous scholars learn how to dismantle, deconstruct and decolonize traditional ways of doing science—what Denzin et al. (2006) term 'letting go'—a backlash against critical qualitative research is gaining momentum. The introduction of new 'gold standards' for reliability and validity (St. Pierre, 2004), the fashion of so-called evidence-based research (Pring, 2004; Thomas, 2005), and the intensified 'rigorous' academic criteria designated by research funding bodies,[5] (Silk and Andrews, 2011) are examples of this backlash. Interestingly, proponents of evidence-based research "fail to recognize that the very act of labeling some research as 'evidence-based' implies that some research fails to mount evidence—a strongly political and decidedly non-objective stance (Denzin et al., 2006, p.770).

In many respects, our approach to the PPB mirrors the (rediscovered) work of Freire (1972) whose approach centered on the import of education and social action as pillars of emancipatory research. His critical pedagogy eschewed what he termed domesticated traditional education, asserting instead that marginalized and oppressed groups needed education for liberation and that research provided opportunity to develop a dynamic understanding informed by critical thought and action—conscienziation—towards a goal of critical consciousness in which the individual is empowered to think and act on the critical conditions around him or her and relate these conditions to the larger contexts of power in society (see Friere, 1972; Giroux, 2001; Kamberelis and Dimitriadis, 2005; Saukko, 2003; Truman et al., 2000). Drawing upon Freire, Christians, Giroux, and Denzin, the epistemology of the PPB is not just about empowering people, rather, it is about helping people to empower themselves, determining what research can do for them (not us), and placing knowledge at their disposal to use in whichever ways they wish. As Christians (2000) proposed:

> research helps persons imagine how things could be different. It imagines new forms of human transformation and emancipation. It enacts these transformations through dialogue. If necessary, it sanctions non-violent forms of civil disobedience, understanding that how this ethic works in any specific situation cannot be given in advance. (p.148)

The epistemological essence then of the PPB in this formulation then is revised into a sacred humanistic discourse on care, solidarity, and universal human rights (Denzin, 2005; Denzin and Giardina, 2006). As opposed to a concern with how to 'get better data,' critical research into, on, and with, coaching becomes about enabling community life to prosper, equipping people to come to mutually held conclusions, about community transformation and participation at all stages of the research process (from design through analysis through interpretation through implementation): a situated and shared morality in which social science is reformulated as a moral and social space that is measured against a universal respect for dignity (Denzin, 2005). This sacred-moral approach, ground in the work of Denzin, Christians, and others, becomes a civic, participatory, collaborative project, a project that joins the researcher with the researched in an ongoing moral dialogue (Kemmis and McTaggart, 2005, p.568). The purpose, then, of PPB becomes a radical democratic practice that is equally pedagogical, political, moral, and ethical, involving the enhancement of moral agency, the production of moral discernment, a commitment to praxis, change, justice, an ethic of resistance, and a performative pedagogy that resists oppression (Denzin 2002; Giroux, 2001; Humphries et al., 2000; Lincoln and Denzin, 2005).

SPORTS COACHING: RESEARCH AS BRICOLAGE, RESEARCHERS AS BRICOLEURS

It is clear that in suggesting the PPB and reconceptualizing the very field of sports coaching we are working with an 'expansionist logic' that necessarily hails interdisciplinarity and alliances with other professions (e.g. art, activists) and academics from disciplines previously closed off to sports coaching research (e.g. urban studies, politics, social policy, health, sociology, (physical) cultural studies, women's studies, critical race theory, and so on). The insights from such fields, the explanatory power, and the possibilities are exciting and challenging at the same time. It is also highly destabilizing. We are suggesting that we need to recognize that we probably do not know as much as we think and that we need to be open to other ways of seeing and thinking to aid us make sense of the various 'sites' of critical investigation. This potentially requires re-schooling, reading, openness, acceptance, admitting we may be wrong, recognizing the blinkers of disciplinarity, and a questioning of what we actually know—these are not the types of considerations many academics like to embrace! It may be that we understand ourselves as bricoleurs and the field characterized by bricolage. Most recently, Denzin and Lincoln (2000) explicated the concept of 'bricolage' in relation to qualitative research. The term is derived from Claude Levi-Strauss' (1966) discussion in *The Savage Mind*; and is based in the French *bricoleur*, which describes a handyman or handywoman who makes use of the tools available to complete a task (Harper, 1987). As an extension to the notion of evolving criticality in qualitative research, Kincheloe (2001) expresses that "no concept better captures the possibility of the future of qualitative research" (p.680) and signifies the interdisciplinarity and intellectual integration necessary in a *sport coaching without guarantees*. Further, *bricoleurs* also have the potential to contribute to social transformation through seeking a better understanding of both the worldviews of diverse peoples and the forces of domination affecting individuals (Kincheloe and McLaren, 2005). Despite the critique of bricolage by those in the academic community who see interdisciplinarity by nature as superficial, madness, knowing nothing well and misguided (Friedman, 1998; McLeod, 2000; Palmer, 1996), bricolage holds profound implications for critical research through the notion of a critical ontology (Kincheloe, 2003):

> Bricoleurs maintain that this object of enquiry [the event] is ontologically complex in that it can't be described as an encapsulated entity. In this more open view, the object of inquiry is always part of many contexts and processes; it is culturally inscribed and historically situated. The complex view of the object of inquiry accounts for the historical efforts to interpret its meanings in the world and how such efforts continue to define its social, cultural, political, psychological, and educational effects. (Kincheloe and McLaren, 2005, p.319)

Bricoleurs attempt to understand the fabric or web of this complexity and the processes that shape it in as thick a way as possible (Blommaert, 1997). This ontological complexity undermines traditional notions of triangulation, because inter-researcher reliability becomes far more difficult to achieve due to its in-process (processual) nature: "process-sensitive scholars watch the world flow by like a river in which the exact contents of the water are never the same" (Kincheloe and McLaren, 2005, p.319). As all observers view the object of enquiry from their own vantage points in the web of reality, no portrait of a social phenomenon is ever exactly the same as another:

> Because all physical, social, cultural, psychological, and educational dynamics are connected in a larger fabric, researchers will produce different descriptions of an object of enquiry depending on what part of the fabric they have focused on—what part of the river they have seen. The more unaware observers are of this type of complexity, the more reductionistic the knowledge they produce about it. (Kincheloe and McLaren, 2005, pp.319–320)

A key ontological concern of the bricolage—and a central dynamic to be investigated in social research—is the relationship between individuals and their contexts. The multidimensionality of the relationships might be interpreted differently in terms of its meaning and effects through the multiple methods employed by bricoleurs that recognize relationships' complex ontological importance. In doing so, this alters the basic foundations of the research act and knowledge production process: "thin reduction-ist descriptions of isolated things-in-themselves are no longer sufficient in critical research" (Kincheloe and McLaren, 2005, p.320). In essence, the bricolage is dealing with a double ontology of complexity—the complexity of objects of enquiry and their being-in-the-world, and the nature of the social construction of human subjectivity—where the process of becoming human agents is understood with a new level of sophistication (Kincheloe and McLaren, 2005). This new level of sophistication afforded by a double ontology of complexity results in a multiperspectival process that moves critical researchers beyond the determinism of macrosocial structures:

> The complex feedback loop between an unstable social structure and the individual can be charted in a way that grants human beings insight into the means by which power operates and the democratic process is subverted. In this complex ontological view, bricoleurs understand that social structures do not *determine* individual subjectivity but *constrain* it in remarkably intricate ways. The bricolage is acutely interested in developing an employing a variety of strategies to help specify these ways subjectivity is shaped (Kincheloe and McLaren, 2005, p.320)

At a more practical level what does this actually mean? What does it mean to embrace the PPB? In the first instance, it requires eschewing any pretense of disciplinarity: accepting the conventions of a particular discipline as a natural way of producing knowledge and viewing a particular aspect of the world. Indeed, as Kincheloe (2001) points out, if the traditional disciplines of our current moment are far from fixed, uniform, and monolithic—it is not uncommon for sports coaching researchers to report that we have more in common with others in different fields of study, we live in a scholarly world with faded disciplinary boundary lines—the research work needed involves opening elastic conversations and analytical frames among, across, and outside of, established disciplines. The bricoleur/bricolage transcends reductionism, understand the complexity of the research task, and is con-cerned with multiple methods of inquiry and with diverse theoretical and philosophical notions of the various elements encountered in the research act. This approach is able to surpass the limitations of a single method, the discursive strictures of one disciplinary approach, the historicity of certified modes of knowledge production, the inseparability of the knower and the known, and the complexity and heterogeneity of all human forms (Kinch-eloe, 2001). Somewhat modifying Kincheloe (2001) then, the PPB requires an array of interdisciplinary bricoleurs to operate in the ruins of the dis-ciplinary temple, to produce a post-apocalyptic sports coaching landscape where certainty and stability have long departed for parts unknown and who recognize, among other issues, that research is socially constructed. It involves recognizing that much of what passes as scholarship are value-laden projects that operate under the banner of objectivity. This is an approach that does not allow 'our' methodologies and the knowledge they produce neatly into disciplinary draws. Instead, we are far more likely to employ practices that are interdisciplinary, transgressive, and oppositional, but connected to a broader notion of cultural politics designed to further a multiracial, economic, and political democracy; projects that connects theory to social change, analysis to practical politics, and academic inquiry to public spheres (Denzin, 2005).

As bricoleurs, those operating in the PPB will need to be cognizant that the majority of cultural analyses need to accept their partiality and provide accounts that are openly incomplete, partisan and insist on the political dimensions of knowledge (Frow and Morris, 2000). Of course, these are practices that violate academic neutrality, politicize the educational process and contaminate the virtues of academic civility (Giroux, 2001). Yet if we, as a field, are to make a difference in the world (as opposed to simply reflecting the conjunctural moment of which it is a part), then there is a need to address the need for action and articulate the political goals (of the researcher and the field), be practice oriented, applied, and addresses the relationship between academia and non-academia (and here we are borrowing from Bourdieu's (1977) *'Outline of a theory of Practice'* that revolutionized the manner in which praxis, practice and interaction were defined in anthropology). Rather than purely represent the present order of things, working as unquestioning puppeteers for a neoliberal, corporate, elitist/performance order, we need to interrogate, debate, and deliberate, we need to make visible and challenge the grotesque inequalities and intolerable oppression within sports coaching and operate as agents of change (Giroux, 2001)—no matter if this de-emphasizes the (redundant) quest for medals and performance improvement or indeed questions the role of sport in (international) development initiatives. As socially responsible scholars we will need to operate across, between and beyond approaches to the empirical and face new challenges and oppositions in "representing responsibility" (Fine et al., 2000, p.108) in transforming public consciousness and common sense about the sporting empirical. Boundaries need to be crossed, taken for granted work routines questioned, new environments and outlets investigated. As Grossberg (2006) suggested, this would ensure we are seen as *political intellectuals* who are able to move things forward and embrace other possibilities. For Scott (1999), the challenge becomes having:

> . . . to ask ourselves what the yield will be of continuing to deepen our understanding of a conceptual space whose contours we have now become so familiar with, and whose insights are rapidly on their way to becoming a new orthodoxy. We have to ask ourselves whether it might not be more useful to try to expand the conceptual boundaries themselves by altering the target of our criticism. This, it seems to me, is the challenge of our present . . . a new domain in which a new set of preoccupations become visible, a set of preoccupations defined not so

much by the politics of epistemology as by a renewal of the theoretical question of the political. (p.223)

If then, there is no longer any pretense to epistemological orthodoxy (Clegg, 2002), we can begin to sketch the pathways for sports coaching research to move towards a field of study that is interdisciplinary, transdisciplinary, and counterdisciplinary in nature (Kincheloe and Maclaren, 2005). This would allow for an ever-evolving criticality in the sports coaching research that is devoid of discrete schools of analysis.

PRACTICING THE PHYSICAL PEDAGOGIC BRICOLAGE

Embracing the bricolage, deep-interdisciplinarity, and the ontological, epistemological, and axiological concerns previously addressed will clearly impact upon the type of knowledge that 'counts' in sports coaching research. To garner such knowledge will impact upon the type of methodological practices deployed. As such, how exactly does one 'practice' PPB? We use the term practice rather pointedly, for following Johnson and colleagues (2004), we prefer this term to the scientism of 'method' for it better captures the plurality of approaches, inherent messiness and indeed the potential borders crossed. It is tempting here to eschew responsibility as many have done before (ourselves included) and hide behind the all too easily thrown around 'anything goes' mentality posited by critics and advocates alike. While there is no particular way to "do" PPB, such a position would work against the 'perpetual' unity in difference (Hall, 1992) that characterizes the multiple theoretical influences, methods, and sites of cultural analyses, it is our intent consider a variety of the methodological faces that may be engaged when practicing PPB.

Our methodological approach then, developing the earlier works of McDonald and Birrell (1999), Andrews (2002), and King (2005), is rooted in engaging society as a concrete, historically produced, fractured totality made up of different types of social relations, practices, and experiences.[6] We argue that each instance of the PPB be engaged and interpreted as a fluid, dynamic category, whose definition and composition is contingent on the specificities of the context (both synchronic and diachronic) in question. In this sense, we need to acknowledge that cultural forms (e.g., pedagogic practices, coaching products, governmental institutions, sport organizations and so on) comprise "a rich aggregate of many determinations and relations" (Marx, quoted in McLellan, 1977, p.351). Determinate relations do exist, they just cannot be guaranteed in advance, hence it would be impossible in advance to advocate which contexts or social forces may explain a specific instance of the PPB. Moreover, while instances of 'coaching' are produced from specific social and historic contexts, they are also actively engaged in the ongoing constitution of the conditions out of which they emerge. As such, the method implicit within Hall's articulated conjunc-turalism is about *reconstructing a context* within which an instance of the physical becomes understandable. This is an aggressively non-reductionist (the multiplicity of forces and effects deny the possibility of reducing cau-sality to one factor such as the economic), yet contingently determinate (it acknowledges the notion of determinacy but stresses its multidirectionality, fluidity, and uncertainty), and articulatory theory/method that implores the researcher to actively (re)create context by "forging connections between (forces) practices and effects" (Grossberg, 1992, p.54).

The empirical core then of the PPB becomes the litany of physical *events* or practices with which the researcher is interested; the negotiated engage-ment with which contributes to the formation of individual subjectivities. From this point of relative abstraction, it is necessary to map the various dimensions and directions of determinacy, acknowledging that, in each case, these are largely—no wholly—arbitrary, connections. These will include, among others, *forces* that point to broader socio-historic trajecto-ries (such as neoliberalism or neoconservatism and how they shape sports policy), *institutions*, entities, or sites (in Frow and Morris' [2000] terms) at which social actions and experiences are organized and directed in par-ticular ways (such as institutions responsible for coaching policy/curricula, various sites at which instruction may take place), *processes* that represent the various operations through which the compulsions of social forces and institutions becomes actualized and operationalized, and, *discourses* that can be the conduit linking forces, institutions, processes, and subjective experiences, since they can provide both the ideological rationale for the trajectories of social forces, and the operations of institutions, while also incorporating subjectivity through which the process of self-identification (and indeed, self-governance), are engaged and experienced. To practice PPB then means recognizing that physical cultural forms (e.g., practices, products, institutions) can only be understood by the way in which they are *articulated* into a particular set of complex social, economic, political, and technological relationships that comprise the social context; recogniz-ing that "there are no necessary correspondences in history, but history is always the production of such connections or correspondences" (Grossberg, 1992, p.53). It is through this theory/method that the PPB aims to provide a context within which a physical *"event"* becomes understandable. In this way, PPB scholarship does not fall back on some form of teleological deter-minism, based on a priori assumptions about the effectivity and direction of power. Rather, the aim is to discern the state of conjunctural power relations, directions, and effects: the "state of play in (physical) cultural relations" (Hall, 1981b, p.235).

Despite our necessary differences in empirical focus and theoretical arsenal, PPB is predicated on a "performative (physical cultural) peda-gogy" (Giroux, 2001, p.7) in which empirical theorizing becomes the basis for "intervening into contexts and power . . . in order to enable people to act more strategically in ways that may change their context for the better" (Grossberg, 1996, p.143 in Giroux, 2001). As alluded to earlier in this chapter, the PPB is thus political in the sense of identifying, and analyzing—and thereby seeking to intervene into—the operation and experience of power, power relations (sometimes liberatory, oftentimes repressive, frequently both) through the examination of the (contested) realm of everyday physical. Hence, the practice/method of PCS involves identifying an "event," almost in an abstract sense, that represents a potential important focus of critical inquiry (in as much as it is implicated in hierarchical, iniquitous, unjust power relations and effects). Thus follows a process of connecting/articulating this "event" to the multiple material and ideological determinations which suture the event—in a dialectic sense—into the conjuncture of which it is a constituent element. The commitment to, and practice of, articulation thus involves: "starting with the particular, the detail, the scrap of ordinary or banal existence, and then working to unpack the density of relations and of intersecting social domains that inform it" (Frow and Morris, 2000, p.354). This is a practice that involves what Fine (1994) has termed 'working the hyphen'; thinking critically about the various points of critical consciousness that can attach the lives of the private individuals, the texts, the institutions who form the essence of our scrap of ordinary to structures (e.g., racial, gendered, economic, national, global) in our efforts to understand the physical, transform public consciousness, and, common sense.

As we attempt to understand and intervene in the disparate structures that meet in and flow through the *event* or *site*, we are likely to encounter an array of contexts that will need investigation. Somewhat adapting Frow and Morris (2000), this is likely to involve: an account of the local and global economic context; the aesthetic context; the political context that addresses the mundane and the politics of physically active bodies in space, gendered and racialized context (such as the organization of gender and racial relations); the historical context; a consideration of physical forms, structures, and experiences as a textual construct and as a form of popular culture directly interrelated with other cultural forms and with an economy of representations and practices that make up a way of life; and, in an effort to get at the particularities of lived experience, deployment of various strategies of inquiry. This, likely far from exhaustive list points to the interplay between physical lived experiences (lived realities), texts (discourses / discursive mediation), and, the social context (Saukko, 2003). Within each of these spheres or surfaces that we engage, we need a diverse methodological arsenal—from discourse analysis to participatory action research, survey work to writing as a method of inquiry—that will range, in our various projects, across the spectrum of (non)preferred approaches. At this juncture, and in an effort not to be prescriptive, Saukko (2003) suggests we be sensitive to three methodological currents that she translates into validities: (1) a contextual validity that analyzes social and historical processes to ensure we are sensitive to local realities; (2) dialogic validity that captures the depth, breadth, balanced nuance, self-reflexive awareness, and is dialogically entwined with the discourses and social contexts that shape experiences; and, (3) a self-reflexive validity that recognizes how discourses shape or mediate how we experience or shape ourselves and our environment. If we are faithful to these 'validities' in each of the connections we forge in articulation, the physical event will not only become more visible to us, but will be opened up to provide instances of interpretation and thus, intervention. That is, as we critically interrogate the banal, the ordinary instance of 'coaching,' connecting it to wider social forces, we will deploy a series of strategies ground within a sacred-moral epistemology. If ours is a moral project, and we think it is, in which we have an obligation to create radical, utopian spaces within our institutions, and indeed, if this is a project that works with, for, of, oppressed and marginalized groups, then we are likely utilize forms of research strategies that offer opportunity for advocacy and empowerment; an approach that is likely to encompass a variety of *dialogical* (Denzin, 2005) methodological practices.

Through reinvigorating the ontological core of the field, we can open PPB to a plurality of approaches to garnering knowledge. Following Johnson et al. (2004), this will be dependent on who we are (our own forms of partiality and positionality), the process of questioning (what we want to know) and our relationship to our participants (who we wish to dialogue with, the differences and similarities of our situations). However, and no matter what strategies we deploy, physical pedagogic bricoleurs will likely have to negotiate the I-thou dialogue. That is, there exists a continuum of methodological strategies ranging from textual analysis through full scale autobiographies, from oral history to interview-based methods, from ethnography to auto-ethnography, all of which involve recognition of the nature of differences and forms of power that circle around the self and other (Johnson et al., 2004). Our approaches then are dialogic, they involve dialogue "between the researching self and sources of different kinds"; but, dialogue is also internal, it happens "within the researcher" as we revise, critique and reformulate our understandings (Johnson et al., 2004, p.77). That we hover between self and other, between text and self, and between interpretation and self, and maintain an 'in-betweeness' (Johnson et al., 2004) throughout the research process is perhaps a necessary consequence, if not feature, of our self-reflexive dialogic methodologies.

It is thus clear that the PPB requires an "expansive and flexible methodological arsenal" (Andrews, 2002, p.115). As Kincheloe (2001) suggested, the intellectual power of bricolage emerges through the use of different methodological and interpretive perspectives in the analysis of an artifact or event:

> Historians, for example, who are conversant with the insights of hermeneutics, will produce richer interpretations of the historical processes

they encounter in their research. In the deep interdisciplinarity of the bricolage the historian takes concepts from hermeneutics and combines them with historiographical methods. What is produced is something new, a new form of hermeneutical historiography or historical hermeneutics. Whatever its name, the methodology could not have been predicted by examining historiography and hermeneutics separately, outside of the context of the historical processes under examination. The possibilities offered by such interdisciplinary synergies are limitless. (p.686)

Bearing in mind that Kincheloe (2001) proposes that bricoleurs use any methods necessary to gain new perspectives on objects of enquiry, Denzin and Lincoln (2000) describe the bricoleur as multicompetent, skilled at using interviews, observation, and personal documents. The bricoleur will explore the use of "ethnography, Pinarian currere,[7] historiography, genre studies, psychoanalysis, rhetorical analysis, content analysis, ad infinitum" (Kincheloe, 2001, p.687). Through further conceptualization of the bricolage, Kincheloe (2005) further adds textual analysis, semiotics, hermeneutics, phenomenology, discourse analysis, philosophical analysis, literary analysis, aesthetic criticism, and theatrical and dramatic ways of observing and making meaning as constituting the methodological bricolage—there is little wonder why Kincheloe (2001, pp.690–691) states that "learning to become a bricoleur is a lifelong process". There is no question that conducting sports coaching research at the interdisciplinary frontier requires the development of expertise in different disciplines and research methodologies. Developing the necessary expertise requires more than a casual acquaintance with the literature of the domain (Kincheloe, 2001), and although Denzin and Lincoln (2005b) intimate that the researcher-as-methodological bricoleur should have a working familiarity with a broad range of methods of collecting and analyzing empirical materials, it is clearly not feasible to demonstrate expertise in the whole range outlined by Kincheloe (2001; 2005).

What is clearer however in this conceptualization is that in the bricoleur views research methods *actively* rather than passively. This is particularly helpful for thinking about how to practice PPB for it points to the notion that our research practices are actively constructed from the tools at hand rather than passively receiving the 'correct,' universally applicable methodologies (Kincheloe, 2005) is an important consideration when practising PCS. As such, while all of our research is necessarily dialogic in type and while we would likely adapt practices for the specific issue at hand, certain methodological practices, ground within the ontological, axiological and epistemological positions advocated above, are perhaps the better *starting points* for dealing with the type of pressing social issues we are likely to encounter in a reconceptualized PPB—from health and healing, human rights and cultural survival, environmentalism, violence,

criminality, deviance, war, genocide, immigration, poverty, racism, equality, justice, abuse, and peace—of our time. Methodologies that can heal
the split between the public and private worlds by connecting the autobiographical impulse with the ethnographic (the inward and outward gazes),
recognizing ourselves as the conduits through which we make sense of our
own, and others, social worlds, are those that appear best suited to the PPB.
As Abu-Lughod (1993) proposed; no longer can [our field] hide behind a
false border between the self and other; rather the time is ripe to bridge
this gap, and reveal both parties as vulnerable experiencing subjects working to coproduce knowledge. In this sense, this is a PPB "on location," a
space in which to use personal stories to create calculated disturbances
in social, cultural and political networks of power (Holman Jones, 2005,
p.782). Such critical, self-reflexive scholarship, runs throughout all strategies of inquiry, asking of us that we hold self and culture together, that we
critique the situatedness of self with others in social contexts. These are
methodologies of "the heart, a prophetic, feminist postpragmatism that
embraces an ethics of truth grounded in love, care, hope and forgiveness"
(Denzin et al., 2006, p.770).

Critical, self-reflexive PPB scholarship then asks, at a methodological
level, that we hold self and culture together, that we critique the situatedness of self with others in social contexts. We are likely then to deploy a
variety of *(auto)biographical* or the *(auto)ethnographic* strategies that can
reveal the self-other; such practices are indeed pressing already at 'legitimate' forms of coaching knowledges, especially in the work of (Douglas,
2009; Jones, 2006, Jones, 2009). Further, various forms of *ethnographic
methods*, such as *performance ethnographies* that can combine political, critical, and expressive actions centered on lived physical experiences
locally and globally (Denzin, 2005), *public ethnography* that understand
and artistically portrays the pleasure and sorrows of coaches / athletes
/ others in a variety of locations through passionately inscribing, trans-
lating and performing research to the general public (Tedlock, 2005) or
indeed, *sensory ethnography* (see Pink, 2009). Further, we are not suggesting that the PPB abandon some of the hallmarks of the approaches
that many of our practitioners have been trained in. Rather, it calls for
these approaches to sit (un)happily and perhaps (un)comfortably alongside
newer and perhaps more *avant garde* approaches. It, thus, asks for a contextualism in our *textual 'readings'* (Johnson et al., 2004) through investigating the ways in which certain texts (ranging from policy documents to
representations of 'coaching' in films such as Miracle, Any Given Sunday,
Million Dollar Baby, or Remember the Titans, Hollywood depictions for
sure, but, in their different ways, clearly point to the role of the coach
beyond a performance agenda) emerge from and play a role in the changing historical, political, and social context (Saukko, 2003, p.99), and, at
the same time, for a focus on interpretations of the meanings of actors

and the cultural forms they use, or that use them (Johnson et al., 2004). And to be clear, such texts are deployed; in May 2011 to 'motivate' players prior to a local football derby with Plymouth, Exeter coaching staff played a clip of Robert De Niro motivating players in a key speech from the film *Any Given Sunday*. As such, the PPB asks that we open up often 'innocent' physical texts—film, television commentary, written, electronic media— to reveal relations of power as we read of, and for, dominance (Johnson et al., 2004). It asks that *meetings*—methods that involve direct engagement between the self and others, or indeed, between different aspects of the self (relational or dialogic aspect of the engagement), including *thematic interview* and *focus groups*, and the longer, less structured conversations that are the features of *oral and life history*—are aware of the role of the self and relations with others (Johnson et al., 2004). Further, the PPB is dialogic with regard to conversation between our different researcher selves, the multitude of self-possibilities (Lincoln, 2001; Plummer, 2005). As such, in practicing the PPB, we engage in a dialogue between ourselves as participant and the self who can stand back, recall, listen around, be self-critical, and develop understanding and explanations; in essence, the self who can achieve conscious partiality; critical distance and (partial) identification (Johnson et al., 2004). There are also a variety of *visual methodologies* which can aid in producing work that connects to coaches, athletes, communities, the public, policy makers and so forth and contribute to change; work which can richly communicate through visual forms such as film production, photography, exhibitions, design, photo-diaries, child-drawing, digital-stories, social media and so on (see e.g. Azzarito, 2010; Margolis and Pauwels, 2011; Pink, 2007). We even envisage uprooting of those methodologies that have been appropriated by other disciplines and institutions—such as by marketing firms—and thus seen to lie outside of the remit of this approach. As Kamberelis and Dimitriadis (2005) revealed in their revitalization of *focus group* work, a genealogy of such methods can disrupt the supposed foundation and pretended community of research. In this example, and drawing on Freire and Kozol, focus group research can be recast as a tool for enacting emancipatory politics, decentering the power of the researcher. This is *participatory research* that can help people feel in control of their own sporting words and exist in spaces in which to exercise power over the material and ideological conditions of their own lives, raise critical consciousness and encourage engagement in praxis—political action in the real world (Kamberelis and Dimitriadis, 2005).

Through making such connections between the physical and the social totality, we feel that PPB scholarship is that which engages in social critique and moral dialogue within specific physical cultural contexts (Denzin, 2005; see also Denzin and Giardina, 2006; Truman et al., 2000). Further, such work asks us to be fluent across methods—and those named above, autobiographies, autoethnographies, ethnographies, textual analyses, interviews, focus groups, life histories, participatory action research, visual research methods are likely just starting points—that engage with community struggles, and theorize conditions of social injustice; that is work that recognizes that flickers and movements for social change do not exclusively happen in the classroom and the academy but in various sites (church groups, community-based organizations, in the locker room, on the playing field, in the sports hall) and texts (Fine et al., 2000). That said, we do not suggest an abandonment of the lecture theatre. Rather, we agree with Said (in Rizvi and Lingard, 2006), we learn through teaching: the presence of students provokes thinking and learning in a productive mediation absent from the often-solitary work of the scholar.

Of course, such calls are likely easier to make than actualize. Our students may well push us to such strategies, and we may feel compelled to do so. Yet, we may also need to retrain in order to effectively aid our students come to terms with such a conception of PPB (yet we may not have the time to do so for we are meant to be writing funding applications!). Often when we deliver our graduate research methods courses we realize that we are woefully out of touch with that which is at the 'cutting edge' in the field of research, learning instead from the resources / scholarship that students bring to our attention. Indeed, a cursory, and thankfully very unscientific, glance at the texts used in such classes at our own institutions confirms such suspicions. Despite the concerns over time (and perhaps our 'authority' in the classroom), we need to be in a position to enable, question, and challenge to ensure rigor, quality, and, aid in dealing with potential issues in practice. How, for example, do we (aid students) identify groups in "need" without essentializing that very group and thus legitimating their social control? Similarly, at what point do we, or our students, leave a setting in which we have been participating? How do we ensure we do not just extract knowledge, leave the community behind, or offer no benefit beyond the research? Worse still, how do we ensure the lack of harm once the support mechanism and level of appropriate support for participants has been disengaged (Phellas, 2000)? Indeed, following Dockery (2000), why would 'locals' co-operate if they gain no benefit, have no control over the focus, the planning, the conduct, recommendations; and, who has the power to respond to, or act, upon findings? Finally, we may even question the premise on which we allow students to engage with methodologies ground within such ontological, epistemological and axiological approaches when the benefits of such approaches are so contested within a corporatized University predicated on evidence-based epistemologies. We can only hope that a continued assault on scientific-based, biomedical models of research, and, a commitment to social justice will prevail. We will then be in a position to be proud of those students who graduate with such sensibilities and confident of a maturing physical pedagogic bricolage.

EXPRESSING AND (RE)PRESENTING THE PHYSICAL PEDAGOGIC BRICOLAGE

As with our methodological choices, there are no prescriptions for how we express or represent PPB scholarship; inevitably though the processes of analysis, interpretation, and, expression are politicized. We are going to make choices—practical, situational, moral, ethical, political—throughout our immersion in the field, in our empirical disembedding, in our 'double-dialogues' with our record of a person's (including ourselves) words, in our theoretical abstractions (see Johnson et al., 2004), and, with regard to how we express our research to multiple communities. Clearly, PPB scholarship has to move beyond what Sparkes (1995) termed persuasive fictions, a stripped down, abstracted, detached form of language, an impersonal voice, a conclusion of propositions, or formulae involving a realist or externalizing technique that objectify through depersonalized and supposedly inert representations of the disengaged analyst. Rather, our work needs more self-conscious texts that struggle with a whole set of claims related to authorship, truth, validity, and reliability, and that bring to the fore some of the complex political/ideological agendas hidden in our writing (Richardson, 2000a, Richardson, 2000b). The genre of representation has "blurred, enlarged and altered to include an accepted place for fictions, poetry, drama, conversations, readers' theatre and so on" (Richardson, 2000b, p.9), yet, these developments are sparsely represented within the major journals in our fields. It is clear that "messy," uncertain, multivoiced texts, cultural criticism, and new alternative works are required to displace classic forms of representation as the "only" legitimate form (e.g., Altheide and Johnson, 1994; Atkinson, 1992; Clifford and Marcus, 1986; Clough, 2001; James et al., 1997; Richardson, 2000a, Richardson, 2000b, Sparkes, 1992; Sparkes, 1995). Indeed, reflexive forms of fieldwork, analysis, and intertextual representation (Tedlock, 2000) offer the potential to open up the PPB to a plethora of intimate and previously 'taboo' topics—friendship, love, physical violence, rape, body habitus, sexuality, ethnicity, physicality, misogyny, gender politics, (marginal) sub-identities, power, disempowerment, diaspora, postcolonial narratives of race, nationalism and international politics, exercise disorder behavior (a far from exhaustive list)—providing space for marginalized voices in important steps towards the democratization of 'coaching' knowledge (Tedlock, 2000) and provide the route by which our own sporting cultures can be made strange to us, allowing for new descriptions of the world to be generated which can offer the possibility of improvement of the human condition (Barker, 2000). This would include 'other' voices from those stakeholders in the coaching constellation who have been conspicuously silent or silenced: parent, official, performance director, coach employers, social worker, community coach, volunteer coach, sports science support subdisciplinarians (nutritionist, biomechanist, physiotherapists etc.), teacher, and politician, peace worker amongst many others. When combining these 'unheard' voices, the possibility then exists of being able to represent the complexity of the PPB. Further, such discussion opens the field to representations that can begin to address the theory-practice gap alluded to Trudel and Gilbert (2006); that is, by it can allow for representing or expressing sports coaching research in a manner that is accessible to coaching practitioners and those with an interest in the practice of coaching, and which is not necessarily written primarily for a scientific audience.

Further, and in embracing such forms of expression, we should heed Giroux's (2001) warning that the performative cannot be a mere "textual gesture," outside of the context of history, power and politics. Rather, the "political and ethical character of the performative are enhanced when politics is not seen as merely symbolic but is inserted into societal contexts and linked to collective struggles over knowledge, resources, and power" (p.10). Expressing the PPB—and we use the term 'expression' markedly to distinguish it from the rather limiting and outdated 'written' product— cannot hide behind any form of pretense of an "invisible author" (Ferguson et al., 1992). Given the epistemological grounding of the research, the researcher's moral and political values are not something messy and untidy, to be taken care of by tight method, or even by attempts to bracket assumptions. As discussed above, there is a need to consciously acknowledge our dialogic positionalities (Harrison, et al., 2001). Yet, we need to ensure that situating ourselves in our work does not lead, at best, to esoteric or narcissistic navel gazing scholarship (e.g., Anderson, 1999; Sparkes, 1995), and at worst, to subtler forms of what Fine (1992) terms 'ventriloqy.' Fine (1992) suggests ventriloqy occurs when we appear to let the 'other' speak, yet, all the while, we hide, unproblematically, under the covers of the marginal, now 'liberated' voices. Similarly, Johnson et al. (2004) point to the dangers of the slip from authorship to orchestration in hiding the power of authorial function. Rather than let voices act as confabulatory camouflage, there is a need to be committed to positioning ourselves as self-conscious, critical, and participatory analysts, engaged but still distinct from our informants; an agenda committed to the study of change, the move toward change, and/or committed to change (Harrison et al., 2001). This is an agenda that addresses issues that concern questioning the hierarchies of the researched and the researcher, calling for us to reflect on that relationship as we minimize status difference, show our human side, answer questions raised in the field instead of hiding behind a cloak of anonymity, and, recognize that our research products are co-produced accomplishments (see Fontana and Frey, 2005; Harrison et al., 2001). Further, it requires us stepping back from the desire to 'get good data;' we are enjoined to move beyond a concern for more and better data to think about how we can work to empower the researched. Perhaps, as an emergent field, we could learn from Bauman (2005,) who, building on Derrida, has argued that we require intimacy and distance. The trick, he argues, is "to be at home in many homes but to be inside and outside at the same time, to combine intimacy with the critical look of an outsider, involvement with detachment" (p.1091). Indeed, we may well need to be aware of what Said (1994) termed the extraordinary persistent residual of our own exilic marginality: an exile from our rigid professional affiliations and a recognition of detachment from those with whom we engage in order to produce resistive academic work that can "write back" to imperial power, can read contrapuntally, can speak to justice, and can challenge injustice (Rizvi and Lingard, 2006; Said, 1994).

Expressing our scholarship then requires decentering, if not wholeheartedly displacing, that form of scientific writing that we would argue still holds onto, even if by a thread, the center within the major journals in our field. There are a variety of approaches from which we may choose. The work of Jones (2009; 2007; 2006), Denison (2007) provides clear examples of the ways in which PPB research can make visible the voices of those athletes and coaches who have been, thus far, silenced, within the field of sports coaching. Indeed, there has been a growing interest among a small but significant group of qualitative researchers in the domains of sport, sport coaching and physical education regarding representational issues (Sparkes et al., 2003). "New territories of expression; [that] also offer new spaces of relationship" (Gergen and Gergen, 2002, p.14) are being 'experimented' with in the various domains of sport have led to the production of confessional tales, autoethnographies, poetic representations, ethnodramas, reflexive conversations, and fictional representations (see Bush and Silk, 2012; Denison, 2007; Denison and Markula, 2002; Denison and Rinehart, 2000; Jones, 2006; Lee et al., 2009; Nilges, 2001; Purdy et al., 2008; Sparkes, 2002a; Sparkes, 2002b; Sparkes, 1995; Sparkes et al., 2003; Sparkes and Silvennoinen, 1999). Further, there are a multitude of texts that provide guidance in such writing practices (e.g. Anderson, 2006; Aultman, 2009; Bartleet, 2009; Douglas and Carless, 2008; Lapadat, 2009; Sparkes, 2002a; Sparkes, 2002b; Sparkes at al., 2003), and most recently these have been applied to physical culture more generally (see Markula and Silk, 2011). Building on such momentum, we thus envision a PPB in which expressions do not simply record a multiplicity of viewpoints, but those where dominant versions, including the researchers' version, are challenged, extended, or repositioned (Johnson et al., 2004). Following Richardson and St Pierre (2005), we need to encourage writing as a method of data collection (sensual data, emotional data, response data; data which were not where data were supposed to be) that elicits points that would have escaped entirely had they not been written (they are 'collected' only in writing). Further, we need to use writing as a method of data analysis— using writing to think, to make connections—that provides the conditions for thought to happen *in* writing (Richardson and St Pierre, 2005). This is an approach that does not allow for conventional practices of coding and sorting then grouping and then section headings that organize and sort writing into an outline in advance. Further, it renders audit trails, member checking, data verification, triangulation, data saturation, peer debriefing, as absurd (Richardson and St Pierre, 2005). Such a democratization of writing practices may open our critical work on the PPB to those scholars who have been unable, or find themselves too uncomfortable, to contribute. This could indeed bring about a critique of Western ethnocentric practices in our field, give voice and space to marginalized peoples, and, provide the basis for epistemologies from previously silent groups (Tedlock, 2000). In this way, a democratization of expression can lead towards the democratization of physical knowledge, providing the field an opportunity to realize the political potential in *disrupting inequality*.

If expressing PCS scholarship then requires that we 'come clean at the hyphen' that separates and merges personal identities with our inventions of others, thereby offering a series of self-reflective points of critical consciousness around questions of how to represent responsibly, transform public consciousness and common sense about social injustice (see Fine, 1992; Harrison et al., 2001), critical questions remain over where we target our efforts. As indicated earlier, to make a difference, to take sides, to be 'true' to a communitarian ethic, does require accessible and public forms of expression (see Denison and Rinehart, 2000; Markula and Denison, 2005; Sykes et al., 2005). Indeed, we agree with Ladson-Billings and Donnor (2005) that we must transcend disciplinary boundaries if we are to have impact upon those who reside in subaltern sites or on policy makers. This means that we cannot spend our time talking to each other in the netherworld of the academy or just write in obscure journals and publish books in languages that do not translate to the lives and experiences of real (physical in at least two senses of the word) people (and we are perhaps more guilty than others in this regard). Indeed, following Fine et al. (2000) we do have an ethical responsibility to retreat from the stance of academic dispassion and aid in educating our students in the languages of policy talk, in the voices of empiricism, through the murky swamps of self-reflective story writing, and in the more accessible language of pamphlets, fliers, and community booklets. Yet, as we remind ourselves of our locations in neoliberal corporatized Universities—the McUniversity—and of 'accepted' forms of scholarship preferred by tenure review committees, Doctoral advisors, journal editors, and, funding bodies, we have to caution against a wholesale evacuation of 'traditional' forms of expression. Rather, there is a need for multiple genres to co-exist, however unhappily, alongside each other, for each to be valued, held to multiple criteria, and, to educate students to analyze, express, and publish differential works in differential spaces (that is, a paper to be delivered at a public meeting may well, but is certainly not preordained to be, differentially conceived than that for a formal Doctoral thesis in an arcane academic discipline). This is perhaps not the way it ought to be, and it is indeed, the very point of disrupting disciplines. Yet, our ethical responsibilities surely must still extend to those who are being trained for a life of scholarship. Perhaps there is future hope in the scholarship of Richardson (e. g., Richardson 2000a/b; Richardson and St. Pierre, 2005) who has not been afraid to situate herself within storied writing and address abuses of power inherent in disciplinary constraints, academic debates, departmental politics, social movements, community structures, research interests, familial ties, and personal history. No matter how we continue to exist within institutional constraints, Richardson and St Pierre (2005) point towards a PPB whose expression needs to adapt to the kind of social / political world we inhabit—a world of uncertainty. It will require us to engage in self-reflexivity, will need us to abandon our preferences and give in to synchronicity, and not flinch from where the writing takes one emotionally or spiritually. In short, we hope that expressing the physical can be a field of 'play where anything can happen' (Richardson and St Pierre, 2005) that will allow for intervention in ways that make political action and change possible.

THE PROMISE OF THE PHYSICAL PEDAGOGIC BRICOLAGE

Research characterized as PPB clearly holds much promise. But, to what standards should it be held? How such work should be judged, for this is work that, dependent on the definition one holds, should be regarded as scholarly, yet also that purports to *make a difference*. As such, inherent within the PPB is a promise to other communities, participants, peoples and places. As such, what judgment criteria might PPB research adhere to? We can, of course, problematize the notion of applying criteria to make judgments about scholarly activity that "reflects the desire to contain freedom, limit possibilities, and resist change" (Bochner, 2000, p.266). Indeed, the word *criteria* itself is a term found problematic to some as it separates modernists from postmodernists, foundationalists from antifoundationalists, empiricists from interpretivists, and scientists from artists (Bochner, 2000):

> It is not that one side thinks judgments have to be made and the other side does not. Both agree that inevitably they make choices about what is good, what is useful, and what is not. The difference is that one side believes that "objective" methods and procedures can be applied to determine the choices we make, whereas the other side believes these choices are ultimately and inextricably tied to our values and our subjectivities. (p.266)

The term criteria then is clearly contested, yet it is all too easy to opt out from application of criteria to PPB at this juncture. Rather, we need to recognize the problematic nature of the term *criteria* and that, as a research community, we do not need to necessarily agree on standards to comply with their own humanly developed conventions (Bochner, 2000). That said, our call for PPB scholarship that is capable of taking sides, that affirms the contextual and the specific, and that is always searching for more social justice, finds itself butting up against an intensified set of 'rigorous' academic 'criteria designated by the National Research Council (NRC) in the United States and bodies such as the Evidence for Policy and Practice Information (EPPI) in the U.K. and the Research Quality Framework (RQF) in Australia (Cheek, 2006). Rigor as defined by such bodies takes us back to the methodological fundamentalism (House, 2005) of evidence-based progress, policies and programs, the epistemological sovereignty of high-science. The EPPI, for example, suggests that criteria for judging qualitative work include an explicit account of the theoretical framework and or inclusion of a literature review; clearly stated aims and objectives, a clear description of context, a clear description of sample, a clear description of fieldwork methods including systematic data collection, an analysis of data by more than one researcher, and, sufficient original data to mediate between evidence and interpretation (House, 2006; Morse, 2006). Such systematic data collection, the existence of a supposed 'clear' sample (to who?), the 'logic' of two interpretations being better than one (presumably a reference to the chimerical notion of triangulation and with no comprehension of the deconstructive and diffractive potentialities of crystallization)[8] could not be further distanced from the ontological, epistemological, and methodological boundaries we have alluded to above (see House, 2005 for a detailed discussion of these EPPI standards). Yet, these 'standards' remind us that criteria are not fixed, are the products of time and place contingent social process, are ensconced in the power and political relations of our present conjuncture (cf. Atkinson and Delamont, 2005). We, thus, are in a moment in which we need to make and defend judgments when there can be no appeal to foundations, to methods, to something outside of place and time constrained social processes of knowledge construction (Atkinson and Delamont, 2005). So, how, exactly, do we judge 'good' quality PPB?

Inevitably, a question such as this raises more questions, in the first instance, than answers. We wonder if we should discuss multiple expressive genres and ways of judgment for fear it will potentially take time away from learning that which 'matters' within disciplinary boundaries. Yet, our fears are somewhat allayed here by Richardson (2000a; 2000b) who argues that learning such techniques, like a new language, will not necessarily deskill you; rather, it will give more to the academics armory. Second, we struggle with a number of questions surrounding whether stories, poems, plays, or performances are 'good' enough by themselves? Should more be added to make it 'scholarship? Does holding work up to 'aesthetic criteria' and 'reflexive criteria' do enough to convince us that this is 'scholarship' (Richardson 2000a; Richardson, 2000b; see also Richardson and St. Pierre, 2005). With Richardson (2000a; 2000b) we feel that such scholarly works make a 'substantive contribution' to understanding social life and to advancing academic knowledge. However, as with any form of expression, there are further academic, moral, and ethical criteria: such narratives are not an 'easier' proposition, they may well be held to even more 'rigorous' standards than their more 'traditional' counterparts. The 'rigor' to which we are referring, anchored within a sacred-moral epistemology, are whether instances of PPB investigation are informed, at every step of the way (see for example our discussion of Saukko's methodological validities), by commitment to a civic agenda, with the aim of enhancing moral discernment, and, with the desire to promote social transformation and critical consciousness (Denzin, 2005). In this way, criteria for judging a politics of liberation are neither mechanical nor terminal. Rather, they embody the emancipatory notion of praxis in which knowledge is not only about finding out about the world, but also about changing it. Of course, evaluation criteria in this formulation are necessarily political and moral and require a debunking of the traditional criteria of validity, generalizability, credibility, and believability of our research—as assessed by the academy, our communities, and our participants—as we judge on how we serve the interests of those who are researched, and how those research participants have more of a say at all points of the project (Denzin, 2002; Harrison et al., 2001; Madiz, 2000).

Adapting Fine et al. (2000), a set of (partial) self-reflexive points of critical consciousness might be useful in providing a roadmap of what such judgment criteria might look like, feel like, and embody. Fine et al. (2000, pp. 126–127) ask the researcher to consider whether they have connected the voices and stories of individuals back to the set of historic, structural, and economic relations in which they are situated (is the physical empirical addressed in context). Further, they ask if research has deployed multiple methods so that very different kinds of analysis have been constructed. They ask whether we have described the mundane (as opposed to the unique or startling) and provided the opportunity for some informants/constituencies/participants to review the material and interpret, dissent, or challenged interpretations. They ask us to consider how such disagreements in perspective would be reported and how we have thought through the theorizing of informant's words. Furthermore, has the research considered how these data could be used for progressive, conservative, repressive social policies? Has there been consideration of falling into the passive voice and has the researcher decoupled responsibility for interpretations. Has there been thought given to who the researcher would be afraid will see these analyses and who is rendered vulnerable/responsible or exposed by these analyses. Finally, they ask if consideration has been given to the extent to which analysis offers an alternative to the commonsense or dominant discourse and the challenges different audiences might pose.

While each instance of PPB research will be different, will appeal to different constituents and will therefore likely be subject to situational, academic, aesthetic, and moral scrutiny—in different ways, and indeed, we hope, for a blurring of criteria across this range—we can begin to sketch the types of questions we can, and should, ask of our projects. In producing in-depth, intimate stories of problematic everyday life, lived up close, offering stories that create moral compassion and help citizens make intelligent decisions and take public action on private troubles (Denzin, 2000), we can ask if the research presents a civic discourse, offers the writer as deeply knowledgeable about the local community, and exposes complacency, bigotry, and wishful thinking. Further, in thinking about quality, we can draw on criteria of accuracy, nonmaleficence, the right to know, making one's moral position public, demonstration of "interpretive sufficiency" (depth, detail, emotion, nuance, coherence, and representational adequacy), and freedom from racial, class, and gender stereotyping (see Amis and Silk, 2008). For example, Denzin (2002) characterizes high quality research by its ability to decloak the seemingly race neutral and color-blind ways of administrative policy, political discourse, and organizational structures and experiences. Holman-Jones (2005) somewhat extends these criteria through asking whether the relationships between authors and participants are reciprocal, if we have created a space for meaningful dialogue among different hearts and bodies, if we have enacted our ethical obligation to critique subject positions, acts and received notions of expertise and justice, if we have produced a self-referential tale that connects to other stories, discourses and contexts, and, if we have offered a charged atmosphere as incitement to act within and outside the context of the work.

There is clearly momentum afoot within the work of a number of scholars who have begun to conceptualize alternative, and more progressive, criteria through which we can judge PPB. We feel it is perhaps best to think of this particular juncture, given this momentum (and indeed given the wider political and economic context within which we operate), to look at this as an invitation of sorts to scholars in this embryonic field to think through the parameters of how our work should be judged. We feel this is an invite that we are not sure we can, ethically, refuse. It is a moment for PPB, as an emergent, even marginalized, (sub-)field, to ensure we do not produce scholarly enquiry into, of, on, that ignores, for the most part, the most pressing social problems of our time and produces a politics that offers nothing but more of the same (Giroux, 2001). Thus, and no matter where we aim to make a difference—in the classroom, through public ethnography, in the academic journal, in the community, on the street, through poetry—we do need think about how we want to live the lives of a social inquirer (Schwandt, 2000). Following Denzin's (2005) exploration of the Kaupapa Maori epistemology, we, as researchers, may want to ask the following about each instance of the PCS project: What research do we want done? Who is it for? What difference will it make? Who will carry it out? How do we want the research done? How will we know it is worthwhile? Who will own the research? Who will benefit? (Denzin, 2005).

The 'quality' of PPB scholarship then becomes part of the essence of the research design; it becomes *internalized* within the ontological, epistemological and methodological contingencies of PPB rather than being something to be 'tested' at the completion of the research (Amis and Silk, 2008). Like Harrison et al. (2001) discussion of reciprocity this is a situated trustworthiness that surpasses validity, credibility, and believability, but not just in regard to assessment by the academy. Rather, trustworthiness is bound with reciprocity and a concern with how research is perceived by the community and by research participants. Judging quality then is reframed, encompassed with social criticism, engendering resistance, and, helping persons imagine how things could be different (Denzin, 2002). Further, given that it is personally and contextually situated, understanding how this ethic works in any specific situation cannot be given in advance, yet, we can argue that the project of PPB should become a contextualized civic, participatory, collaborative project committed to community development, a project that joins the researcher with the researched in an ongoing moral dialogue (Christians, 2000; Denzin, 2002).

We are sure many will disagree with the propositions in this chapter; those in a position of privilege who have built academic careers in sports coaching as experts, in writing sacrosanct coaching texts, those who are comfortable with a 'performance' agenda, those who do not like change, challenge, and indeed those who have preserved academe as a neo-colonial, gendered institution, or, those who privilege the classroom as the only, as opposed to one of many, places in which we can make an impact. The work of avant garde scholars such as Denzin, Giroux, and Richardson has gone far from critiqued, yet we are convinced enough by their arguments to offer our tentative exploration through how we may ensure that PPB can produce meaningful research and adequately capture the complexities and magnitude of 'coaching.' There are many questions that remain unresolved. Scholars such as Atkinson and Delamont (2005) may well argue that we have privileged the graphos—the written word—in our research and our vision of what the PPB research should be. Maybe we have, and maybe others will aid us in thinking through sensibilities and contingencies of PPB, envisioning other ways of thinking, practising, expressing that are yet to be imagined. Some may argue that the source of experience—the data, the face to face co-presence—may be lost in our political and moral emphasis (see Manning, 2002) and call for relocating the task to the study of everyday sense making rather than 'cinematic glimpses,' 'postcards from exotic venues,' or 'deeply self-ruminating poetry' (Manning, 2002; Snow, 2002). Some may go further than this, suggesting our goals should not be political or moral, but that we should aim "at the more reasonable goal of securing a close approximation of the empirical world" (Snow and Morrill 1993, p.10) and indeed of a high-performance elitist coaching agenda. Finally, there will be those who warn of the dangers in assimilating 'coaching' research into literary forms such as poetry and fiction and the subsequent potential to firmly and sometimes exclusively, recenter the author thereby creating a new basis for authorial privilege (Atkinson and Delamont, 2005). We expect, deserve and welcome criticism; a healthy academic field is one in which contestation is a functional necessity and there are 'valid' arguments to be made among many of these critics, some of which we envision will be furthered by scholars in our field as we debate the nature, scope, and purpose of the PPB research. Indeed, as may be expected, this is far from a neat and tidy narrative, we have had many debates among ourselves in writing this manuscript, we are far from agreed on many of the points of emphasis, on the influence of certain scholars on our thinking, and some of arguments are, thankfully, far from solipsistic as a result. We feel this is to be expected, and we believe that messier, less coherent texts with competing points of view will form a central part of the project. We hope that there will be disagreements, rejections, rejoinders that force us to reconsider part of the argument and that others take up and extend other parts of the argument, all of which will expand, contend, and push the boundaries and horizons of an emergent and impactful PPB.

CONCLUSION

In this chapter we have offered a suggestive and generative directional purview of the ontological, epistemological, and methodological boundaries framing the putative intellectual project that is the PPB. Ground in the theoretical contingencies of physical cultural studies, this is a project that is motivated towards progressive social change and producing knowledge that will enable scholars—*bricoleurs*—to intervene into the broader social world and make a difference. In attempting to do so, it is envisaged that bricoleurs will undertake critical, self-reflexive scholarship, deploy an "expansive and flexible methodological arsenal" (Andrews, 2002, p.115), move beyond persuasive fictions (Sparkes, 1995) or 'classic' forms of representations, enter new territories of expression (Gergen and Gergen, 2002) and produce more self-conscious texts. The concluding chapter summarizes the key components of the reconceptualized field of sports coaching research—the PPB—and considers the contextual and conceptual challenges to the project.

7 Conclusion and Contextual and Conceptual Challenges to PPB

Do you really believe that the sciences would ever have originated and grown if the way had not been prepared by magicians, alchemists, astrologers, and witches whose promises and pretensions first had to create a thirst, a hunger, a taste for *hidden* and *forbidden* powers. Indeed, infinitely more had to be promised than could ever be fulfilled in order that anything at all might be fulfilled in the realm of knowledge. (Nietzsche, 1882, p.300)

. . . it is surely essentialist to presume that only women can/should "do" gender; only people of colour can/should do race work; only lesbians and gays can/should "do" sexuality; only women in violence can tell stories of violence. (Fine, 1994, p.152)

The purpose of offering this directional purview for the 'field' of sports coaching is not to present a form of scholarship that privileges certain forms of intellect over others, but is concerned with the progressive potential of a 'field in tension' (Silk and Andrews, 2011) in which an evolving dialogue surrounding ontology, epistemology, methodology, interpretation, expression, and impact can be held. In essence, we do not suggest discarding that which currently holds the center, but *displacing* it as the only *legitimate* form that falls under the narrowly defined banner of scholarship. Indeed, reconceptualizing the 'field' of sports coaching seeks to *displace, decenter*, and, *disrupt* the established field of research and result in an environment where *anything can happen*. It is important to emphasize that the 'nirvana' sought for the environment of sports coaching research where *anything can happen* is not to be confused with an environment in which *anything goes* (Amis and Silk, 2008).

Although the borders or boundaries of a reconceptualized 'field' of sports coaching are going to be fluid and malleable, it is of fundamental importance to identify the sites of critical engagement if the intellectual project is to achieve its emancipatory, intellectual, political, and, moral ends. *Sport* is a vague and imprecise noun (Andrews, 2008), and to alleviate criticism of the conceptual weakness presented by this signifier (Coalter, 2007); it seems prudent to embrace the evolution of *sport* to physical culture and therefore the mobilization of the nomenclature of PCS. The broader domain of physical culture encompasses various dimensions of physicality, including, but not restricted to sport, exercise, fitness, dance, wellness, health, movement practices, 'Activities of Daily Living' (ADL), recreation, work, and the pedagogic. Each of these 'spheres' incorporates different motivations for, and practices of, organizing and regulating human movement and for each of them the *active body* is something that can be experienced (by the instrumental subject) or observed (as a representational object) (Andrews, 2008). In adopting a PCS sensibility, this creates the opportunity for the very essence of a reconceptualized 'field' of sports coaching—with its multiple iterations of experiencing, communicating, instructing, teaching, and learning—to be captured.

Therefore, as a consequence of the impreciseness of the noun 'sport' and also the richer description of the act of 'coaching' afforded by encompassing the motivations and practices of organizing and regulating, experiencing and observing, teaching and learning, and, communicating and instructing the active body, it seems critical for the reconceptualized 'field' to move away from the limiting and somewhat misleading terms 'sport' and 'coaching'. It is not enough for this project to merely *adopt* a PCS sensibility. To invoke and paraphrase Silk and Andrews (2011), there is a need for the reconceptualized 'field' to embrace the conceptual underpinnings that understand physicality focused on bodily movement and activity. By mobilizing the terminology inherent in PCS, the term 'physical' more accurately portrays the various dimensions of physicality that congeal to form the complex and diverse cultural space for inquiry, and the term 'pedagogic' more fully explicates the organizing and regulating of the teaching, learning, education and instructional approach undertaken in the cultural space. What is proposed then is for the reconceptualized 'field' to replace the limiting and misleading ascribed label of 'sports coaching', and deploy the moniker of the 'Physical Pedagogic Bricolage' (PPB). The immediate and noticeable impact of ascribing PPB to the 'field' is that it opens up the reconceptualized 'field' to spheres of inquiry that might have been discarded[1] or not seen as relevant by practitioners under the old moniker of 'sports coaching'. Spheres of enquiry that sit comfortably within the PPB that might have been 'discarded' or left to scholars in other fields of enquiry might be the practitioner attempting to engage older populations in some sort of physical activity to tackle obesity or the practitioner attempting to illuminate the underrepresentation of particular ethnic identities in recreation programs.

Throughout sports coaching texts, the intimation is made that at the definitional core of the practice is improving the sporting *performance* of others (Jones, 2005a). For example, Kidman and Hanrahan (2004, p.145, emphasis added) state that "one of the primary roles of a coach is to help athletes improve their *performance*", whereas Borrie and Knowles (2003) refer to the process of coaching as helping a player/athlete learn and improve a particular skill. Having articulated that the PPB encompasses broader spheres of enquiry that have traditionally been discarded by the 'field', the very essence of PPB—with its multiple iterations of experiencing, communicating, instructing, teaching, and learning—necessitates a radical reconceptualization of 'performance' as we understand it.

Analogies between teaching and coaching are frequently made. Jones (2005b, p.xiv) articulates that "coaching is fundamentally intertwined with teaching and learning within given situational constraints". Importantly, measuring effectiveness solely against results [performance] "has an impoverishing effect on the education process, sharply narrowing it down to rote learning and teaching predominantly to the test. The test shapes the syllabus and all that happens in the classrooms" (ACSSO, 2009, p.1). Pineau (1994) articulates that educators, and by association sports coaches, have been encouraged to "conceive of themselves as 'actors' engaged in instructional dramas, as 'artists' operating on intuition and creativity, and as 'directors' who orchestrate learning experiences" (p.6). Therefore, by adapting research in to 'live performances' and the cumulative benefits to individuals, families and communities of having those experiences available night after night, year after year, could illuminate a broader base to capture the essence at the definitional core of 'coaching' in the PPB. Instead of offering a single, solitary measure of impact 'performance'— which has led to "an overtly reductive interpretation of something that is multi-dimensional" (Brown and Novak, 2007, p.9), the PPB proposes seven key intrinsic constructs that capture the essence of coaching: Captivation, intellectual stimulation, kinesthetic (physical) stimulation, emotional resonance, spiritual value, aesthetic growth, and social bonding (adapted from Brown and Novak, 2007). It is important to remember that not all coaching [pedagogic] episodes should be expected to generate impact across all seven areas. The constructs merely enable the reader to better understand the dimensionality of impacts in the PPB (Brown and Novak, 2007).

Universities have actively positioned themselves within the context of the new economy—a process termed 'academic capitalism' (Slaughter and Rhoades, 2004)—and are *driving* corporate dispositions (Barnett, 2000a; Clark, 1998; Dimitriadis, 2006). The resultant hyper-professionalism of academics work towards specialized knowledge in the service of funding 'niches' (such as EBR) is driving academics to have greater individual responsibility, greater autonomy, and a reduction in social responsibility (Dimitriadis, 2006). Embracing a PCS sensibility in the reconceptualized field of PPB research means viewing Said's (1994) call for 'amateurism in intellectual life' sympathetically. Indeed, there is a need to displace the notion of the 'universal intellectual' and also the 'specific intellectual' and develop Giroux's (1995) notion of the 'border intellectual' who is not constrained by paradigms and disciplinary boundaries. To this, the deployment of the concept of bricolage (Denzin and Lincoln, 2000) signifies the multidisciplinary, interdisciplinarity and intellectual integration necessary for scholarly activity in the reconceptualized field of PPB.

Currently, scholarly activity in the field of 'sports coaching' can be seen to be underpinned by four approaches (Jones, 2005a)—psychological, sociological, modeling, and pedagogical—however, in the reconceptualized theme field of PPB, the physical pedagogic bricolage, seeks to avoid the reductionist, monological, one-dimensional knowledge that results from external impositions of disciplinary boundaries (Kincheloe, 2005). *Bricoleurs* attempt to account for the complex relationship between material reality and human perception (Kincheloe, 2005) by adopting a multiperspectival process—employing methodological, theoretical, interpretive, political, and narrative bricolage—to get beyond the *determinism* of reductionist notions of macro-social structures (Kincheloe, 2005). In reconceptualizing the concept of 'determinancy' and reworking the concepts of 'Marxism without guarantees' (Hall, 1996b) and 'sport without guarantees' (Andrews, 2002), a *sports coaching without guarantees* or more accurately redefined, a *physical pedagogic approach without guarantees* allows for a truly contextual sensibility to unpick the complex, multi-layered field. The physical pedagogic bricolage engages with the numerous overlapping systems and discourses (for example: economic, political, technological, aesthetic, demographic, regulatory, and spatial) and reflects societies fundamental divisions along hierarchically ordered lines of division (for example: class, ethnic, gender, ability, generational, national, racial, and sexual norms). In meeting the call to draw from a theoretical base that is multidisciplinary, the *physical pedagogic bricolage* could see psychology, sociology and pedagogy supplemented by the academic disciplines of history, philosophy, religion, languages and linguistics, literature, visual arts, applied arts, performing arts, anthropology, area studies, economics, education, ethnic studies, gender and sexuality studies, geography, political science, social work, systems science, health science, journalism, media and communication, and law.[2]

Adding to the theoretical eclecticism of the bricolage, each of these academic disciplines include multiple subdisciplinary areas—for example: cultural history, cultural anthropology, Black studies, political history, public finance, child welfare, social policy, cultural geography, complexity theory, media studies, and sports law—that would further explicate the context and therefore the understanding of the 'moment' or 'event'. Indeed, it is incumbent on the PPB practitioner to remember that the bricolage is a way of naming and organizing existing impulses that influence the understanding of the contextual practices of 'sports coaching' [*sic*]. Reworking Kincheloe (2005), the physical pedagogic bricolage serves to promote understanding and communication and create structures that allow for a better informed more rigorous mode of knowledge production. Interestingly, it was posited earlier that the intellectual project to reconceptualize the field did not suggest discarding that which currently holds the center. This humility should not be misread:

> I strongly believe in the power of the [physical pedagogic] bricolage to move the field in a positive direction; it is concurrently important,

however, to understand its constructions and limitations in the context of contemporary social research. The appreciation of the complexity of everyday life and the difficulty of understanding it brings with it demands humility on the part of the [PPB] researchers. (Kincheloe, 2005, p.332)

Invoking Giroux (2001), PPB practitioners must facilitate the call for cultural workers—academics, journalists, social workers, teachers, lawyers, performance artists, representatives of the media and others—to become 'border crossers' and engage in intertextual negotiations across different sites of cultural production. It is important to remember that using isolated disciplines/subdisciplines does not make for an integrated academic area, and that a collection of cross-disciplinary areas that simply coexist together does not constitute intellectual integration (Gill, 2007). What is needed is the deep interdisciplinarity of the bricolage, for example where the historian takes concepts from hermeneutics and combines them with historiography or historical hermeneutics (Kincheloe, 2001). Not only does the physical pedagogic bricolage challenge researchers to undergo a process that is critical, self-reflexive and dialogic—an internal dialogue that happens "within the researcher" (Johnson et al., 2004, p.77)—it also necessitates academics to develop new collaborations and networks, in addition to the theoretical insights to be gained from engaging with previously unimagined disciplines.

These *new circuits of knowledge* (Slaughter and Rhoades, 2004) operate at a number of levels in the physical pedagogic bricolage to further the understanding of the 'moment'; intellectual integration from dialogue *between* academics from the myriad of cross-disciplinary areas, the engagement of the academics with the multiple iterations of the individual actors involved in the praxis of the PPB (sports coaches or physical pedagogues, instructors, teachers, athletes, parents, officials, dietary advisors, and others), and also engagement at an institutional/organizational level.[3]

To demonstrate how this would manifest in the PPB, for example by examining one dynamic [amongst many others]—the coach-athlete relationship—it can be illuminated how contemporary iterations of examining fail to address the power relationship from an athlete's perspective (Purdy et al., 2008). Typically, studies have been from the coach's perspective (Johns and Johns, 2000; Jones et al., 2003, 2004), however embracing the PPB would result in an increase in research that begins to examine the relationship that exists between coach and athlete from an athlete's perspective [amongst numerous other stakeholder perspectives]. Therefore, Purdy et al. (2008) autoethnographic approach is an example in contemporary sports coaching research of work that would be encouraged within the reconceptualized field. Indeed PPB research that deploys autoethnography and other complementary *avant garde* approaches can seek to help in the understanding of sports coaching as a complex, interactive process, being sensitive to the peculiarities, intricacies and ambiguities of coaching (Jones and Wallace, 2005). In doing so, the PPB addresses the oversimplification and unrealistic conceptions that have led to the dissatisfaction of many coaches with sports coaching research (Bowes and Jones, 2006) and thus can also facilitate in breaking down the theory practice gap.

When the deep interdisciplinarity of the physical pedagogic bricolage is considered working symbiotically with the *new circuits of knowledge*, the field of PPB affords an opportunity to not only aid the understanding of an 'event' and thus make it a far more meaningful and impactful—useful— piece of research, but can also be used as a tool to aid in the understanding the very populations we are pedagogically interacting with [coaching] and therefore surely, aiding the pedagogic [coaching] process in terms of qual- ity and effectiveness. This is highlighted by the example of pedagogically interacting with children with a minority ethnic identity who are socially disadvantaged, the 'event' is only partially understood unless it is under- stood in relation say to family life, criminal activity, issues over migration, issues with English as an additional language (EAL), child welfare, school, religious beliefs, social engineering, the governance of the body, and others. In explicating 'events' in this way, effectively by eroding the fixedness of the categories, relations and social domains that inform it, the PPB practitioner is *working the hyphen* (Fine, 1994). Reworking Fine (1994), the physical pedagogic bricolage is a field of inquiry, into which the PPB practitioner and the 'Others' enter and play with the blurred boundaries that prolifer- ate. In *working the hyphen*, the PPB practitioner must create occasions for a dialogue with the subjects of inquiry about "what is, and is not, 'happening between', within the negotiated relations of whose story is being told, why, to whom, with what interpretation, and whose story is being shadowed, why, for whom, and with what consequence" (Fine, 1994, p.135). In doing this, the PPB practitioner deploys a critical consciousness in relation to the 'moment' or 'event' under inquiry and is therefore capable of unpacking the density of relations and the intersecting social domains that inform it (Frow and Morris, 2000).[4]

The performative power of interdisciplinarity is emphasized by Gir- oux (2001), who uses the example of how a performance artist—Suzanne Lacy—brought together urban youth and the police in Oakland, California to engage in a dialogue about police brutality and urban youth violence. This is a lesson to educators, academics, and other cultural workers who wish for their work to not simply reflect the world, but to *make a dif- ference*. The importance of this for those academics practising within the reconceptualized field of PPB, is that their work should be defined by being dynamic, vibrant, politically engaged, and socially relevant; redefining the educator, academic, or *bricoleur* as an 'oppositional public intellectual' (Giroux, 2001).

Applying the physical pedagogic bricolage requires an "expansive and flexible methodological arsenal" (Andrews, 2002, p.115) and therefore the physical pedagogic bricoleur must be multicompetent and have a work-ing familiarity with a broad range of methods of collecting and analyzing empirical materials. Physical pedagogic bricoleurs will use any methods necessary to gain new perspectives on objects of enquiry, and might explore the use of interviews, observation, personal documents, ethnography, dis-course analysis, content analysis amongst many others, and indeed, they should make use of newer and perhaps more *avant garde* approaches.[5] This sensibility is evident in the manner that scholarly activity, as a result of the physical pedagogic bricolage, is expressed, (re)presented, and ultimately communicated. The methodological advances of the physical pedagogic bri-colage *must* be accompanied by similar advances in expression (Amis and Silk, 2008), and indeed physical pedagogic bricoleurs should break away from traditional modes of expression in the social sciences and experiment with the emerging alternatives such as polyvocality, poetry, pastiche, art, photography, ethnography as drama, fiction, and many more.

However, it should be remembered that writing is still the main form of communication in the social sciences, in PCS, and thus in the PPB (Johnson et al., 2004), so the deployment of the term 'creative analytic practice eth-nography' (Richardson, 2000b)—used to frame work where the author has moved outside conventional social scientific writing—would be prudent to guide the physical pedagogic bricoleur. Invoking and reworking Haraway (1988) and Fine (1994), moving away from conventional social scientific writing would mean moving away from texts produced with the "god trick"; painting subjects of inquiry from "nowhere". The PPB practitioner, through their expression, (re)presentation and communication, should no longer self-consciously shelter themselves in the text as if they were trans-parent. They should carry a voice, body, race, class, gender, interests, and politics into the texts that they produce. Not only would this facilitate tell-ing stories that matter (Clegg, 2002), but through the democratization of writing practices (Silk and Andrews, 2011), it will further open up the field of PPB research to those scholars who have been unable or unwilling to sit within the established disciplinary boundaries. In essence, it will comple-ment the call for the physical pedagogic bricolage to be both multidisci-plinary and interdisciplinary, with intellectual integration fostered through the myriad of possibilities afforded by dialogue across boundaries; physical pedagogic bricoleurs would become 'border crossers' (Giroux, 2001).

In the context of the corporate [Mc]university in tandem with a 'meth-odological fundamentalism'—our 'proto-fascist' present (Giroux, 2005)—there is a need for critical social scientific work that is not only sympathetic to, but embraces the intellectual, political, moral, emancipatory project of PCS. In embracing a PCS sensibility, we have posited that the 'field' of 'sports coaching' is reconceptualized as a field of inquiry that moves beyond the limiting and misleading mythopoeic status given to the terms of 'sport' and 'coaching' and embraces the various instances of the pedagogic approaches to physical activity. Practitioners in this new field—physical pedagogic bricoleurs—through critical interrogations into the physical that are grounded in a 'moral sacred epistemology' (Denzin, 2002), must ensure that the performative and utopian impulses to produce research that confronts inequality, places moral order, ethics, and social transformation as central concerns (Giroux, 2001; Silk and Andrews, 2011). In seeking a better understanding of both the world views of diverse peoples and the forces of domination affecting individuals, this 'radically contextualist' PPB must be *meaningful* to a range of communities, and *make a difference* (Andrews, 2008; Grossberg, 2006; Silk and Andrews, 2011; Kincheloe and McLaren, 2005; Miller, 2001b). Reworking Silk and Andrews (2011), what is proposed is an approach that challenges the practices imposed under neoliberal ideology, one that is characterized by a multiperspectival process and a socially and culturally responsive, communitarian, justice-oriented agenda; in essence, the PPB is an approach that can 'do coaching justice'.

CONCLUDING COMMENTS: CONTEXTUAL AND CONCEPTUAL CHALLENGES TO PPB

There are invariably a variety of challenges that would be faced in embracing the PPB, not limited to the status of such work as 'academic', the location of most researchers in the corporate university, the 'standards' to which academic work is held and judged and so on. All may well (or may well not) agree with our arguments, but find them too dangerous, foolish, or discomforting.[6] For embracing the argument, embracing PPB, may very well require destabilizing self-reflexivity, having conversations with yet to be imagined parties, stepping outside the halls of academe, and a leaving behind of all that is academically agreeable. It will likely require admitting—for we are not sure that no matter how far our heads may be planted in the sand that we hold on to the sanctity of the University as a place of learning and discovery, if, that is, they ever where—that the institutions we inhabit and for which we spent so long (and so much money) preparing, are political and corporate entities that restrict our scholastic horizons.

Indeed, within a present dominated by corporatized Universities—the McUniversity—and 'evidence' what place for an intellectual, political, moral, emancipatory project such as PPB? There is something quite disheartening, yet at the same time perhaps quite comforting, to think of how PPB will be so derided in a context that espouses what Lincoln and Cannella (2004a) have termed a methodological fundamentalism that aggressively pushes evidence-based progress, policies, and programs; in short, a nation of researchers locked into a governmental policy, research that 'serves policy' (Atkinson in Lather, 2006; Denzin and Giardina, 2006; House, 2006), and, the randomized experiment, as the only real 'science' that 'counts'? In tandem with this methodological fundamentalism, our institutes of higher education are increasingly commercialized and vocationalized as a source of profit for corporate interest—what Bauman (1999) calls the latest rendition of a society that has stopped questioning itself—that legitimate, promote, and essentially concretize research that serves industry, government, and funding bodies. Again, in the context of a baleful regime and 'academic' institutions serving as handmaidens for an increasingly blurred line of corporate / governmental interests, how do we carve out a space that can realize the full potentialities of the field of coaching / sport / pedagogy?

We have spent considerable space in this book postulating on what we feel PPB *ought* to look like, a potentially dangerous proposition lest we be accused of declaring a state of affairs that may not be universally shared among PPB practitioners; a presumption that, somewhat ironically, could be taken to privilege certain forms of scholarship over others. This is not our aim. Rather, we are far more interested in—and feel that there is greater progressive potential in—a field in tension, in healthy contestation, and, in which debates surrounding ontology, epistemology, political intent, method, interpretation, expression, and impact will continue to be held and will not be neatly cleared up and tidied away as a result of this propositional and perhaps provocative text. However, we do hope we have been able to raise questions, provide a space for thoughtful reflexivity, outline a set of approaches to the physical that perhaps more accurately represent the distillation of knowledge by those whose work addresses the litany of pedagogical, political, cultural, economic, and discursive forces that shape, train, contour, govern, manage and educate the physically active body.

Further, we hope to have highlighted the potentialities of PPB in terms of the power of those of us in the academy to apply research so that it impacts, and is *meaningful* to a range of communities who it has the potential to touch. It is likely that only through practice, through actually getting out and doing, writing and expressing—as opposed to talking about practice in somewhat esoteric terms, something which we are as complicit in as anyone else—that we will be in a position to really begin to define the parameters of PPB. To those may dismiss us out of hand, we need to be clear, we are not suggesting we leave behind the insights, theoretical development, impacts, and contributions bought to bear on the sports coaching research thus far. It would be a grave error and would be remiss were we not ground within the debates that have informed us to this present juncture. Our preferences, of course, are clear as we muse on the possibilities of PPB. We need critical interrogations into the physical / pedagogic that continually reworks and questions practices in the field in respect to how well, and indeed how we have engaged, private troubles and personal concerns and extended the critical, performative, and utopian impulses to address urgent social issues in the interest of promoting social change (Giroux, 2001). At the very least, we need to use theory as a resource to:

think and act, learning how to situate texts within historical and institutional contexts, and creating the conditions for collective struggles
over resources and power . . . such a gesture not only affirms the social
function of oppositional cultural work (especially within the [corpo-
rate] university) but offers opportunities to mobilize instances of collective outrage, if not collective action, against material inequalities.
(Giroux, 2001, p. 11)

We began this conclusion with a few words of warning, and perhaps we
should end with additional concerns. A critical interrogation of the physi-
cal/pedagogic as contextual, interventionist, multi-methodological and
interdisciplinary is a daunting prospect in and of itself, yet further, it is a
project that is far from stable, perhaps better characterized by a state of
perpetual flux and an urgent (and hopefully proactive) response to a (crip-
pling) socio-political agenda. As we alluded to earlier, not only can such an
approach likely not be realized within the confines of a doctoral program
(a lifetime of scholarly pursuit is perhaps more accurate), the scholar may
face difficulty with publication, tenure, funding, and may face ridicule from
disciplinarians in regard to superficiality, especially when asked to transcend, facilitate, and cultivate, at times as yet unimagined, boundary work
(Kincheloe, 2001; Lincoln, 2001). Yet, if we are truly interested in change,
in mobilizing public opinion and voice, in bringing attention to inequalities,
and producing a better, more just physical pedagogy, then we would question being silent, doing nothing, and conforming to a pre-existing agenda
which we did not set.

Our position is clear. We should not be silent; the voices of the silenced,
the marginalized, the oppressed, have been silent and suppressed for too
long within the critical interrogation of the physical / pedagogic. PPB is
predicated on understanding, critical reflection, and intervention to make
a difference. We need to ensure that PPB scholarship is that which posits a
"spirit in opposition, rather than in accommodation . . . in dissent against
the status quo" (Said, 1994, p.12) lest we be "mistaken for an anonymous
functionary or careful bureaucrat" (Said, 1994, p. 13). For, if we are to
hold true to the commitments of a critical and public pedagogy (Giroux,
2000; Giroux, 2001; Grossberg, 2006; McLaren, 1991), PPB researchers
must remain vigilant in their struggle against "the disconnection" that will
surely occur if we forsake the political imperative and allow our research
to be "inhabited for merely academic purposes" by producing studies in
which the physical / pedagogic are divorced from contextual analyses of
"power and social possibilities" (Johnson, 1996, p.78). We need to make
our practices 'count' despite a climate dominated by evidence and high-
performance agendas, not to be afraid of, indeed, panegyrize practices that
contaminate, and, in the face of likely ridicule, pursue a socially and culturally responsive, communitarian, justice-oriented agenda (Lincoln and
Denzin, 2005). In short, and following Lincoln and Denzin (2005), we

need a PPB that, at its heart, throughout its capillaries, and ingrained as the essence if its bones, is characterized by a sense of interpersonal responsibility and moral obligation on the part of researchers, responsibility and obligation to participants, to respondents and to consumers of research (including undergraduate and graduate students through the classroom), and, to ourselves as field workers and scholars.

Notes

NOTES TO CHAPTER 1

1. Disciplinarians maintain that interdisciplinary approaches result in superficiality; interdisciplinary proponents argue that disciplinarity produces naïve over-specialisation (Kincheloe, 2001).
2. See St. Pierre (2006) for a review of scientifically-based research in education.

NOTES TO CHAPTER 2

1. Margaret Thatcher was the Secretary of State for Education at this time.
2. A second neoliberal transformation occurred in the early 1990s. The neoliberal project metamorphozed into more socially interventionist forms, epitomized by the Third-Way politics of the Clinton and Blair administrations. Peck and Tickell (2002, p.389) refer to this as "roll-out" neoliberalism.
3. Hayek was awarded the Nobel Prize in Economic Sciences jointly with the Swedish economist Gunnar Myrdal in 1974. In 1991 he was bestowed the Presidential Medal of Freedom (the highest civilian award in the United States) by George H.W. Bush.
4. Friedman was awarded the Nobel Prize in Economic Sciences in 1976. In 1988 he was bestowed the Presidential Medal of Freedom by Reagan.
5. See Stuart Hall (1983) 'The great moving right show.'
6. The political centre of gravity shifted towards the Tories well before their return to government in 1951 (Jacques, 1983).
7. Labour governments (1964–1970); Conservative government (1970–1974); Labour governments (1974–1979).
8. Emphasizing the function of market forces and a reduced role of the state.
9. For the pivotal work on the 'end of history' argument, see Fukuyama (1989) 'The end of history.'
10. Not only nuclear holocaust but could be interpreted as a metaphor for any 'armed' struggle (war, ethnic cleansing, acts of terror etc.)
11. See Klein (2007) for an insightful look at how people of power cash in on chaos—the 'shock doctors'—in order to remake our world in their image. Klein (2007) describes this as 'disaster capitalism.'
12. For a detailed look at Third Way politics see Tony Blair's 'The third way: new politics for a new century.'
13. The White Paper (2003) was a precursor to the Higher Education Act 2004.
14. The Russell Group represents twenty leading universities in the United Kingdom.

15. See Personneltoday (2008) for an interesting press release pertaining to Butlins joining with Chichester University to offer degrees. This training scheme is not unique, and joins foundation degrees launched by supermarket giant Tesco and beds retailer Dreams.
16. For an informative analysis of how the increase in tuition fees in England raises issues for university funding in Scotland, see Dearden et al. (2012) '*Higher education finance in the UK.*'
17. Following the general election on May 6, 2010, the United Kingdom has a change of government. With no party winning an overall majority, the Conservatives and Liberal Democrats have formed a coalition government.
18. This proposal was accepted by Parliament in December 2010, with the fee cap to rise in the 2012–2013 academic year.
19. The cap on tuition fees will be raised to £9,000 a year while concomitantly cutting annual public funding for higher education by £2.9 billion.

NOTES TO CHAPTER 3

1. Slaughter and Rhoades (2004) describe that the turn of the century saw the rise of the 'new' global knowledge or information society that called for a fresh account of the relations between higher education institutions and society. They also use the terms knowledge society, information society, and new economy interchangeably in their theory of academic capitalism.
2. Slaughter and Rhoades (2004) use the terms *knowledge society*, *information society*, and *new economy* interchangeably.
3. For an insightful discussion on copyright issues in universities (public and private domains) see McSherry (2006).
4. For a detailed examination of how the expansion of higher education has influenced the funding base, see Greenaway and Haynes (2001) '*Funding higher education in the UK: the role of fees and loans.*'
5. How to prop up failing departments, how to respond to immediate student demands, how to ensure a good RAE score (Frith, 2001).
6. For a detailed report on higher education finance in the UK see Dearden et al. 2012.
7. Original work published 1978.
8. Apart from comments on the significance of pedagogy to his thinking, his thoughts on the role of the intellectual, on the university as an important public space for democratic discussions, and on the significance of developing a disposition of criticality in all our students (Rizvi and Lingard, 2006).
9. This notion of a 'regime' is derived from Foucault's (1980) concept of 'disciplinary regimes.'
10. For an interesting interrogation of performance-based university based research funding systems see Hicks (2012).
11. See Sorheim et al. (2011) for an insightful article on the funding of university spin-off companies.
12. Start-up companies include companies that professors started themselves or companies in which the professors receive stock equity in return for knowledge (Slaughter et al., 2004).
13. "Knowledge, after nearly a thousand years, is divorced from inwardness and is literally dehumanised" (Bernstein, 1990, p.136).
14. Degree holders who work in industry.
15. Based on Mertonian values of communalism, universalism, disinteredness, and organized skepticism. See Merton (1942) '*The normative structure of science.*'

16. This is not to suggest that universities have not been in 'crisis' before. McSherry (2006) highlights that the American research university has gone through at least three distinct 'crises' in the past five decades alone.

17. See Gibbons et al. (1994) *'The new production of knowledge'* for a detailed explanation of the characteristics of a dual conception of the epistemologies of 'Mode 1' (propositional) knowledge and the newly emerging 'Mode 2' knowledge (knowledge-in-use). For a critique of *'The new production of knowledge'* see Pestre (2000).

18. Barnett (2000, p.413) cites "the potential patenting of human genetic material on the one hand, and forbidding the publication in journals of the reporting of new findings (so as to extract the maximum market leverage)" as examples.

19. David (2007) cites some of the recent feminist and gender studies as painting a more optimistic picture of the future for women as academics and researchers in higher education.

20. See Messner-Davidow (1993) *'Manufacturing the attack on liberalised higher education'* for an insightful analysis of the conservative attack on higher education

21. Frith (2001, p.92) refers to these developments as "certificates of Bouncing and Beauty, which are clearly not academic."

22. See Lomas (2002) for a discussion of whether the development of mass education necessarily means the end of quality.

23. In 2007 of the 300,000 university applicants from less affluent social backgrounds just over 1% get into one of the top 13 universities (Sutton Trust, 2007). See Reay et al. (2009) *'Fitting in or standing out: working-class students in UK higher education'* for a detailed understanding of the multilayered notion of student identity in UK higher education.

24. See Leathwood and O'Connell (2003) who unpick the construction of the 'new student' in higher education.

25. As a result of the creation of approximately 20 new universities in the 1960s, and the removal of the 'binary divide' in the early 1990s, this resulted in over 40 polytechnics gaining university status equating to almost 100 universities in the UK (Greenaway and Haynes, 2003). In the year 2012, there are approximately 150 universities and university colleges in the UK.

26. As discussed in Chapter 2 and Chapter 3.

27. In the UK the term Sport(s) Science(s) is used as an umbrella term for academic programmes that focus on the application of scientific principles and techniques with the aim of improving sporting performance. In the United States, the term Kinesiology is used, and in Australia, Human Movement Studies.

NOTES TO CHAPTER 4

1. Data cited is for the soccer World Cup in 1998. Note that these figures cited in Cashmore (2000) have been criticized as being vastly overinflated. (See The Independent, 2007 *'Why Fifa's claim of one billion TV viewers was a quarter right.'*)

2. It is not the purpose of this chapter to give a detailed account of the economic impacts of sport in the UK or indeed its global impact. See Coalter (2007) for an intuitive description of *'The economic impacts of sport: investing in success?'*

3. The persistent assertion that sport was somehow separate from society (Allison, 1993).

4. Recent high level of academic interest has been shown for future analysis of sport policy by utilizing major models and frameworks for analysis adopted in other policy areas. See Houlihan (2005) *'Public sector sport policy.'*
5. Parallels can be drawn between this and the 'audit culture' noted by Apple (2005) permeating education in the 1980s.
6. See the pre-election policy statement from the Labour Party (1996) *'Labour's sporting nation.'*
7. For example *'Sport and social exclusion'* (Collins et al., 1999); *'The role of sport in regenerating deprived urban areas'* (Coalter et al., 2000); *'Game plan'* (DCMS and Strategy Unit, 2002); *'The benefits of sport'* (Coalter, 2005).
8. Coalter (2007) attributes the lack of a strong cumulative body of research evidence from which to inform sport policy and practice to four broad factors: conceptual weaknesses; methodological weaknesses; little consideration of sufficient conditions; limitations of narrative reviews.
9. In line with Coalter's (2007) concerns, there is an abundance of research unpicking the role of [team] sports in promoting a political project of defining acceptable forms of masculinity (see Hargreaves, 1986c; Crosset, 1990; Messner, 2002; Price and Parker, 2003; Harris and Clayton, 2007; Anderson and McGuire, 2010).
10. For some insightful discussion surrounding the power that sport has *impacting* national prestige in other Western countries (Canada, Finland and Austria) see: Jackson and Ponic (2001), Laine (2006) and Horak and Spitaler (2003).
11. See Rowe (2003) for an insightful article about sport and the repudiation of the global. See Ritzer (2007) *'The Globalization of nothing 2'* for a detailed look at the importance of recognizing the local.
12. See Scholte (2002) for a detailed look at the way globality (the condition) and globalization (the trend) are defined. Scholte (2002) identifies globalization as the spread of transplanetary connections between people.
13. For a detailed discussion on the sports–government connection, see Allison, 1993; Houlihan, 1994; Maguire et al., 2002; Wilson, 1994.
14. There is a growing base of academic literature around the sociology of sports-mega events. For an overview of this field of study, see Horne and Manzenreiter (2006) *'An introduction to the sociology of sports mega-events.'*
15. For an insightful discussion on wider issues surrounding hosting the Olympic Games, see Magdalinski (2000) *'The reinvention of Australia for the Sydney 2000 Olympic Games.'*
16. Each of the 'promises' has a range of 'key programme' policies aimed at achieving the 'headline ambitions' stated in the document.
17. See for example Poli (2007) *'The denationalization of sport: de-ethnicization of the nation and identity deterritorialization.'*
18. For a useful discussion on *'Sport, nationalisms and their futures'* see Reid and Jarvie (2000).
19. Particularly in soccer and other team sports (Houlihan, 2004).
20. Also in other countries such as Canada and Australia to a lesser extent (Coalter, 2007).
21. For an articulate discussion on a global role for sport, see Coalter (2007) Chapter 5 *'Sport in development.'*
22. These 8 goals include eradicating extreme poverty and hunger, universal primary education, promoting gender equality and empowering women, combating HIV/AIDS, and reducing child mortality. See United Nations (2005b) *'The Millennium goals report 2005'* for fuller details.
23. Jarvie (2006, p.96) states that "at a minimal illustrative level globalisation can be articulated at the level of politics, culture, economics, technology and society".

24. 1,745 undergraduate sport courses in 2006, of which 192 (11.0%) concentrated on sports coaching, 90 (5.2%) sport education, 67 (3.8%) sport psychology, 18 (1.0%) sport/exercise physiology, 1054 (62.7%) 'sports science' (Bush, 2007).
25. 1,745 undergraduate sports courses commencing in 2009 (UCAS, 2008b).
26. Forty-one different 'sport' programmes commencing in 2008 (UCAS, 2008a).
27. Programs commencing in 2008.
28. In January 2007 'The UK Action Plan for Coaching' was renamed to 'The UK Coaching Framework: A 3–7-11 Action Plan.'
29. The model of Côté et al. (1995) is an example of a model 'of' coaching. It was developed based on high performance gymnastics coaches and has since been *validated* with team and combat sports.
30. Coach Career Development research represents 23.7% of articles that were coded by coaching focus category 1998–2001 (Gilbert and Trudel, 2004).,
31. Lyle (2008) distinguishes three principal contexts in which sport coaching can take place: recreational/community, club/performance, excellence.
32. See Stafford and Balyi (2005) '*Coaching for long term athlete development: improving participation and performance in sport.*'
33. Murray et al. (2007) articulate that in modern opinion, 'theory' tends to be distinguished from 'practice' in the way that 'thinking' is separate from 'doing' (the *vita contemplativa* from the *vita activa*). Murray et al. (2007) posit that this is a false and dangerous binary. See Foucault (1977) for an insightful discussion on how theory and practice are related.
34. For example this tension is also mirrored in education (Bates, 2002b).
35. See Abraham and Collins (1998) '*Examining and extending research in coach development.*'
36. From 1994–1997 qualitative methodology increased 9.1% and from 1998–2001 7.7%. Using the average rise of 8.4% for each of these time periods, and estimate of 45% is reached for the present day.
37. Other stakeholders—the assistant coach, game official, administrators, and parents—also exert an influence on the coaching process.
38. Fewer than 5% of the coaching research articles were devoted exclusively to female coaches (Gilbert and Trudel, 2004).
39. Contemporary research is starting to address scarcity in particular 'minority' groups. See Anderson (2007) '*Coaching identity and social exclusion*' for an insightful discussion on sport and a coach's role in relation to misogyny, homophobia, ableism, racism, and violence.
40. Seven of the top ten sports are team sports with basketball alone present in one third of the studies. Tennis, track and field, swimming, and diving are the individual-type sports in the top ten (Gilbert and Trudel, 2004).
41. See Jones et al. (2002) '*Understanding the coaching process: a framework for social analysis.*'

NOTES TO CHAPTER 5

1. This is the very essence of a reconceptualized field of sports coaching research. See Chapter 6.

NOTES TO CHAPTER 6

1. 80% of main research questions in sports coaching are oriented towards a quantitative methodology (Gilbert and Trudel, 2004a).

2. As an interdisciplinary project, the field of study draws upon a number of disciplines and is multiperspectival in nature. As a transdisciplinary project, it has its own integrity as defined by the practices, methods, and work developing in its tradition. As a counterdisciplinary project, assimilation into standard academic disciplines is refused, and there is openness to a variety of methods and theoretical positions whilst assuming a critical-oppositional stance to the current organization of the field.

3. "I am wise when I can honestly say: 'I know that I know nothing!'" (Murray et al., 2007, p.513).

4. The point of 'no exit.'

5. Examples of the research funding bodies: the National Research Council (NRC) in the United States, the Research Quality Framework (RQF) in Australia, and the Evidence for Policy and Practice Information (EPPI) in the United Kingdom. See House (2005) for a detailed discussion of the EPPI standards.

6. There are a number of texts that deal explicitly with 'method' in cultural studies. Our students have found Saukko (2003); White and Schwoch (2006) and Johnson et al. (2004) most useful.

7. Pinar's (1975) new way of looking at curriculum, through his notion of currere, meaning trip or route taken to extend understanding of not only oneself, but of others, through a reflexive cycle.

8. Richardson proposes the crystal over the triangle—"the crystal combines symmetry and substance with an infinite variety of shapes, substances, transmutations, multidimensionalities, and angles of approach. Crystals grow, change, alter, but are not amorphous. Crystals are prisms that reflect externalities and refract within themselves, creating different colors, patterns, and arrays, casting off in different directions. What we see depends on our angle of repose . . . Crystallization, without losing structure, deconstructs the traditional idea of validity, and crystallization provides us with a deepened, complex, thoroughly partial, understanding of the topic. Paradoxically, we know more and doubt what we know. Ingeniously we know there is always more to know" (Richardson, 2000a, p. 934).

NOTES TO CHAPTER 7

1. The term 'discarded' is used here to emphasise that the scholarly activity undertaken would be located in other fields of enquiry.

2. This list is by no means exclusive of exhaustive.

3. For example: Sport England, UK Sport, British Olympic Association, SportsCoach UK, DCMS, and others.

4. In essence this captures and frames the direction of research in the PPB.

5. Such as performance ethnographies or public ethnographies.

6. We are reminded here of the Semmelweis reflex. The Semmelweis reflex is a metaphor for the reflex-like tendency to reject new knowledge because it contradicts established norms, beliefs, or paradigms (Edwards, 1968).

Bibliography

Abraham, A. and Collins, D. (1998). Examining and extending research in coach development. *Quest*, 50, 59–79.

Abu-Lughod, L., (1993). *Writing women's worlds: Bedouin stories*. Berkeley: University of California Press.

ACSSO. (2009). *Performance pay for teachers* [online]. Available from: http://www.acsso.org.au/ed070612.pdf [Accessed 9 January 2009].

Allison, L. (1993). *The changing politics of sport*. Manchester: Manchester University Press.

Altheide, D. and Johnson, J. (1994). Criteria for assessing interpretive validity in qualitative research. *In*: N.K. Denzin and Y.S. Lincoln (eds.), *Handbook of qualitative research*. Thousand Oaks, CA: Sage, 485–499.

Amis, J.M. and Silk, M.L. (2008). The philosophy and politics of quality in qualitative organizational research. *Organizational Research Methods*, 11(3), 456–480.

Anderson, E. (2007). Coaching identity and social exclusion. *In*: J. Denison (ed.), *Coaching knowledges: Understanding the dynamics of sport performance*. London: A and C Black, 24–50.

Anderson, E. and McGuire, R. (2010). Inclusive masculinity theory and the gendered politics of men's rugby. *Journal of Gender Studies*, 19(3), 249–261.

Anderson, L. (2006). Analytic autoethnography. *Journal of Contemporary Ethnography*, 35(4), 373–395.

Anderson, L. (1999). The open road to ethnography's future. *Journal of Contemporary Ethnography*, 28(5), 451–459.

Andrews, D.L. (2008). Kinesiology's inconvenient truth and the physical cultural studies imperative. *Quest*, 60, 46–63.

Andrews, D.L. (2006). *Sport-commerce-culture: essays on sport in late capitalist America*. New York: Peter Lang.

Andrews, D.L. (2004). Sport in the late capitalist moment. *In*: T. Slack. (ed.), *The commercialisation of sport*. London: Routledge, 3–28.

Andrews, D.L. (2002). Coming to terms with cultural studies. *Journal of Sport and Social Issues*, 26(1), 110–117.

Andrews, D.L., Mason, D.S. and Silk, M.L. (eds.). (2005). *Qualitative methods in sports studies*. Oxford: Berg.

Apple, M.W. (2005). Education, markets, and an audit culture. *Critical Quarterly*, 47(1–2), 11–29.

Apple, M.W. (2001). *Educating the "Right" way: markets, standards, God, and inequality*. New York: Routledge.

Atkinson, M. (2011). Physical cultural studies. *Sociology of Sport Journal*, 28(1), 135–144.

Atkinson, M. (2010). Entering scapeland: yoga, fell and post-sport physical cultures. *Sport in Society: Cultures, Commerce, Media, Politics,* 13(7), 1249–1267.

Atkinson, P. (1992). *Understanding ethnographic texts.* Newbury Park, CA: Sage.

Atkinson, P. and Delamont, S. (2005). Analytic Perspectives. *In:* N.K. Denzin and Y.S. Lincoln (eds.), *The Sage handbook of qualitative research* (3rd ed.). Thousand Oaks, CA: Sage, 821–840.

Atkinson, P. and Hammersley, M. (1994). Ethnography and participant observation. *In:* N. Denzin and Y. Lincoln (eds.), *Handbook of qualitative research.* Thousand Oaks, CA: Sage, 248–261.

Aultman, L.P. (2009). A story of transition: using poetry to express liminality. *Qualitative Inquiry,* 15(7), 1189–1198.

Azzarito, L. (2010). Ways of seeing the body in kinesiology: A case for visual methodologies. *Quest, 62,* 155–170.

Bailey, D. and Hall, S. (1992). The vertigo of displacement. *Ten 8,* 2(3), 15–23.

Ball, S.J. (2012). Performativity, commodification and commitment: an I-Spy guide to the neoliberal university. *British Journal of Educational Studies,* 60(1), 17–28.

Balyi, I. (1992). Beyond Barcelona: a contemporary critique of the theory of periodisation. *In: Beyond Barcelona.* 4th Elite Coaches Seminar. Canberra: Australian Coaching Council.

Barnett, R. (2000a). University knowledge in an age of supercomplexity. *Higher Education,* 40, 409–422.

Barnett, R. (2000b). *Realising the university in an age of supercomplexity.* Ballmoor: Open University Press.

Barnett, R. and Griffin, A. (eds.). (1997). *The end of knowledge in higher education.* London: Cassell.

Bartleet, B. Behind the baton: exploring autoethnographic writing in a musical context. *Journal of Contemporary Ethnography,* 38(6), 713–733.

Bates, R. (2002a). Administering the global trap: the role of educational leaders. *Educational Management and Administration,* 30(2), 139–156.

Bates, R. (2002b). The impact of educational research: alternative methodologies and conclusions. *Research Papers in Education,* 17(4), 403–408.

Bauman, Z. (2005). Afterthought: on writing; on writing sociology. *In:* N.K. Denzin and Y.S. Lincoln (eds.), *The Sage handbook of qualitative research* (3rd ed.). Thousand Oaks, CA: Sage, 1089–1098.

Bauman, Z. (2000). *Globalization: the human consequences.* Cambridge: Polity Press.

Bauman, Z. (1999). *In search of politics.* Stanford, CA: Stanford University Press.

Baker, D. Epstein, G. and Pollin, R. (eds.). (1999). *Globalisation and progressive economic policy.* Cambridge: Cambridge University Press.

Barker, C. (2000). *Cultural studies: theory and practice.* London: Sage.

Bauer, M., Askling, B., Gerard Marton, S., and Marton, F. (1999). *Transforming universities: changing patterns of governance, structure and learning in Swedish higher education.* London: Jessica Kinglsey.

BBC. (2008). *Tory teaching offer to ex-troops* [online]. Available from: http://news.bbc.co.uk/1/hi/uk_politics/7640903.stm [Accessed 02 October 2008].

Beck, U. (2000). *What is globalisation?* Cambridge: Polity Press.

Becker, H. (1967). Whose side are we on? *Social Problems,* 14, 239–247.

Bernstein, B. (1990). *The structuring of pedagogic discourse: vol. iv. Class codes and class control.* London: Routledge.

Bhattacharje, Y. (2008). Democrat: Barack Obama. *Science,* 319, 28–29.

Birrell, S. (1990). Double fault: Renee Richards and the construction and naturalization of difference. *Sociology of Sport Journal,* 7(1), 1–21.

Birrell, S. (1989). Race relations theories and sport: Suggestions for a more critical analysis. *Sociology of Sport Journal,* 6(3), 212–227.

Blair, T. (1998). *The Third Way: new politics for a new century.* London: Fabian Society.

Bleaney, M. (1983). Conservative economic strategy. *In:* S. Hall and M. Jacques (eds.), *The politics of Thatcherism.* London: Lawrence and Wishart.

Blommaert, J. (1997). *Workshopping: notes on professional vision in discourse analysis.* Wilrijk: Antwerp Papers in Linguistics, 91.

Bloom, M., Grant, M. and Watt, D. (2005). *Strengthening Canada: the socio-economic benefits from sports participation in Canada.* Ottawa: Conference Board of Canada.

Bloom, G., Stevens, D. and Wickwire, T. (2003). Expert coaches' perceptions of team building. *Journal of Applied Sport Psychology,* 15(2), 129–143.

Bloyce, D. and Smith, A. (2010). *Sport policy and development: an introduction.* London: Routledge.

Bochner, A.P. (2000). Criteria against ourselves. *Qualitative Inquiry,* 6(2), 266–272.

Bompa, T.O. (1999a). *Periodisation training for sport.* Champaign, IL: Human Kinetics.

Bompa, T.O. (1999b). *Periodisation: theory and methodology of training* (4th edition). Champaign, IL: Human Kinetics.

Bompa, T.O. (1996). *Periodisation of strength.* Toronto: Veritas.

Bone, J. and McNay, I. (2006). *Higher education and human good.* Bristol: Tockington Press.

Borrie, A. and Knowles, Z. (2003). Coaching science and soccer. *In:* T. Reilly and M. Williams (eds.), *Science and soccer* (2nd ed.). London: Cambridge University Press.

Bottery, M. (2000). *Education, policy and ethics.* London: Continuum.

Bourdieu, P. (1997). The forms of capital. *In:* A.H. Halsey, H. Lauder, P. Brown, and A.S. Wells (eds.), (1997). *Education, culture, economy, society.* Oxford: Oxford University Press, 46–58.

Bourdieu, P. (1977). *Outline of a theory of practice.* Cambridge: Cambridge University Press.

Bourdieu, P. and Wacquant, L. (2001). Neoliberal speak: notes on the new planetary vulgate. *Radical Philosophy,* 105, 2–5.

Bowes, I. and Jones, R.L. (2006). Working at the edge of chaos: understanding coaching as a complex, interpersonal system. *The Sport Psychologist,* 20, 235–245.

Bramham, P. (2008). Sports policy. *In:* K. Hylton and P. Bramham (eds.), *Sports development: policy, process and practice* (2nd ed.). London: Routledge, 10–23.

Bramham, P. and Henry, I. (1991). Explanations of the organisation of sport in British society. *International Review for the Sociology of Sport,* 26, 139–150.

Bramham, P. and Henry, I. (1985). Political ideology and leisure policy. *Leisure Studies,* 4(1), 1–19.

Brenner, N. and Theodore, N. (2002a). Cities and the geographies of "actually existing neoliberalism". *Antipode,* 34(3), 349–379.

Brenner, N. and Theodore, N. (2002b). Preface: from the "new localism" to the spaces of neoliberalism. *Antipode,* 34(3), 341–347.

Brewer, C.J. and Jones, R.L. (2002). A five-stage process for establishing contextually valid systematic observation instruments: the case of rugby union. *The Sport Psychologist,* 16(2), 139–161.

Brignell, J. (2000). *Sorry, wrong number!* London: Brignell Associates and European Science and Environmental Forum.

Brown, A.S. and Novak, J.L. (2007). *Assessing the intrinsic impacts of a live performance.* San Francisco: WolfBrown.

Brown, D. (2006). Pierre Bourdieu's "masculine domination" thesis and the gendered body in sport and physical culture. *Sociology of Sport Journal,* 23(2), 162–188.

Browne, J. (2010) *Securing a sustainable future for higher education: an independent review of higher education funding and student finance.* London, The UK Government.

Brown, N. and Szeman, I. (2002). The global coliseum: on Empire. *Cultural Studies,* 16(2), 177–192.

Brown, P. (2006). The opportunity trap. *In:* H. Lauder, P. Brown, J. Dillabough, and A.H. Halsey (eds.), *Education, globalization and social change.* Oxford: Oxford University Press, 381–397.

Brown, P. and Lauder, H. (2001). *Capitalism and social progress: the future of society in a global economy.* Basingstoke: Palgrave.

Bruni, A. (2006). "Have you got a boyfriend or are you single?" On the experiences of being "straight" in organizational research. *Gender, Work and Organization,* 13, 299–316.

Burgan, M. (2006). *What ever happened to the faculty? Drift and decision in higher education.* Baltimore, MD, John Hopkins University Press.

Bush, A.J. (2007). What is coaching? *In:* J.Denison (ed.), *Coaching knowledges: understanding the dynamics of sport performance.* London: AandC Black, 3–23.

Bush, A.J. and Silk, M.L. (2012). Politics, power and the podium: coaching for Paralympic performance. *Reflective Practice: International and Multidisciplinary Perspectives* [online]. Available from: http://dx.doi.org/10.1080/14623943.201 2.670109.

Bush, A.J. and Silk, M. L., 2010. Towards an evolving critical consciousness in coaching research: the physical pedagogic bricolage. *International Journal of Sports Science and Coaching,* 5(4), pp. 551–565.

Bush, A.J., Brierly, J., Carr, S., Gledhill, A., Mackay, N., Manley, A., Morgan, H., Roberts, W. and Willsmer, N. (2012). *Foundations in sports coaching.* Oxford: Pearson.

Cannella, G.S. (2011). Political possibility, hypercapitalism, and the "conservative reeducation machine". *Cultural Studies <=> Critical Methodologies,* 11(4), 364–368.

Carr, D. (2003). *Making sense of education: an introduction to the philosophy and theory of education and teaching.* London: Routledge Falmer.

Carrington, B. (2010). *Race, sport and politics: The sporting black diaspora.* London: Sage.

Carrington, B. (2001). Decentering the Centre: Cultural Studies in Britain and its legacy. *In:* T. Miller, (ed.), *A companion to cultural studies.* Oxford: Blackwell, 275–297.

Carrington, B., and MacDonald, I. (2009). *Marxism, cultural studies and sport.* London: Routledge.

Carter, P. (2005). *Review of national sport effort and resources.* London: Sport England.

Cashmore, E. (2000). *Making sense of sports* (3rd ed.). London: Routledge.

Cassidy, T., Jones, R.L. and Potrac, P. (2004). *Understanding sports coaching: the social, cultural and pedagogical foundations of coaching practice.* London: Routledge.

Cerny, P.G., Menz, G., and Soederberg, S. (2005). Different roads to globalization: neoliberalism, the competition state, and politics in a more open world. *In:* S. Soederberg, G. Menz, and P.G. Cerny (eds.), *Internalizing globalization.*

The rise of neoliberalism and the decline of national varieties of capitalism. Basingstoke: Palgrave, 1–30.

Chakraborty, S. and Lahiri, A. (2007). Costly intermediation and the poverty of nations. *International Economic Review*, 48(1), 155–183.

Chen, K. (1994). Positioning positions: a new internationalist localism of cultural studies. *Positions: East Asia Cultures Critique*, 2(3), 680–710.

Chossudovsky, M. (1996). *The globalization of poverty.* Sydney: Pluto.

Christians, C.G. (2005). Ethics and politics in qualitative research. *In*: N.K. Denzin and Y.S. Lincoln (eds.), *The Sage handbook of qualitative research* (3rd ed.). Thousand Oaks, CA: Sage, 139–164.

Christians, C. (2000). Ethics and politics in qualitative research. *In*: N.K. Denzin and Y.S. Lincoln (eds.), *Handbook of qualitative research* (2nd ed.). Thousand Oaks, CA: Sage, 133–155.

Clark, B. (1998). *Creating entrepreneurial universities.* Oxford: Pergamon.

Clarke, J. (1991). *New times and old enemies: essays on cultural studies and America.* London: Harper Collins.

Clarke, J. (1975). The skinheads and the magical recovery of community. *Working Papers in Cultural Studies*, 7–8 (Summer), 99–105.

Clarke, J. (1973). Football hooliganism and the skinheads. *Centre for Contemporary Cultural Studies: Stencilled Occasional Papers Series*, 42, 1–21.

Clegg, S.R. (2002). "Lives in the balance": a comment on Hinings and Greenwood's "disconnects and consequences in organization theory?" *Administrative Science Quarterly*, 47, 428–441.

Clifford, J. and Marcus, G.E. (eds.). (1986). Writing culture: the poetics and politics of ethnography. Santa Fe, NM: University of California Press

Clough, P. (2001). On the relationship of the criticism of ethnographic writing and the cultural studies of science. *Cultural Studies <=> Critical Methodologies*, 1(2) 240–270.

Coakley, J. (2001). *Sport in society: issues and controversies* (7th edition). New York: McGraw Hill.

Coalter, F. (2010). *'What is sport, what is development'? Fuzzy snapshots or clear videos?* Keynote speech at 'Sport for Sport' Symposium. Hatfield: Hertfordshire University, 9 September 2010.

Coalter, F. (2007). *A wider social role for sport: who's keeping the score?* London: Routledge.

Coalter, F. (2005). The social benefits of sport: an overview to inform the community planning process, *Research Report*, 98, Edinburgh: Sportscotland.

Coalter, F., Allison, M. and Taylor, J. (2000). *The role of sport in regenerating deprived urban areas.* Edinburgh: Scottish Executive.

Cohen, L., Hancock, P. and Tyler, M. (2006). Beyond the scope of the possible: art, photography, and organizational abjection. *Culture and Organization*. 12(2), 109–125.

Cole, C. L. (2007). Bounding American democracy: sport, sex, and race. *In*: N. Denzin and M. Giardina (eds.), *Contesting empire, globalizing dissent: cultural studies after 9/11.* Boulder: Paradigm, 152–166.

Collins, M. (2010). *Examining sports development.* London: Routledge.

Collins, M., Henry, I., Houlihan, B. and Buller, J. (1999). *Sport and social inclusion: a report to the department of culture, media and sport, institute of sport and leisure policy.* Loughborough: Loughborough University.

Collins, P.H. (1991). Black feminist thought. New York: Routledge.

Connell, R. (1985). *Teachers' Work.* London: Allen and Unwin.

Côté, J. (2006). The development of coaching knowledge. *International Journal of Sports Science and Coaching*, 1(3), 217–222.

Côté, J., Sammela, J., Trudel, P., Baria, A. and Russell, S. (1995). The coaching model: a grounded assessment of expert gymnastic coaches knowledge. *Journal of Sport and Exercise Psychology*, 17(1), 1–17.

Cox, C.B. and Dyson, A.E. (1969). *Black Paper: the crisis in education*. London: Critical Quarterly Society.

Critcher, C. (1977). Fads and fashions. *Centre for Contemporary Cultural Studies: Stencilled Occasional Papers Series, 63.*

Critcher, C. (1974). Football since the war: Study in social change and popular culture. *Centre for Contemporary Cultural Studies: Stencilled Occasional Papers Series, 29.*

Critcher, C. (1971). Football and cultural values. *Working Papres in Cultural Studies*, 1(Spring), 103–119.

Crosset, T. (1990). Masculinity, sexuality, and the development of early modern sport. *In*: M. Messner and D. Sabo (eds.), *Sport, men and the gender order: critical feminist perspectives*. Champaign, IL: Human Kinetics, 23–45.

Cross, N. and Lyle, J. (1999). *The coaching process: principles and practice for sport*. Oxford: Butterworth-Heinemann.

Cushion, C., Armour, K.M. and Jones, R.L. (2006). Locating the coaching process in practice: models 'for' and 'of' coaching. *Physical Education and Sport Pedagogy*, 11(1), 83–99.

d'Arripe-Longueville, F., Fournier, J.F. and Dubois, A. (1998). The perceived effectiveness of interactions between expert French judo coaches and elite female athletes. *The Sport Psychologist*, 12, 317–332.

Dallmayr, F. (2002). Lessons of September 11. *Theory, Culture, and Society*, 19(4), 137–145.

Daniels, R., Blasch, L., and Caster, P. (2000). Resisting corporatization of the university. *In*: G. D. White and F. C. Hauck (eds.), *Campus, Inc.: Corporate power in the ivory tower*. Amherst, NY: Prometheus Books, 61–84.

Darder, A. and Mirón, L.F. (2006). Critical pedagogy in a time of uncertainty: a call to action. *Cultural Studies <=> Critical Methodologies*, 6(1), 5–20.

David, M. (2007). Equity and diversity: towards a sociology of higher education for the twenty-first century? *British Journal of Sociology of Education*, 28(5), 675–690.

Davies, B. (2005). The (im)possibility of intellectual work in neoliberal regimes. *Discourse: Studies in the Cultural Politics of Education*, 26(1), 1–14.

Davies, L.E. (2002). Consumer's expenditure on sport in the UK: increased spending or underestimation? *Managing Leisure*, 7, 83–102.

Dearden, L., Goodman, A. and Wyness, G. (2012). Higher education finance in the UK. *Fiscal Studies*, 33(1), 73–105.

Dearlove, J. (2000). Globalisation and the study of British politics. *Politics*, 20(2), 111–118.

De Knopp, P., Engström, L-M., Skirstad, B. and Weiss, M.R. (eds.). (1996). *Worldwide trends in youth sport*. Champaign, IL: Human Kinetics.

Delanty, G. (2001). *Challenging knowledge: the university in the knowledge society*. Buckingham: Open University Press and SRHE.

Delanty, G. (1998). The idea of the university in the global era: from knowledge as an end to the end of knowledge? *Social Epistemology*, 12(1), 3–26.

Denison, J. (2007). Social theory for coaches: a Foucauldian reading of one athlete's poor performance. *International Journal of Sports Science and Coaching*, 2(4), 369–383.

Denison, J. and Markula, P. (2002). Introduction: moving writing. *In*: J. Denison and P. Markula. (eds.). *'Moving writing': crafting movement and sport research*. New York: Peter Lang, 1–24.

Denison, J. and Rinehart, R. (2000). Introduction: imagining sociological narratives. *Sociology of Sport Journal*, 17(1), 1–4.

Denzin, N.K. (2005). Emancipatory discourses and the ethics and politics of interpretation. *In:* N.K. Denzin and Y.S. Lincoln (eds.), *The Sage Handbook of Qualitative Research* (3rd ed.). Thousand Oaks, CA: Sage, 933–958.

Denzin, N.K. (2004). The war on culture, the war on truth. *Cultural Studies <=> Critical Methodologies*, 4(2), 137–142.

Denzin, N.K. (2003). *Performative ethnography: critical pedagogy and the politics of culture.* Thousand Oaks, CA: Sage.

Denzin, N.K. (2002). Cultural studies in America after September 11th, 2001. *Cultural Studies <=> Critical Methodologies*, 2, 5–8.

Denzin, N.K. (1997). *Interpretive ethnography: ethnographic practices for the 21st century.* Thousand Oaks, CA: Sage.

Denzin, N.K. (1989). *Interpretive biography.* Newbury Park, CA: Sage.

Denzin, N.K. and Lincoln, Y.S. (2005a). The art and practices of interpretation, evaluation, and representation. *In:* N.K. Denzin and Y.S. Lincoln (eds.), *The Sage handbook of qualitative research* (3rd ed.). Thousand Oaks, CA: Sage, 909–914.

Denzin, N.K. and Lincoln, Y.S. (2005b). Methods of collecting and analyzing empirical materials. *In:* N.K. Denzin and Y.S. Lincoln (eds.), *The Sage handbook of qualitative research* (3rd ed.). Thousand Oaks, CA: Sage, 641–650.

Denzin, N.K. and Lincoln, Y.S. (2005c).Introduction: the discipline and practice of qualitative research. *In:* N.K. Denzin and Y.S. Lincoln (eds.), *The Sage handbook of qualitative research* (3rd ed.). Thousand Oaks, CA: Sage, 1–32.

Denzin, N.K. and Lincoln, Y.S. (2000). Introduction: the discipline and practice of qualitative research. *In:* N.K. Denzin and Y.S. Lincoln (eds.), *Handbook of qualitative research* (2nd ed.). Thousand Oaks, CA: Sage, 1–28.

Denzin, N.K., Lincoln, Y.S. and Giardina, M.D. (2006). Disciplining qualitative research. *International Journal of Qualitative Studies in Education*, 19(6), 769–782.

Denzin, N.K. and Giardina, M.D. (eds.). (2006). *Qualitative inquiry and the conservative challenge: confronting methodological fundamentalism.* Walnut Creek, CA: Left Coast Press.

Department for Business, Innovation and Skills (BIS). (2011). *Higher Education: Students at the Heart of the System.* London: HMSO.

Department for Culture, Media and Sport (DCMS). (2012). *Creating a sporting habit for life.* London: DCMS.

Department for Culture, Media and Sport (DCMS). (2008a). *Before, during and after: making the most of the London 2012 Games.* London: DCMS.

Department for Culture, Media and Sport (DCMS). (2008b). *Playing to win: a new era for sport.* London: DCMS.

Department for Culture, Media and Sport (DCMS). (2006a). *Sport: Coaching* [online]. Available from: http://www.culture.gov.uk/sport/coaching.htm [Accessed 19 April 2006].

Department for Culture, Media and Sport (DCMS). (2006b). *Sport: Coaching* [online]. Available from: http://www.culture.gov.uk/sport/coaching.htm [Accessed 24 July 2006].

Department for Culture, Media and Sport (DCMS). (2006c). *UK Sport press release* [online]. Available from: http://www.culture.gov.uk/global/press_notices/archive_2006/dcms_uksport.htm [Accessed 19 April 2006].

Department for Culture, Media and Sport and the Strategy Unit. (2002). *Game plan: a strategy for delivering government's sport and physical activity objectives.* London: Cabinet Office.

Department for Culture, Media and Sport (DCMS). (2000). *A sporting future for all*. London: DCMS.

Department for Education and Science (DES). (1991). *Higher education: a new framework*. London: HMSO.

Department for Education and Skills (DfES). (2003). *The future of higher education*. London: HMSO.

Derrida, J. (1978). *Writing and difference* (A. Bass, ed.). Chicago: University of Chicago Press.

Descartes, R. (1637). *A discourse on method*. Translated by J. Veitch., 1949. London: Temple.

Dick, F.W. (1989). *Sports training principles* (2nd ed.). London: AandC Black.

Dimitriadis, G. (2006). On the production of expert knowledge: revisiting Edward Said's work on the intellectual. *Discourse: Studies in the Cultural Politics of Education*, 27(3), 369–382.

DIUS. (2007a). *The functions of the new department* [online]. Available from: http://www.dius.gov.uk/functions.htm [Accessed 17 August 2007].

DIUS. (2007b). *The role of the new department* [online]. Available from: http://www.dius.gov.uk/role.htm [Accessed 17 August 2007].

DIUS. (2007c). *Increased support for students in higher education* [online]. Available from: http://www.dius.gov.uk/pressreleases/press-release-20070705.htm. [Accessed 16 August 2007].

Dockery, G. (2000). Participatory research: whose roles, whose responsibilities. *In*: C. Truman, D. Mertons and B. Humphries (eds.), *Research and inequality*. London: Routledge, 95–110.

Donnelly, P. (1988). Sport as a site for 'popular' resistance. *In*: R. S. Gruneau (ed.), *Popular culture and political practices*. Toronto: Garamond Press, 69–82.

Donnelly, P. (1983). Resistance through sports: Sport and cultural hegemony *Sports et societies contemporaines: International committee for the 8th sociology of sport symposium*. Paris: Societe Francais de Sociology du Sport, 397–406.

Douge, B. and Hastie, P. (1993). Coach effectiveness. *Sport Science Review*, 2, 14–29.

Douglas, K. (2009). Storying myself: negotiating a relational identity in professional sport. *Qualitative Research in Sport and Exercise*. 1(2), 176–190.

Douglas, K. and Carless, D. (2008). Using stories in coach education. *International Journal of Sports Science and Coaching*, 3(1), 33–49.

DuGay, P., Hall, S., Janes, L., Mackay, H. and Negus, K. (1997). *Doing cultural studies: the story of the Sony Walkman*. London: Sage.

Duncan, M.C. (2007). Bodies in motion: the sociology of physical activity. *Quest*, 59(1), 55–66.

DWP. (2007). *Working for children*. London: HMSO.

Edwards, W. (1968). Conservatism in human information processing. *In*: B. Kleinmutz (ed.), *Formal representation of human judgment*. New York: John Wiley and Sons, 17–52.

Etzkowitz, H.A., Webster, A. and Healey, P. (1998). *Capitalizing knowledge: new interactions of industry and academe*. Albany: State Universitiy of New York Press.

Evans, M. (2005). Neoliberalism and policy transfer in the British competition state: the case of welfare reform. *In*: S. Soederberg, G. Menz, and P.G. Cerny (eds.), *Internalizing globalization. The rise of neoliberalism and the decline of national varieties of capitalism*. Basingstoke: Palgrave, 69–89.

Evans, M. (2004/5). *Killing thinking: the death of the universities*. London: Continuum.

Ferguson, P.M., Ferguson, D.L. and Taylor, S.J. (1992). Conclusion: the future of interpretivism in disability studies. *In*: P.M. Ferguson, D.L. Ferguson and S.J.

Taylor (eds.), *Interpreting disability: a qualitative reader.* New York: Teachers College Press, 295–302.

Fine, M. (1994). Working the hyphens: reinventing self and other in qualitative research. *In:* N.K. Denzin and Y.S. Lincoln (eds.), *Handbook of qualitative research.* Newbury Park, CA: Sage, 70–82.

Fine, M. (1992). Passions, politics and power: feminist research possibilities. *In:* M. Fine (ed.), *Disruptive voices: the possibilities of feminist research.* Ann Arbor: The University of Michigan Press.

Fine, M., Weis, L., Weseen, S. and Wong, L. (2000). For whom? Qualitative research, representations and social responsibilities. *In:* N.K. Denzin and Y.S. Lincoln (eds.), *Handbook of qualitative research* (2ⁿᵈ ed.). Thousand Oaks, CA: Sage, 167–207.

Fontana, A. and Frey, J.H. (2005). The interview: from neutral stance to political involvement. *In:* N.K. Denzin and Y.S. Lincoln (eds.), *The Sage handbook of qualitative research* (3ʳᵈ ed.). Thousand Oaks, CA: Sage, 695–727.

Foucault, M. (1997). *The politics of truth.* New York: Semiotext(e).

Foucault, M. (1980). *Power/knowledge: selected interviews and other writings, 1972–1977.* New York: Pantheon Books.

Foucault, M. (1977). Intellectuals and power: a conversation between Michel Foucault and Gilles Deleuze. *In:* D.F. Bouchard (ed.), *Language, counter-memory, practice: selected essays and interviews.* Ithaca, NY: Cornell University Press, 205–217.

Foucault, M. (1969). *The archaeology of knowledge.* A. M. Sheridan Smith. (trans.). 1972. New York: Pantheon.

Fowler, F.C. (1994). The international arena: The global village. *In:* J.D. Scribner and D.H. Layton (eds.), *The study of educational politics.* London: Falmer.

Frank, D.J. and Gabler, J. (2006). *Reconstructing the university: worldwide shifts in academia in the 20ᵗʰ century.* Stanford, CA: Stanford University Press.

Fréchette, L. (2000). *Opening address of the World Sport's Forum* [online]. Available from: http://www.un.org/News/Press/docs/2000/20000317.dsgsm88.doc. html [Accessed 6 June 2008].

Freire, P. (1972). *Pedagogy of the oppressed.* Harmondsworth, UK: Penguin.

Freshwater, D. and Rolfe, G. (2004). *Deconstructing evidence based practice.* New York: Routledge.

Frith, S. (2001). Checking the books: what are universities for? *Critical Quarterly,* 43(1), 88–93.

Friedman, M. and Schwartz, A.J. (1982). *Monetary trends in the United States and the United Kingdom: their relation to income, prices, and interest rates, 1967–1975.* Chicago: Chicago University Press.

Friedman, M. and Schwartz, A.J. (1963). *A monetary history of the United States, 1867–1960.* Princeton: Princeton University Press.

Friedman, M. (1959). *A program for monetary stability.* New York: Fordham University Press.

Friedman, M. (1956). *Studies in the quantity theory of money.* Chicago: University of Chicago Press.

Friedman, M. (1953). *Essays in positive economics.* Chicago: University of Chicago Press.

Friedman, M. (1948). A monetary and fiscal framework for economic stability. *American Economic Review,* 38(3), 245–264.

Friedman, M.T. and Van Ingen, C. (2011). Bodies in space: spacializing physical cultural studies. *Sociology of Sport Journal,* 28(1), 85–105.

Friedman, S. (1998). (Inter) disciplinarity and the question of the women's studies Ph.D. *Feminist Studies,* 24(2), 301–325.

Frow, J. and Morris, M. (2000). Cultural studies. *In:* N.K. Denzin and Y.S. Lincoln (eds.), *Handbook of qualitative research* (2nd ed.). Thousand Oaks, CA: Sage, 315–346.

Fukuyama, F. (2006). *America at the Crossroads: Democracy, Power, and the Neoconservative Legacy.* New Haven: Yale University Press.

Fukuyama, F. (1989). The end of history? *The National Interest,* 16 (Summer), 3–18.

Fukuyama, F. (1992). *The end of history and the last man standing.* London: Penguin.

Gamble, A. (1988). *The free economy and the strong state.* London: Macmillan.

Gergen, M. and Gergen, K. (2002). Ethnographic representation as relationship. In: A. Bochner and C. Ellis (eds.), *Ethnographically speaking.* Walnut Creek, CA: AltaMira Press, 11–33.

Giardina, M.D. (2005). *Sporting pedagogies: Performing culture and identity in the global arena.* New York: Peter Lang.

Giardina, M.D., and Newman, J.I. (2011a). Physical cultural studies and embodied research acts. *Cultural Studies <=> Critical Methodologies,* 11(6), 523–534.

Giardina, M.D., and Newman, J.I. (2011b). What is this "physical" in physical cultural studies? *Sociology of Sport Journal,* 28(1), 36–63.

Gibbons, M., Limoges, C., Nowotny, H., Schwartzman, S., Scott, P. and Trow, M. (1994). *The new production of knowledge: the dynamics of science and research in contemporary societies.* London: Sage.

Giddins, A. (1998). *The third way.* Cambridge: Polity.

Gilbert, W., Côté, J., and Mallett, C. (2006). The talented coach: developmental paths and activities of successful sport coaches. *International Journal of Sports Science and Coaching,* 1(1), 69–76.

Gilbert, W. and Trudel, P. (2004a). Analysis of coaching science published from 1970–2001. *Research Quarterly for Exercise and Sport,* 75(4), 388–399.

Gilbert, W. and Trudel, P. (2004b). The role of the coach: how model youth team sport coaches frame their roles. *The Sport Psychologist,* 18, 21–43.

Gill, D.L. (2007). Integration: the key to sustaining kinesiology in higher education. *Quest,* 59(3), 270–286.

Gill, S. (1995). Globalisation, market civilisation and disciplinary neoliberalism. *Millennium,* 24, 399–423.

Giroux, H.A. (2010). Bare pedagogy and the scourge of neoliberalism: rethinking higher education as a democratic public sphere. *The Educational Forum,* 74(3), 184–196.

Giroux, H.A. (2009). Democracy's nemesis: The rise of the corporate university. *Cultural Studies <=> Critical Methodologies,* 9(5), 669–695.

Giroux, H.A. (2008). The militarization of US higher education after 9/11. *Theory, Culture and Society,* 25(5), 56–82.

Giroux, H.A. (2005a). *The terror of neoliberalism: authoritarianism and the eclipse of democracy.* Boulder: Paradigm Publishers.

Giroux, H.A. (2005b). The terror of neoliberalism: rethinking the significance of cultural politics. *College Literature,* 32(1), 1–19.

Giroux, H.A. (2004a). War talk, the death of the social, and disappearing children: remembering the other war. *Cultural Studies <=> Critical Methodologies,* 4(2), 206–211.

Giroux, H.A. (2004b). Beyond belief: religious fundamentalism and cultural politics in the age of George W. Bush., *Cultural Studies <=> Critical Methodologies,* 4(4), 415–425.

Giroux, H.A. (2003). *Public spaces, private lives: democracy beyond 9/11.* Lanham: Rowman and Littlefield.

Giroux, H.A. (2002). Terrorism and the fate of democracy after September 11th. *Cultural Studies <=> Critical Methodologies,* 2(1), 9–14.

Giroux, H.A. (2001). Cultural studies as performative politics. *Cultural Studies <=> Critical Methodologies*, 1(1), 5–23.

Giroux, H.A. (2000). Public pedagogy as cultural politics: Stuart hall and the 'crisis' of culture. *Cultural Studies*, 14(2), 341–360.

Giroux, H.A. (1999). *Corporate culture and the attack on higher education and public schooling.* Bloomington: Phi Delta Kappa Educational Foundation, Fastback 442.

Giroux, H.A. (1995). Is there a place for cultural studies in colleges of education? *Review of Education, Pedagogy, and Cultural Studies*, 17(2), 127–142.

Giulianotti, R. and Robertson, R. (2004). The globalization of football: a study in the glocalization of the 'serious life'. *The British Journal of Sociology*, 55(4), 545–568.

Goldberg, M. (2006). *Kingdom coming: the rise of Christian nationalism.* New York, W.W. Norton.

Goldenberg, M.J. (2006). On evidence and evidence-based medicine: lessons from the philosophy of science. *Social Science and Medicine*, 62, 2621–2632.

Green, M., 2006. From 'Sport for all' to not about 'Sport' at all? Interrogating sport policy interventions in the United Kingdom. *European Sport Management Quarterly*, 6, 217–238.

Green, M. and Houlihan, B. (2006). Governmentality, modernization, and the "disciplining" of national sporting organisations: athletics in Australia and the United Kingdom. *Sociology of Sport Journal*, 23, 47–71.

Green, M., and Jenkins, C. (eds.). (1982). *Sporting fictions.* Birmingham: C.C.C.S.

Greenaway, D. and Haynes, M. (2003). Funding higher education in the UK: the role of fees and loans. *The Economic Journal*, 113 (February), 150–166.

Grix, J. and Carmichael, F. (2011). Why do governments invest in elite sport? A polemic. *International Journal of Sport Policy and Politics*, 4(1), 73–90.

Grossberg, L. (2010). *Cultural studies in the future tense.* Durham, NC: Duke University Press.

Grossberg, L. (2006). Does cultural studies have futures? Should it? (or what's the matter with New York?): cultural studies, contexts and conjunctures. *Cultural Studies*, 20(1), 1–32.

Grossberg, L. (1997a). Cultural studies, modern logics, and theories of globalisation. *In*: A. McRobbie (ed.), *Back to reality? Social experience and cultural studies.* Manchester: Manchester University Press, 7–35.

Grossberg, L. (1997b). *Bringing it all back home: essays on cultural studies.* Durham, NC: Duke University Press.

Grossberg, L. (1997c). The circulation of cultural studies *Bringing it all back home: Essays on cultural studies.* Durham, NC: Duke University Press, 234–244.

Grossberg, L. (1996). Toward a genealogy of the state of cultural studies: The discipline of communication and the reception of cultural studies in the United States. *In*: C. Nelson and D. P. Gaonkar (eds.), *Disciplinarity and dissent in cultural studies.* New York: Routledge, 131–147.

Grossberg, L. (1992). *We gotta get out of this place: popular conservatism and postmodern culture.* New York: Routledge.

Grossberg, L. (1989). The circulation of cultural studies. *Critical Studies in Mass Communication*, 6(4), 413–420.

Grubb, N.W. and Lazerson, M. The globalization of rhetoric and practice: the education gospel and vocationalism. *In*: H. Lauder, P. Brown, J. Dillabough and A.H. Halsey (eds.), (2006). *Education, globalization and social change.* Oxford: Oxford University Press, 295–307.

Gruneau, R. S. (1988). Modernization or hegemony: Two views on sport and social development. In J. Harvey and H. Cantelon (eds.), *Not just a game: essays in Canadian sport sociology.* Ottawa: University of Ottawa Press, 9–32.

Gruneau, R. S. (1983). *Class, sports, and social development.* Amherst: University of Massachusetts Press.

The Guardian. (2008). *Postgraduate course search 2008* [online]. Available from: http://guardian.uk.studylink.com/results/results.html?page=1andkeywords=sportandlevels-of-study=andstudy-locations=andsubject-areas=andcourses-per-page=25andresults-list-mode=summary-of-courses-by-provider [Accessed 13 May 2008].

Guthman, J. (2009). Teaching the Politics of Obesity: Insights into Neoliberal Embodiment and Contemporary Biopolitics. *Antipode,* 41(5), 1110–1133.

Haleem, H., Jones, R.L., Potrac, P. (2004). Investigating the coach-athlete relationship: The case for autoethnography. In J. Wright. (ed.). *Researching in sport, physical and health education.* Wollongong, Australia: University of Wollongong Press, 93–104.

Hall, S. (2007). Richard Hoggart, The Uses of Literacy and the cultural turn. *International Journal of Cultural Studies,* 10(1), 39–49.

Hall, S. (1996a). On postmodernism and articulation: An interview with Stuart Hall (edited by Lawrence Grossberg). *In*: D. Morley and K.H. Chen (eds.), *Stuart Hall: critical dialogues in cultural studies.* London: Routledge, 131–150.

Hall, S. (1996b). The problem with ideology: Marxism without guarantees. *In*: D. Morley and K-H. Chen (eds.) *Stuart Hall: critical dialogues in cultural studies.* London: Routledge, 25–46.

Hall, S. (1992). Cultural studies and its theoretical legacies. *In*: L. Grossberg, C. Nelson and P. Treichler (eds.), *Cultural studies.* London: Routledge, 277–294.

Hall, S. (1985). Signification, representation, ideology: Althusser and the post-structuralist debates. *Critical Studies in Mass Communication,* 2, 91–114.

Hall, S. (1983). The great moving right show. *In*: S. Hall and M. Jacques (eds.) *The politics of Thatcherism.* London: Lawrence and Wishart.

Hall, S. (1981a). Cultural studies: Two paradigms. *In*: T. Bennett, G. Martin, C. Mercer and J. Woollacott (eds.), *Culture, ideology and social process.* Milton Keynes: Open University, 19–37.

Hall, S. (1981b). Notes on deconstructing "the popular". *In:* R. Samuel (ed.), *People's history and socialist history.* London: Routledge and Kegan Paul, 227–240.

Halsey, A.H. and Webb, J. (eds). (2000). *Twentieth century British social trends.* Basingstoke: Macmillan.

Halsey, A.H., Lauder, H., Brown, P. and Wells, A.S. (eds.). (1997). *Education, culture, economy, society.* Oxford: Oxford University Press.

Hamilton, E. and Cairns, H. (eds.). (1961). *Plato: the collected dialogues.* Princeton: Princeton University Press.

Hammersley, M. (2000). *Taking sides in social research: essays on partisanship and bias.* London: Routledge.

Haraway, D.J. (1988). Situated knowledges: the science question in feminism and the privilege of partial perspective. *Feminist Studies,* 14, 575–599.

Hardt, M., and Negri, A. (2000). *Empire.* Cambridge: Harvard University Press.

Hargreaves, J. (1987). The body, sport and power relations. *In*: J. Horne, D. Jary and A. Tomlinson (eds.), *Sport, leisure and social relations.* London: Routledge and Kegan Paul, 139–159.

Hargreaves, J. (1986a). *Sport, power and culture.* New York: St. Martin's Press.

Hargreaves, J. (1986b). Where's the virtue? Where's the grace? A discussion of the social production of gender through sport. *Theory, Culture and Society,* 3(1), 109–121.

Hargreaves, J. (1986c). *Sport, power and culture: a social and historical analysis of popular sports in Britain.* Cambridge: Polity Press.

Hargreaves, J. (1984). Women and the Olympic phenomenon. *In*: A. Tomlinson and G. Whannel (eds.), *Five ring circus: Money, power and politics at the Olympic Games*. London: Pluto Press, 53–70.

Hargreaves, J. (1982a). *Sport, culture and ideology*. London: Routledge and Kegan Paul.

Hargreaves, J. (1982b). Theorising sport: An introduction. *In*: J. Hargreaves (ed.), *Sport, culture and ideology*. London: Routledge and Kegan Paul, 1–29.

Hargreaves, J., and Vertinsky, P. (eds.). (2007). *Physical culture, power, and the body*. London: Routledge.

Harper, D. (1987). *Working knowledge: skill and community in a small shop*. Chicago: Chicago University Press.

Harris, J. and Clayton, B. (2007). The first meterosexual rugby star: rugby union, masculinity, and celebrity in contemporary Wales. *Sociology of Sport Journal*, 24, 145–164.

Harrison, J., MacGibbon, L. and Morton, M. (2001). Regimes of trustworthiness in qualitative research: the rigors of reciprocity. *Qualitative Inquiry*, 7(3), 323–345.

Harvey, D. (2005). *A brief history of neoliberalism*. Oxford: Oxford University Press.

Harvey, D. (2003). *The new imperialism*. Oxford: Oxford University Press.

Hastie, P.A. (1992). Towards a pedagogy of sports coaching: research directions for the 1990s. *International Journal of Physical Education*, 29(3), 26–29.

Hayek, F.A. (1988). *The fatal conceit: the errors of socialism*. Chicago: University of Chicago Press.

Hayek, F.A. (1973). *Law, legislation and liberty: volume 1, Rules and order*. London: Routledge.

Hayek, F.A. (1976). *Law, legislation and liberty: volume 2, The mirage of social justice*. London: Routledge.

Hayek, F.A. (1976). *Law, legislation and liberty: volume 3, The political order of a free people*. London: Routledge.

Hayek, F.A. (1960). *The constitution of liberty*. London: Routledge.

Hayek, F.A. (1952). *The counter-revolution of science, studies on the abuse of reason*. London: George Allen and Unwin.

Hayek, F.A. (1948). *Individualism and Economic order*. Chicago: University of Chicago Press.

Hayek, F.A. (1944). *The road to selfdom*. Chicago: University of Chicago Press.

Hayek, F.A. (1941). *The pure theory of capital*. Chicago: University of Chicago Press.

Hayek, F.A. (1933). *Monetary theory and the trade cycle*. New York: Sentry Press.

Hayes, D. and Wynyard, R. (eds.). (2002). *The McDonaldization of higher education*. Westport, CT: Greenwood Press.

Haywood, L., Kew, F. and Bramham, P. (1995). *Understanding leisure*. Cheltenham: Stanley Thornes.

Henry, I. (2001). *The politics of leisure policy*. Basingstoke: Palgrave.

Hicks, D. (2012). Performance-based university research funding systems. *Research Policy*, 41, 251–261.

Hinings, C.R. and Greenwood, R. (2002). Disconnects and consequences in organization theory? *Administrative Science Quarterly*, 47, 411–421.

Hirst, P. and Thompson, G. (1999). *Globalisation in question* (2nd ed.). Cambridge: Polity Press.

HMCS. (2007). *Working together: annual report and accounts 2006/07*. London: HMSO.

Hobsbawm, E. (2005). *In defence of history* [online]. The Guardian. Available from: http://books.guardian.co.uk/news/articles/0,,1391079,00.html [Accessed 11 July 2007].

Hodge, M. (2002). Labour's plans for lifelong learning in the second term. *Speech by Margaret Hodge, MP at The Social Market Foundation*, London, 11 April.

Hollands, R. G. (1988). English-Canadian sports novels and cultural production. *In*: J. Harvey and H. Cantelon (eds.), *Not just a game: essays in Canadian sport sociology*. Ottawa: University of Ottawa Press, 213–226.

Hollands, R. G. (1984). The role of cultural studies and social criticism in the sociological study of sport. *Quest, 36*, 66–79.

Holman-Jones, S. (2005). Autoethnography: making the personal political. *In*: N. Denzin and Y. Lincoln (eds.), *The Sage handbook of qualitative Research* (3rd ed.). Thousand Oaks, CA: Sage, 763–791.

Horak, R. and Spitaler, G. (2003). Sport space and national identity: soccer and skiing as formative forces: on the Austrian example. *American Behavioral Scientist, 46*, 1506–1518.

Horne, J. and Manzenreiter, W. (2006). An introduction to the sociology of sports mega-events. *The Sociological Review, 54* (2), 1–24.

Houlihan, B. (2005). Public sector sport policy. *International Review for the Sociology of Sport, 40* (2), 163–185.

Houlihan, B. (2004). Sports globalisation, the state and the problem of governance. *In*: T. Slack. (ed.). (2004). *The commercialisation of sport*. London: Routledge, 52–71.

Houlihan, B. (1994). *Sport and international politics*. Hemel Hempstead: Harvester-Wheatsheaf.

Houlihan, B. (1991). *Government and the politics of sport*. London: Routledge.

Houlihan, B. and White, A. (2002). *The politics of sport development: development of sport or development through sport?* London: Routledge.

House, E.R. (2006). Methodological fundamentalism and the quest for control(s). *In*: N.K. Denzin and M.D. Giardina (eds.), *Qualitative inquiry and the conservative challenge: confronting methodological fundamentalism*. Walnut Creek, CA: Left Coast Press, 93–108.

House, E.R. (2005). Qualitative evaluation and changing social policy. *In*: N. Denzin and Y. Lincoln (eds.), *The Sage handbook of qualitative research* (3rd ed.). Thousand Oaks, CA: Sage, 1069–1081.

House, E.R. (2003) Bush's neo-fundamentalism and the new politics of evaluation. *In*: O. Karlsson (ed.), *Studies in educational policy and Educational Philosophy*, 2. Sweden: Uppsala University.

Howe, P.D. (2011). Cyborg and supercrip: The paralympics technology and the (dis)empowerment of disabled athletes. *Sociology, 45*(5), 868–882.

Howell, O. (2008). Skatepark as neoliberal playground: Urban governance, recreation space, and the cultivation of personal responsibility. *Space and Culture, 11*(4), 475–496.

Howell, J.W., and Ingham, A.G. (2001). From social problem to personal issue: The language of lifestyle. *Cultural Studies, 15*(2), 326–351.

Hughson, J. (2008). Ethnography and `physical culture'. *Ethnography, 9*(4), 421–428.

Humphries, B., Mertens, D.M. and Truman, C. (2000). Arguments for an emancipatory research paradigm. *In*: C. Truman, D.M. Mertens and B. Humphries (eds.), *Research and inequality*. London: UCL Press, 3–24.

Hytten, K. (2006). Education for social justice: provocations and challenges. *Educational Theory, 56*(2), 221–236.

The Independent. (2007). *Why Fifa's claim of one billion TV viewers was a quarter right* [online]. Available from: http://www.independent.co.uk/sport/football/

news-and-comment/why-fifas-claim-of-one-billion-tv-viewers-was-a-quarter-right-438302.html [Accessed 6 June 2008].

Ingham, A. G. (1985). From public issue to personal trouble: Well-being and the fiscal crisis of the state. *Sociology of Sport Journal,* 2(1), 43–55.

Ingham, A.G. (1997). Toward a department of physical cultural studies and an end to tribal warfare. *In:* J. Fernandez-Balboa (ed.), *Critical postmodernism in human movement, physical education, and sport.* Albany: State University of New York Press, 157–182.

Ingham, A., and Hardy, S. (1984). Sport: Structuration, subjugation and hegemony. *Theory, Culture and Society,* 2(2), 85–103.

Ingham, R., Hall, S., Clarke, J., Marsh, P., and Donovan, J. (1978). *Football hooliganism: the wider context.* London: Inter-Action Imprint.

Jackson, S.J. and Ponic, P. (2001). Pride and Prejudice: reflecting on sport heroes, national identity, and crisis in Canada. *Sport in Society,* 4(2), 43–62.

Jacques, M. (1983). Thatcherism–Breaking out of the impasse. *In:* S. Hall and M. Jacques (eds.), *The politics of Thatcherism.* London: Lawrence and Wishart.

James, A., Hockey, J. and Dawson, A. (eds.). (1997). *After writing culture: epistemology and praxis in contemporary anthropology.* London: Routledge.

Jarvie, G. (2006). *Sport, culture and society: an introduction.* London: Routledge.

Jessop, B. (2002). Liberalism, neoliberalism, and urban governance: a state-theoretical perspective. *Antipode,* 34(3), 452–472.

Jiwani, N., and Rail, G. (2010). Islam, hijab and young Shia muslim Canadian women's discursive constructions of physical activity. *Sociology of Sport Journal,* 27(3), 251–267.

Johns, D.P. and Johns, J.S. (2000). Surveillance, subjectivism and technologies of power: an analysis of the discursive practice of high-performance sport. *International Review for the Sociology of Sport,* 35(2), 219–234.

Johnson, R. (1996). What is cultural studies anyway? In: J. Storey (ed.), *What is cultural studies? A reader.* London: Hodder, 75–114.

Johnson, S. (1998). Skills, Socrates and the Sophists: learning from history. *British Journal of Education Studies,* 46, 201–214.

Johnson, R., Chambers, D., Tincknell, E. and Raghuram, P. (2004). *The practice of cultural studies.* London: Sage.

Jones, R.L. (2009). Coaching as caring (the smiling gallery): accessing hidden knowledge. *Physical Education and Sport Pedagogy,* 14(4), 377–390.

Jones, R.L. (2007). Coaching redefined: An everyday pedagogical endeavour. *Sport, Education and Society,* 12(2), 159–174.

Jones, R.L. (2006). Dilemmas, maintaining 'face' and paranoia: An average coaching life. *Qualitative Inquiry,* 12(5), 1012–1021.

Jones, R.L. (2005a). *Higher education academy network for hospitality, leisure, sport and tourism: resource guide to sports coaching.* Available from: http://www.hlst.heacademy.ac.uk/Resources/coaching.pdf [Accessed 10 April 2006]

Jones, R.L. (ed.) (2005b). *The sports coach as educator: reconceptualising sports coaching.* London: Routledge.

Jones, R.L. (2000). Toward a sociology of coaching. *In:* R.L. Jones and K.M. Armour (eds.), *Sociology of sport: theory and practice.* London: Pearson, 33–43.

Jones, R.L. and Wallace, M. (2005). Another bad day at the training ground: coping with ambiguity in the coaching context. *Sport, Education and Society,* 10(1), 119–134.

Jones, R.L., Armour, K.M. and Potrac, P. (2004). *Sports coaching cultures: from practice to theory.* London: Routledge.

Jones, R.L., Armour, K.M. and Potrac, P. (2003). Constructing expert knowledge: a case study of a top-level professional soccer coach. *Sport, Education and Society,* 8(2), 213–229.

Jones, R.L., Armour, K.M. and Potrac, P. (2002). Understanding the coaching process: a framework for social analysis. *Quest*, 54, 34–48.

Kahan, D. (1999). Coaching behaviour: a review of the systematic observation research literature. *Applied Research in Coaching and Athletics Annual*, 14, 17–58.

Kamberelis, G. and Dimitriadis, G. (2005). Focus groups: strategic articulations of pedagogy, politics, and inquiry. *In:* N.K. Denzin and Y.S. Lincoln (eds.), (2005). *The Sage handbook of qualitative research* (3rd ed.). Thousand Oaks, CA: Sage, 887–907.

Kaplan, E. (2004). *With God on their side: George W. Bush and the Christian Right*. New York: New York Press.

Kemmis, S. and McTaggart, R. (2005). Participatory action research: communicative action and the public sphere. *In:* N.K. Denzin and Y.S. Lincoln (eds.), *The Sage handbook of qualitative research* (3rd ed.). Thousand Oaks, CA: Sage, 559–603.

Kennedy, V. (2000). *Edward Said: A critical introduction*. Cambridge: Polity Press.

Kennedy-Wallace, G. (2000). Plato.com: the role and impact of corporate universities in the third millennium. In: P. Scott (ed.), *Higher education re-formed*. London: Falmer.

Kidman, L. (ed.). (2001). *Innovative coaching: empowering your athletes*. Christchurch, NZ: Innovative Communications.

Kidman, L. and Hanrahan, S. (2004). *The coaching process: a practical guide to improving your effectiveness* (2nd ed.). Palmerston North: Dunmore.

Kincheloe, J.L. (2005). On to the next level: continuing the conceptualisation of the bricolage. *Qualitative Inquiry*, 11(3), 323–350.

Kincheloe, J.L. (2003). Critical ontology: visions of selfhood and curriculum. *Journal of Curriculum Theorizing*, 19(1), 47–64.

Kincheloe, J.L. (2001). Describing the bricolage: conceptualizing a new rigor in qualitative research. *Qualitative Inquiry*, 7(6), 679–692.

Kincheloe, J.L. and McLaren, P. (2005). Rethinking critical theory and qualitative research. *In:* N.K. Denzin and Y.S. Lincoln (eds.), *The Sage handbook of qualitative research* (3rd ed.). Thousand Oaks, CA: Sage, 303–342.

Kincheloe, J.L. and Steinberg. (2006). An ideology of miseducation: countering the pedagogy of empire. *Cultural Studies <=> Critical Methodologies*, 6(1), 33–51.

King, S. J. (2006). *Pink ribbons, inc.: breast cancer and the politics of philanthropy*. Minneapolis: University of Minnesota Press.

King, S.J. (2005). Methodological contingencies in contextual sports studies. *In:* D.L. Andrews, D. Mason and M.L. Silk (eds.), *Qualitative research in sports studies*. Oxford: Berg, 21–38.

Kirk, D. (1999). Physical culture, physical education and relational analysis. *Sport, Education and Society*, 4(1), 63–73.

Klein, N. (2007). *The shock doctrine*. London: Penguin.

Krizek, R. (1998). Lessons: what the hell are we teaching the next generation anyway? *In:* A. Banks and S. Banks (eds.), *Fiction and social research*. London: Altamira, 89–113.

Kuhn, T. (1970). *The structure of scientific revolutions*. Chicago: University of Chicago Press.

Labour Party. (1996). *Labour's sporting nation*. London: Labour Party.

Ladson-Billings, G. and Donnor, J. (2005). The moral-activist role of critical race theory scholarship. *In:* N.K. Denzin and Y.S. Lincoln (eds.), *The Sage handbook of qualitative research* (3rd ed.). Thousand Oaks, CA: Sage, 279–302.

Lakoff, G. (2006). *Whose freedom? The battle over America's most important idea*. New York: Farrar, Straus and Giroux.

Laine, T. (2006). Shame on us: shame, national identity and the Finnish doping scandal. *International Journal of the History of Sport*, 23(1), 67–81.

Landes, D. (1999). *The wealth and poverty of nations*. London: Abacus.

Lapadat, J.C. (2009). Writing our way into shared understanding: collaborative autobiographical writing in the qualitative methods class. *Qualitative Inquiry*, 15(6), 955–979.

Larner, G. (2004). Family therapy and the politics of evidence. *Journal of Family Therapy*, 26, 17–39.

Lather, P. (2006). This *is* your father's paradigm: Government intrusion and the case of qualitative research in education. *In*: N. K. Denzin and M.D. Giardina (eds.), *Qualitative inquiry and the conservative challenge*. Walnut Creek, CA: Left Coast Press, 31–56.

Lather, P. (1991). *Getting smart: feminist research and pedagogy with/in the postmodern*. New York: Routledge.

Lauder, H., Brown, P., Dillabough, J. and Halsey, A.H. (2006). *Education, globalization and social change*. Oxford: Oxford University Press.

Lawton, D. (1992). *Education and politics in the 1990's: conflict or Consensus?* London: Routledge.

Leathwood, C. and Hutchings, M. (2003). Entry routes to higher education: pathways, qualifications and social class. *In*: L. Archer, M. Hutchings, and A. Ross (eds.), *Higher education and social class: issues of exclusion and inclusion*. London: RoutledgeFalmer, 138–154.

Leathwood, C. and O'Connell, P. (2003). 'It's a struggle': the construction of the 'new student' in higher education. *Journal of Education Policy*, 18(6), 597–615.

Lee, R. C. (2003). *Life and times of cultural studies: The politics and transformation of the structures of knowledge*. Durham, NC: Duke University Press.

Lee, S., Shaw, D.J., Chesterfield, G. and Woodward, C. (2009). Reflections from a world champion: an interview with Sir Clive Woodward, Director of Olympic performance, the British Olympic Association. *Reflective Practice*, 10(3), 295–310.

Levi-Strauss, C. (1966). *The savage mind*. Chicago: University of Chicago Press.

Lincoln, Y.S. (2011). "A well-regulated faculty . . .": the coerciveness of accountability and other measures that abridge faculties' right to teach and research. *Cultural Studies <=> Critical Methodologies*, 11(4), 369–372.

Lincoln, Y.S. (2005). Institutional review boards and methodological conservatism: the challenge to and from phenomenological paradigms. *In*: N.K. Denzin and Y.S. Lincoln (eds.), *The Sage handbook of qualitative research* (3rd ed.). Thousand Oaks, CA: Sage, 165–181.

Lincoln, Y.S. (2001). An emerging new bricoleur: promises and possibilities—a reaction to Joe Kincheloe's "describing the bricoleur." *Qualitative Inquiry*, 7(6), 693–705.

Lincoln, Y.S. and Cannella, G.S. (2004a). Qualitative research, power, and the radical right. *Qualitative Inquiry*, 10(2), 175–201.

Lincoln, Y.S. and Cannella, G. (2004b). Dangerous discourses, methodological fundamental- ism, and governmental regimes of truth. *Qualitative Inquiry*, 10(1), 5–14.

Lincoln, Y.S. and Denzin, N. (2005). Epilogue: the eighth and ninth moments: qualitative research in/and the fractured future. *In*: Denzin, N. and Lincoln, Y (eds), *The sage handbook of qualitative research* (3rd ed.). Thousand Oaks, CA: Sage.

Lomas, L. (2002). Does the development of mass education necessarily mean the end of quality? *Quality in Higher Education*, 8(1), 71–79.

Lombardo, B.J. (1987). *The humanistic coach: from theory to practice*. Springfield, Ill: C.C. Thomas.

Lyle, J. (2008). Sports development and sports coaching. *In*: K. Hylton and P. Bramham (eds.), *Sports development: policy, process and practice* (2nd ed.). London: Routledge, 214–235.

Lyle, J. (2007). A review of the research evidence for the impact of coach education. *International Journal of Coaching Science*, 1(1), 19–36.

Lyle, J. (2002). *Sports coaching concepts: a framework for coaches' behaviour.* London: Routledge.

Lyle, J. (1986). Coach education: preparation for a profession. *In: Proceedings of the 8th Commonwealth and international conference on sport, physical education, dance, recreation and health.* London: E. and F.N. Spon.

Lyotard, J-F. (1984). *The postmodern condition: a report on knowledge.* Manchester: Manchester University Press.

MacKinnon, D. (2000). Managerialism, governmentality and the state: a neo-Foucauldian approach to local economic governance. *Political Geography*, 19(3), 293–314.

MacLeod, D. (2003). *New universities' record ignored by access plans* [online]. *The Guardian.* Available from: http://www.education.guardian.co.uk/Print/0,3858,4644333,00.html (Accessed 29 July 2003).

MacLeod, G. (2002). From urban entrepreneurialism to a "revanchist city"? On the special injustices of Glasgow's renaissance. *Antipode*, 34(3), 602–624.

Madriz, M. (2000). Focus groups in feminist research. *In*: N.K. Denzin and Y.S. Lincoln (eds.), *Handbook of qualitative research* (2nd ed.). Thousand Oaks, CA: Sage, 835–850.

Magdalinski, T. (2000). The reinvention of Australia for the Sydney 2000 Olympic Games. *International Journal of the History of Sport*, 17(2), 305–322.

Maguire, J., Jarvie, G., Mansfield, L. and Bradley, J. (2002). *Sports worlds: a sociological perspective.* Champaign, IL: Human Kinetics.

Maguire, J. (1999). *Global sport: identities, societies, civilizations.* Cambridge: Polity Press.

Manning, P. (2002). The sky is not falling. *Journal of Contemporary Ethnography*, 31(4), 490–498.

Margolis, E. and Pauwels, L. (2011). *The Sage Handbook of Visual Research Methods.* London: Sage.

Markula, P. and Denison, J. (2005). Sport and the personal narrative. . *In*: D.L. Andrews, D. Mason and M.L. Silk (eds.), *Qualitative research in sports studies.* Oxford: Berg, 165–184.

Markula, P. and Silk, M. (2011). *Qualitative Research for Physical Culture.* New York: Palgrave Macmillan.

Martin, H. and Schumann, H. (1997). *The global trap: globalisation and the assault on democracy and prosperity.* Sydney: Pluto.

Martindale, R.J.J., Collins, D. and Daubney, J. (2005). Talent development: a guide for practice and research within sport. *Quest*, 57, 353–375.

McDonald, M. G. (2008). Rethinking Resistance: The Queer Play of the Women's National Basketball Association, Visibility Politics and Late Capitalism. *Leisure Studies*, 27(1), 77–93.

McDonald, M.G. and Birrell, S. (1999). Reading sport critically: a method for interrogating power. *Sociology of Sport Journal*, 16, 283–300.

McDonald, M. G., and Toglia, J. (2010). Dressed for success? The NBA's dress code, the workings of whiteness and corporate culture. *Sport in Society: Cultures, Commerce, Media, Politics*, 13(6), 970–983.

McLaren, P.L. (2003). *Life in schools: an introduction to critical pedagogy in the foundations of education* (4th Ed). Boston: Allyn and Bacon.

McLaren, P.L. (1991). Schooling the postmodern body: critical pedagogy and the politics of enfleshment. *In*: H.A. Giroux. (ed.). *Postmodernism, feminism and cultural politics: redrawing educational boundaries.* Albany: State University of New York Press, 144–173.

McLellan, D. (1977). *Karl Marx: selected writings.* Oxford: Oxford University Press.

McLeod, J. (2000). *Qualitative research as bricolage.* Paper presented at the Society for Psychotherapy Research Annual Conference, June 2000, Chicago.

McNay, I. (1999). The paradoxes of research assessment and funding. *In*: M. Henkel and B. Little. (eds.). (1999). *Changing relationships between higher education and the state.* London: Jessica Kinglsey.

McNay, L. (1994). *Foucault: a critical introduction.* London: Polity Press.

McSherry, C. (2006). Building an epistemic regime. *In*: H. Lauder, P. Brown, J. Dillabough, and A.H. Halsey. (eds). (2006). *Education, globalization and social change.* Oxford: Oxford University Press, 866–874.

Menz, G. (2005). Making Thatcher look timid: the rise and fall of the New Zealand model. *In*: S. Soederberg, G. Menz, and P.G. Cerny (eds.), *Internalizing globalization. The rise of neoliberalism and the decline of national varieties of capitalism.* Basingstoke: Palgrave, 49–61.

Merton, R.K. (1942). The normative structure of science. *In*: R.K.Merton. *The sociology of science: theoretical and empirical investigations.* Chicago: University of Chicago Press.

Messner, M. (2002). *Taking the field: women, men and sports.* Minneapolis: University of Minnesota Press.

Messner-Davidow, E. (1993). Manufacturing the attack on liberalised higher education. *Social Text*, 36, 40–80.

Miller, T. (2009). Michel Foucault and the critique of sport. *In*: B. Carrington and I. MacDonald (eds.), *Marxism, cultural studies and sport.* London: Routledge, 181–194.

Miller, T. (2001a). *Sportsex.* Philadelphia: Temple University Press.

Miller, T. (2001b). What it is and what it isn't: introducing . . . cultural studies. *In*: T. Miller (ed.), *A companion to cultural studies.* Malden, MA: Blackwell, 1–20.

Michie, J. and Grieve-Smith, J. (eds.). (1999). *Global instability: the political economy of world economic governance.* London: Routledge.

Mitchell, M.F. (1992). A descriptive analysis and academic genealogy of major contributors to JTPE in the 1980s. *Journal of Teaching in Physical Education*, 11, 426–442.

Moody, K. (1997). *Workers in a lean world.* New York: Verso.

Morgan, H. (2012). Sports development: coaching in context. *In*: A.J. Bush et al. (eds.), *Foundations in sports coaching.* Oxford: Pearson, 14–26.

Moran, J. (2006). Milk bars, Starbucks, and the uses of literacy. *Cultural Studies*, 20(6), 552–573.

Morse, J.M. (2006). The politics of evidence. *In*: N.K. Denzin and M.D. Giardina (eds.), *Qualitative inquiry and the conservative challenge: confronting methodological fundamentalism.* Walnut Creek, CA: Left Coast Press, 79–92.

Murray, S.J., Holmes, D., and Rail, G. (2008). On the constitution and status of 'evidence' in the health sciences. *Journal of Research in Nursing*, 13(4), 272–280.

Murray, S.J., Holmes, D., Perron, A., and Rail, G. (2007). No exit? Intellectual integrity under the regime of 'evidence' and 'best-practices'. *Journal of Evaluation in Clinical Practice*, 13, 512–516.

Naidoo, R. and Jamieson, I. (2006). Empowering participants or corroding learning? Towards a research agenda on the impact of student consumerism in higher education. *In*: H. Lauder, P. Brown, J. Dillabough and A.H. Halsey (eds.), *Education, globalization and social change.* Oxford: Oxford University Press.

Nash, C. and Collins, D. (2006). Tacit knowledge in expert coaching: science or art? *Quest*, 58(4), 465–477.

Newman, J.I., and Giardina, M. (2011). *Sport, spectacle, and NASCAR nation: consumption and the cultural politics of neoliberalism.* New York:Palgrave Macmillan.

Nietzsche, F. (1882). *The gay science.* W. Kaufmann. (trans.). 1974. New York: Vintage Books.

Nilges, L. (2001). The twice told tale of Alice's physical life in Wonderland: writing qualitative research in the 21ˢᵗ century. *Quest*, 53, 231–259.

Nelson, C., Treichler, P.A. and Grossberg, L. (1992). Cultural studies: an introduction. *In:* L. Grossberg, C. Nelson, and P. Treichler (eds.), *Cultural studies.* New York: Routledge.

Noddings, N. (2007). *Philosophy of education* (2ⁿᵈ ed.). Boulder, Colorado: Westview.

Obama, B., and Biden, J. (2008). *Investing in America's future* [online]. Available from: http://www.barackobama.com/pdf/issues/FactSheetScience.pdf [Accessed 18 February 2008].

Ohmae, K. (1990). *The borderless world: power and strategy in the interlinked economy.* London: HarperCollins.

Olssen, M. and Peters, M.A. (2005). Neoliberalism, higher education and the knowledge economy: from the free market to knowledge capitalism. *Journal of Education Policy*, 20(3), 313–345.

Palmer, C. (1996). Information work at the boundaries of science: linking library services to research practices. *Library Trends*, 44(2), 165–192.

Peabody, N. (2009). Disciplining the body, disciplining the body-politic: physical culture and social violence among north Indian wrestlers. *Comparative Studies in Society and History*, 51(2), 372–400.

Peck, J. and Tickell, A. (2002). Neoliberalizing space. *Antipode*, 34(3), 380–404.

Personneltoday. (2008). *Butlins joins with Chichester University to offer degrees* [online]. Available from: http://www.personneltoday.com/articles/2008/09/01/47265/butlins-joins-with-chichester-university-to-offer-degrees.html [Accessed 16 September 2008].

Pestre, D. (2000). The production of knowledge between academies and markets: a historical reading of the book 'The new production of knowledge'. *Science, Technology and Society*, 5(2), pp. 169–181.

Peters, R. (1976). Television coverage of sport. *Centre for Contemporary Cultural Studies: Stencilled Occasional Papers Series.*

Phellas, C. (2000). Cultural and sexual identities in in-depth interviewing. In C. Truman, D. Mertons, and B. Humphries (eds.), *Research and inequality.* London: Routledge, 52–64.

Pinar, W.F. (1975). Currere: toward reconceptualization. *In:* W. F. Pinar (ed.), *Curriculum theorizing: the reconconceptualists.* Berkeley: McCutchan Publishing, 396–414.

Pineau, E.L. (1994). Teaching is performance: reconceptualising a problematic metaphor. *American Educational Research Journal*, 31(1), 2–25.

Pink, S. (2009). *Doing sensory ethnography.* London: Sage.

Pink, S. (2007). *Doing Visual Ethnography: images, media and representation in research* London: Sage.

Plummer, K. (2005). Critical humanism and queer theory: living with the tensions. *In:* N.K. Denzin and Y.S. Lincoln (eds.), *The Sage handbook of qualitative research* (3ʳᵈ ed.). Thousand Oaks, CA: Sage, 357–373.

Poli, R. (2007). The denationalization of sport: de-ethnicization of the nation and identity deterritorialization. *Sport in Society*, 10(4), 646–661.

Potrac, P., Jones, R.L. and Cushion, C. (2007). Understanding power and the coach's role in professional English soccer: a preliminary investigation of coach behaviour. *Soccer and Society*, 8(1), 33–49.

Potrac, P., Jones, R.L. and Armour, K.M. (2002). It's all about getting respect: the coaching behaviours of an expert English soccer coach. *Sport, Education and Society*, 7(2), 183–202.

Potrac, P., Brewer, C., Jones, R.L., Armour, K. and Hoff, J. (2000). Toward a holistic understanding of the coaching process. *Quest*, 52, 186–199.

Price, M. and Parker, A. (2003). Sport, sexuality, and the gender order: amateur rugby union, gay men and social exclusion. *Sociology of Sport Journal*, 20, 108–126.

Pring, R. (2004). Conclusion: evidence-based policy and practice. In: G. Thomas and R. Pring (eds.), *Evidence-based practice in education*. Buckingham: Open University Press, 201–212.

Pronger, B. (1998). Post-sport: Transgressing boundaries in physical culture. *In*: G. Rail (ed.), *Sport and postmodern times*. New York: State University of New York Press, 277–300.

Pullo, F.M. (1992). A profile of NCAA division 1 strength and conditioning coaches. *Journal of Applied Sport Science Research*, 6(1), 55–62.

Purdy, L., Potrac, P. and Jones, R.L. (2008). Power, consent and resistance: An autoethnography of competitive rowing. *Sport, Education and Society*, 13(3), 319–336.

Quail, C.B., Razzano, K.A., and Skalli, L.H. (2004). *Tell me more: rethinking daytime talk shows*. New York: Peter Lang.

Readings, B. (1996). *The university in ruins*. Cambridge, MA: Harvard University Press.

Reay, D., Crozier, G. and Clayton, J. (2009). 'Fitting in' or 'standing out': working-class students in UK higher education. *British Educational Research Journal*, 36(1), 107–124.

Reid, I.A. and Jarvie, G. (2000). Sport, nationalisms and their futures. *In*: R.L. Jones and K.M. Armour (eds.), *Sociology of sport: theory and practice*. London: Pearson, 33–43.

Reynolds, B. (2005). Mind the gap between rich and poor. *NICVA Conference: Poverty: will the poor always be with us?* 8 July 2005, Belfast.

Rich, E. (2011). Exploring the relationship between pedagogy and physical cultural studies: the case of new health imperatives in schools. *Sociology of Sport Journal*, 28, 64–84.

Richardson, L. (2000a). Evaluating ethnography. *Qualitative Inquiry*, 6(2), 253–255.

Richardson, L. (2000b). Writing: a method of inquiry. *In*: N. Denzin and Y. Lincoln (eds.), *Handbook of qualitative research* (2nd ed.). London: Sage, 923–948.

Richardson, L. (1993). Poetic representation, ethnographic presentation and transgressive validity: the case of the skipped line. *Sociological Quarterly*, 34, 695–710.

Richardson, L. and St. Pierre, E.A. (2005). Writing: a method of inquiry. *In*: N.K. Denzin and Y.S. Lincoln (eds.), *The Sage handbook of qualitative research* (3rd ed.). Thousand Oaks, CA: Sage, 959–978.

Riordan, J. and Krüger, A. (1999). *The international politics of sport in the twentieth century*. London: Taylor & Francis.

Riordan, J. (ed.). (1978). *Sport under Communism*. London: Hurst.

Ritzer, G. (2007). *The globalization of nothing 2*. Thousand Oaks, California: Pine Forge Press.

Ritzer, G. (2004). *The McDonaldization of society* (Revised New Century Edition ed.). London: Sage.

Ritzer, G. (2002). Enchanting McUniversity: towards a spectacularly irrational university quotidian. *In*: D. Hayes & R. Wynyard (eds.), *The McDonaldization of higher education*. Westport, CT: Greenwood Press, 19–32.

Rizvi, F. and Lingard, B. (2006). Edward Said and the cultural politics of education. *Discourse: Studies in the Cultural Politics of Education*, 27(3), 293–308.

Rojek, C. and Turner, B. (2000). Decorative sociology: towards a critique of the cultural turn. *The Sociological Review*, 48(4), 629–648.

Rose, N. (2000a). Community, citizenship and the third way. *American Behavioural Scientist*, 43, 1395–1411.

Rose, N. (2000b). Government and control. *British Journal of Criminology*, 40(2), 321–339.

Rouse, M.J. and Daellenbach, U.S. (1999). Rethinking research methods for the resource-based perspective: isolating sources of sustainable competitive advantage. *Strategic Management Journal*, 20, 487–494.

Rowe, D. (2003). Sport and the repudiation of the global. *International Review for the Sociology of Sport*, 38(3), 281–294.

Roy, A. (2003). The loneliness of Noam Chomsky. *In*: A. Roy (ed.), *War talk*. Cambridge, MA: South End Press, 77–101.

Roy, A. (2001). War is peace. *In*: A. Roy (ed.), *Power politics*. Cambridge, MA: South End Press, 125–145.

Rutherford, J. (2005). Cultural studies in the corporate university. *Cultural Studies*, 19(3), 297–317.

Rysst, M. (2010). "Healthism" and looking good: Body ideals and body practices in Norway. *Scandinavian Journal of Public Health*, 38(5), 71–80.

Sagaria, M.A.D. (2007). *Women, universities and change: gender equality in the European Union and the U.S.* London: Palgrave Macmillan.

Said, E.W. (2003). *Orientalism*. London: Penguin.

Said, E. (1994). *Representations of the intellectual*. New York: Pantheon.

Said, E.W. (1983). *The world, the text and the critic*. Cambridge, MA: Harvard University Press.

Said, E. (1978). *Orientalism*. London: Routledge.

Sam, M.P. and Jackson, S.J. (2004). Sport policy development in New Zealand. *International Review for the Sociology of Sport*, 39 (2), 205–222.

Saukko, P. (2005). Methodologies for cultural studies: an integrative approach. *In*: N.K. Denzin and Y.S. Lincoln (eds.), *The Sage handbook of qualitative research* (3rd ed.). Thousand Oaks, CA: Sage, 343–356.

Saukko, P. (2003). *Doing research in cultural studies: an introduction to classical and new methodological approaches*. Thousand Oaks, CA: Sage.

Scholte, J.A. (2002). *What is globalization? The definitional issue—again*. Centre for the Study of Globalisation and Regionalisation (CSGR), Working Paper 109/02.

Scholte, J.A. (2000). *Globalization: a critical introduction*. Basingstoke: Palgrave.

Schuster, J.H. and Finkelstein, M. J. (2006). *The American faculty: the restructuring of academic work and careers*. Baltimore, MD: John Hopkins University Press.

Schwandt, T. (2000). Three epistemological stances for qualitative inquiry: interpretivism, hermeneutics, and social constructionism. *In*: N.K. Denzin and Y.S. Lincoln. (eds.) *Handbook of qualitative research* (2nd ed.). Thousand Oaks, CA: Sage, 189–214.

Scott, S. (2010). How to look good (nearly) naked: The performative regulation of the swimmer's body. *Body and Society*, 16(2), 143–168

Scott, D. (1999). *Refashioning futures: criticism after postcoloniality*. Princeton: Princeton University Press.

Shavit, Y., Arum, R. and Menahem, G. (eds.). (2007). *Stratification in higher education: a comparative study*. Stanford, CA: Stanford University Press.

Sherman, C., Crassini, B., Maschette, W. and Sands, R. (1997). Instructional sport psychology: a reconceptualisation of sports coaching as sports instruction. *International Journal of Sport Psychology*, 28(2), 103–125.

Silk, M.L. and Andrews, D. L. (2011). Toward a physical cultural studies. *Sociology of Sport Journal*, 28(1), 4–35.

Silk, M.L., Bush, A.J., and Andrews, D. (2010). Contingent intellectual amateurism, or, the problem with evidence based research. *Journal of Sport and Social Issues*, 34(1), 105–128.

Silver, H. (1990). *Education, change and the policy process*. London: Falmer.

Simpson, P. (2008). Chronic everyday life: Rhythmanalysing street performance. *Social and Cultural Geography*, 9(7), 807–829.

Skalli, L. (2004). Loving Muslim women with a vengeance: the West, women, and fundamentalism. *In*: J. Kincheloe and S.R. Steinberg (eds.), *The miseducation of the West: constructing Islam*. New York: Greenwood, 43–58.

SkillsActive. (2011). *Sport and recreation* [online]. Available from: http://www.Skillsactive.com/sport [Accessed 23 March 2011].

Slack, J. D. (1996). The theory and method of articulation in cultural studies. *In*: D. Morley and K.H. Chen (eds.), *Stuart Hall: critical dialogues in cultural studies*. London: Routledge, 112–127.

Slaughter, S. and Leslie, L. (1997). *Academic capitalism: politics, policies and the entrepreneurial university*. Baltimore: John Hopkins University Press.

Slaughter, S. and Rhoades, G. (2004). *Academic capitalism and the new economy: markets, state, and higher education*. London: John Hopkins University Press.

Slaughter, S., Archerd, C.J. and Campbell, T.I.D. (2004). Boundaries and quandaries: how professors negotiate market relations. *The Review of Higher Education*, 28(1), 129–165.

Smith, J.K. and Hodkinson, P. (2005). Relativism, Criteria, and Politics. *In*: N.K. Denzin and Y.S. Lincoln (eds.), *The Sage Handbook of Qualitative Research* (3rd ed.). Thousand Oaks, CA: Sage, 915–932.

Smith, L.T. (2006). Choosing the margins: the role of research in indigenous struggles for social justice. *In*: N.K. Denzin and M.D. Giardina (eds.), *Qualitative enquiry and the conservative challenge: confronting methodological fundamentalism*. Walnut Creek, CA: Left Coast Press.

Snow, D. (2002). On the presumed crisis in ethnographic representation: observations from a sociological and interactionist standpoint. *Journal of Contemporary Ethnography*, 31, 498–507.

Snow, D. and Morrill, C. (1993). Reflections on anthropology's ethnographic crisis of faith. *Contemporary Sociology*, 32, 8–11.

Soederberg, S., Menz, G., and Cerny, P.G. (eds.). (2005). *Internalizing globalization. The rise of neoliberalism and the decline of national varieties of capitalism*. Basingstoke: Palgrave.

Sorheim, R., Widding, L.O., Oust, M. and Madsen, O. (2011). Funding of university spin-off companies: a conceptual approach to financing challenges, *Journal of Small Business and Enterprise Development*, 18(1), 58–73.

Sparkes, A.C. (2002a). *Telling tales in sport and physical activity: a qualitative journey*. Champaign, IL: Human Kinetics Press.

Sparkes, A.C. (2002b). Fictional representations: on difference, choice, and risk. *Sociology of Sport Journal*, 19, 1–24.

Sparkes, A.C. (1995). Writing people: reflections on the dual crisis of representation and legitimation in qualitative inquiry. *Quest*, 47, 158–195.

Sparkes, A.C. (1992). Writing and the textual construction of realities: some challenges for alternate paradigms in physical education. *In*: A. Sparkes (ed.),

Research in physical education and sport: exploring alternate visions. London: The Falmer Press, 271–297.

Sparkes, A.C., Nilges, L., Swan, P. and Dowling, F. (2003). Poetic representations in sport and physical education: insider perspectives. *Sport, Education and Society*, 8(2), 153–177.

Sparkes, A.C. and Silvennoinen, M. (eds.). (1999). *Talking bodies: men's narratives of the body and sport*. SoPhi: University of Jyvaskylal, Finland.

Sperling, J. and Tucker, R.W. (1997). *For-profit higher education: developing a world-class workforce*. New Brunswick: Transaction Publishers.

Sports coach UK. (2008). *Research in Sports coach UK* [online]. Available from: http://www.sportscoachuk.org/research/Research.htm [Accessed 18 August 2008].

Sports coach UK. (2006). *UK action plan for coaching* [online]. Available from: http://www.sportscoachuk.org/About+Us/UKAPC/introduction.htm [Accessed 20 April 2006].

Sport England. (2007). *Economic importance of sport: summary report England 2003* [online]. Available from: http://www.sportengland.org/england_summary_econ_importance.pdf [Accessed 6 June 2008].

St. Pierre, E.A. (2006). Scientifically based research in education: epistemology and ethics. *Adult Education Quarterly*, 56(4), 206–239.

St. Pierre, E.A. (2004). Refusing alternatives: a science of contestation. *Qualitative Inquiry*, 10(1), 130–139.

St. Pierre, E.A. and Roulston, K. (2006). The state of qualitative inquiry: a contested science. *International Journal of Qualitative Studies in Education*, 19(6), 673–684.

Stables, A. (2003). *Education for diversity*. Aldershot: Ashgate.

Stafford, I. and Balyi, I. (2005). *Coaching for long term athlete development: improving participation and performance in sport*. Leeds: Coachwise.

Steinmetz, G. (2003). The state of emergency and the revival of American imperialism: toward an authoritarian post-Fordism. *Public Culture*, 15(2), 323–345.

Sutton Trust. (2007). *University admissions by individual schools*. London: Sutton Trust.

Sykes, H., Chapman, C. and Swedberg, A. (2005). Performed ethnographies. *In*: D.L. Andrews, D. Mason and M.L. Silk (eds.), *Qualitative research in sports studies*. Oxford: Berg, 185–202.

Tamboukou, M. (1999). Writing genealogies: an exploration of Foucault's strategies for doing research. *Discourse: Studies in the Cultural Politics of Education*, 20(2), 201–217.

Targett, S. (1998). *Government gets its sums wrong over move to charge university tuition fees* [online]. The Financial Times. Available from: http://www.bl.uk/welfarereform/issue1/eduhigh.html [Accessed 6 August 2007].

Tedlock, B. (2005). The observation of participation and the emergence of public ethnography. *In*: N.K. Denzin and Y.S. Lincoln (eds.), *The Sage handbook of qualitative research* (3rd ed.). Thousand Oaks, CA: Sage, 467–481.

Tedlock, B. (2000). Ethnography and ethnographic representation. *In*: N.K. Denzin and Y.S. Lincoln (eds.), *Handbook of qualitative research* (2nd ed.). Thousand Oaks, CA: Sage, 455–486.

Thangaraj, S. (2010). Ballin' Indo-Pak style: pleasures, desires, and expressive practices of "South Asian American" masculinity. *International Review for the Sociology of Sport*, 45(3), 372–389.

The Telegraph. (2008). *Premier league wages break the one billion pounds barrier* [online]. Available from: http://www.telegraph.co.uk/sport/main.jhtml?xml=/sport/2008/05/29/sfnpre129.xml [Accessed 29 May 2008].

Thomas, G. (2005). Introduction: evidence and practice. *In*: G. Thomas and R. Pring. (eds.). *Evidence-based practice in education*. Buckingham: Open University Press, 1–18.

Thorpe, H. (2009). Bourdieu, feminism and female physical culture: gender reflexivity and the habitus-field complex. *Sociology of Sport Journal*, 26(4), 491–516.

Thorpe, H., Barbour, K. and Bruce, T. (2011). "Wandering and wondering": theory and representation in feminist physical cultural studies. *Sociology of Sport Journal*, 28(1), 106–134.

Tomlinson, A. (1989). Whose side are they on? Leisure studies and cultural studies in Britain. *Leisure Studies*, 8, 97–106.

Tomlinson, A., and Whannel, G. (eds.). (1984). *Five ring circus: money, power and politics at the Olympic Games*. London: Pluto Press.

Tomlinson, S. (2001). *Education in a post-welfare society*. Buckingham: Open University Press.

Torrance, H. (2006). Research quality and research governance in the United Kingdom: from methodology to management. *In*: N.K. Denzin and M.D. Giardina (eds.), *Qualitative inquiry and the conservative challenge: confronting methodological fundamentalism*. Walnut Creek, CA: Left Coast Press, 127–148.

Trudel, P. and Gilbert, W. (2006). Coaching and coach education. In D.Kirk, M. O'Sullivan and D. McDonald (eds.), *Handbook of physical education*. London: Sage, 516–539.

Truman, C., Mertens, D.M. and Humphries, B. (eds.). (2000). *Research and inequality*. London: UCL Press.

Trudel, P. (2006). What the coaching science literature has to say about the roles of coaches in the development of elite athletes. *International Journal of Sports Science and Coaching*, 1(2), 127–130.

Trudel, P. and Gilbert, W. (2006). Coaching and coach education. *In*: D. Kirk, M. O'Sullivan, and D. McDonald (eds.), *Handbook of physical education*. London: Sage, 516–539.

Tsang, T. (2000). Let me tell you a story: a narrative exploration of identity in high performance sport. *Sociology of Sport Journal*, 17, 44–59.

Turner, G. (1990). The British tradition: A short history. *British cultural studies: An introduction*, 41–84. Boston: Unwin Hyman.

UCAS. (2008a). *Universities and Colleges Admissions Service course search 2008: sport* [online]. Available from: http://search.ucas.co.uk/cgi-bin/hsrun/search/search/StateId/D07br39hrcW0YsRLbjHORrx7RXdIA-U3KF/HAHTpage/search.HsKeywordSuggestion.whereNext?query=677andword=SPORTandsingle=N [Accessed 13 May 2008].

UCAS. (2008b). *Universities and Colleges Admissions Service course search 2009: sport* [online]. Available from: http://search.ucas.co.uk/cgi-bin/hsrun/search/search/StateId/D07sFG9hfpY0Yd8AbjH4XQC8RXd8y-VNLf/HAHTpage/search.HsKeywordSuggestion.whereNext?query=677andword=SPORTandsingle=N [Accessed 13 May 2008].

UCAS. (2008c). *Universities and Colleges Admissions Service course search 2008: sport foundation degrees* [online]. Available from: http://develop.ucas.com/cgi-bin/hsrun.exe/General/FDCourseSearch/StateId/D07rb39hfNK0Ydu5bjHSM6amD1D_1–4qNd/HAHTpage/FDCourseSearch.HsForm.mapFormToCmd [Accessed 13 May 2008].

UNICEF. (2007). *A steady eye on children* [online].UNICEF annual report 2006. Available from: http://www.unicef.org/about/annualreport/files/Annual_Report_2006.pdf [Accessed 16 July 2007].

United Nations. (2005a). *Business plan international year of sport and physical education*. New York: United Nations.

United Nations. (2005b). *The Millennium development goals report* 2005. New York: United Nations.

United Nations. (2005c). *Sport for development and peace: towards achieving the Millennium development goals.* New York: United Nations.

Van Maanen, J. (1988). *Tales of the field: on writing ethnography.* Chicago: University of Chicago Press.

Van Neutegem, A. (2006). Bridging the athlete-coach transition: a reflective note on long-term coach development. *Coaches Plan,* 13(2), 41–46.

Vannini, A., and Fornssler, B. (2011). Girl, interrupted: interpreting Semenya's body, gender verification testing, and public discourse. *Cultural Studies <=> Critical Methodologies,* 11(3), 243–257.

Watson, D. (2006). New Labour and higher education [online]. *AUA Conference, Queens University Belfast,* 11 April 2006. Available from: http://www.aua.ac.uk/publications/conferenceproceedings/2006belfast/davidwatson.doc [Accessed 6 August 2007].

Watson, R. (1973). The public announcement of fatality. *Working Papers in Cultural Studies: Centre for Contemporary Cultural Studies,* 4(Spring), 5–20.

Way, R. and O'Leary, D. (2006). Long-term coach development concept. *Perspective,* 12(13), 24–31.

Weber, M. (1958). *The protestant ethic and the spirit of capitalism.* New York: Charles Scribner's Sons.

Wesson, L. and Weaver, J. (2001). Administration-educational standards: using the lens of post-modern thinking to examine the role of the school administrator. *In*: J. Kincheloe and D. Weil (eds.), *Standards and schooling in the United States: an encyclopaedia.* Santa Barbara, CA: ABC-Clio.

Weiss, L. (1997a). Globalization and the myth of the powerless state. *New Left Review,* old series 225, 3–27.

Weiss, C.H. (1997b). How can theory-based evaluation make greater headway? *Evaluation Review,* 21(4), 501–524.

Whannel, G. (1992). *Fields in vision: Television sport and cultural transformation.* London: Routledge.

Whannel, G. (1986). The unholy alliance: Notes on television and the remaking of British sport 1965–1985. *Leisure Studies,* 5, 129–145.

Whannel, G. (1983). *Blowing the whistle.* London: Comedia.

White, M. and Schwoch, J. (2006). (eds.). *Questions of method in cultural studies.* Oxford: Blackwell.

Whitson, D. (1986). Structure, agency and the sociology of sport debates. *Theory, Culture and Society,* 3(1), 99–107.

Whitson, D. (1984). Sport and hegemony: On the construction of the dominant culture. *Sociology of Sport Journal,* 1(1), 64–78.

Whitson, D., and Macintosh, D. (1990). The scientization of physical education: Discourses of performance. *Quest,* 42(1), 40–51.

Williams, J. (1997). The discourse of access: the legitimation of selectivity. *In*: J. Williams (ed.), *Negotiating access to higher education: the discourse of selectivity and equity.* Buckingham: SRHE and the Open University Press, 24–46.

Willis, P. (1974). Women in sport (2). *Working Papers in Cultural Studies (C.C.C.S.),* 5(Spring), 21–36.

Wilson, J. (1994). *Playing by the rules: sport, society, and the state.* Detroit: Wayne State University Press.

Wilson, J. (1988). *Politics and leisure.* London: Allen and Unwin.

Woodman, L. (1993). Coaching: a science, an art, an emerging profession. *Sport Science Review,* 2(2), 1–13.

Woodward, K. (2008). Hanging out and hanging about: Insider/outsider research in the sport of boxing. *Ethnography, 9*(4), 536–560.

Wright, H. K. (2001). "What's going on?" Larry Grossberg on the status quo of Cultural Studies: An interview. *Cultural Values, 5*(2), 133–162.

Zweiniger-Bargielowska, I. (2006). Building a British superman: physical culture in interwar Britain. *Journal of Contemporary History,* 41(4), 595–610.

Index